The Vietnam Veteran

The Vietnam Veteran

A History of Neglect

by David E. Bonior
Steven M. Champlin
Timothy S. Kolly

*Foreword by Robert O. Muller
and Jan C. Scruggs*

PRAEGER

PRAEGER SPECIAL STUDIES • PRAEGER SCIENTIFIC

New York • Philadelphia • Eastbourne, UK
Toronto • Hong Kong • Tokyo • Sydney

Library of Congress Cataloging in Publication Data

Bonior, David E.
      The Vietnam veteran.

      Includes index.
      1. Veterans—United States. 2. Veterans—
United States—Public opinion. 3. Public opinion—
United States. 4. Vietnamese Conflict, 1961-1975—
United States. I. Champlin, Steven M. II. Kolly,
Timothy S. III. Title
UB357.B64 1984   355.1'15'0973   84-15154
ISBN 0-03-070279-8 (alk. paper)
ISBN 0-03-008162-9 (pbk.)

Published in 1984 (hb) and 1986 (pb) by Praeger Publishers
CBS Educational and Professional Publishing
a Division of CBS Inc.
521 Fifth Avenue, New York, NY 10175 USA

© 1984 by Praeger Publishers

6789 052 987654321

Printed in the United States of America
on acid-free paper

Foreword

by Robert O. Muller and Jan C. Scruggs

March 29, 1984

Vietnam was America's longest war. Begun in the early 1960s, the last American combat unit left in 1973. The war was never officially declared and the legal technicality of declaring the war "era" over would wait until 1975, but 11 years ago today the last American combat soldier left Vietnam.

Twenty-seven million men came of age during the Vietnam War. Some nine million served, nearly one in three. Of those, nearly three million served in the combat theater. This book is their story.

Volunteer or not, high draft number or low, the war also shaped the lives of the eighteen million who did not serve. Faced with the war, they made difficult decisions that shaped their future.

The war also changed the lives of sisters and wives, some of whom are veterans in the legal sense, all of whom are veterans of those confusing years and hard choices. It shaped the lives of parents, especially those whose children never returned. Marked by dissent at home, followed by Watergate, the war started a cycle that profoundly influenced American society.

The decade since the war's end is a long time; the two decades since its beginning longer still. Those twenty years span an era in our history. In this book the story of the Vietnam homecoming becomes a story of our times and a measure of our national character.

For societies, as for individuals, some decisions have to count. We have to honor them despite changes in circumstances, for better or worse. War is one of those decisions that should be neither easily undertaken nor quickly pushed aside.

Yet for ten years this nation waged a war with one hand while denying it with the other. The national indecision affected the conduct of the war and attitudes toward its veterans. When the war ended, the nation sought to forget it all. The soldiers were left to bear the worst by themselves.

This is not the stuff of proud tales, to be passed from one generation to another through Memorial Day speeches. Now, as in the past, it is tempting to cover the facts with easy rationalizations. But we play with our past at heavy expense.

vii

Many veterans — many of our brothers and sisters — are still stuck in Vietnam, unable to move past the nightmares and the scarred values. The nation is stuck with them, struggling to overcome a deep cynicism, seemingly unable to find any shared values, no matter how basic.

We are a people divided. Antiwar activists and proud veterans are separated by more than the war itself. They are divided by a contentiousness that threatens to become the only permanent legacy of the Vietnam War.

There must be something better to be won from the war years. There must be an alternative to continued bickering. If we, as one people — as one nation — will go back, however hard the task, to bring our Vietnam veterans home, then perhaps we all will be better for the trip.

"The nation did not honor its debt to Vietnam veterans," the authors conclude and then suggest that this "failure should be written deep in our history books." Out of such honesty might come the humility to accept our history — the better and the worse — and move forward together.

This is a book about a deep and embarrassing national failure, but it is also a book with a message of hope. Somehow, despite all the pettiness, despite all the institutional failures, despite the failed leadership, the nation and its Vietnam veterans have found a road home. It just remains to complete the trip.

If we have one complaint with this book, it is this: The book tells almost nothing of the role played by its three authors, most importantly, by Dave Bonior. Perhaps that is as it should be, but we remember.

Robert O. Muller
President
Vietnam Veterans of
    America

Jan C. Scruggs
President
Vietnam Veterans Memorial
    Fund

Preface

A damp late afternoon November chill drops onto the Washington streets, and the clouds are massing overhead. It is too warm for snow, but too cold to mistake this day for autumn.

I cross Wisconsin Avenue from my apartment building and begin my short walk to the Washington National Cathedral, America's answer to those wondrous monuments of Rheims and Paris, of Vienna and Cologne.

The cavernous expanses of the cathedral's main nave make it seem incredible to remember that there once was a moment when this shrine could hold no more pilgrims.

On January 20, 1973, I had stood outside in the rain listening over hastily placed loudspeakers to Haydn's "Missa in Tempore Belli" (Mass in Time of War). The occasion was Richard M. Nixon's second inaugural, and 15,000 to 18,000 worried citizens had been drawn to the cathedral for a counter-inauguration.

Meanwhile, in the Kennedy Center on the shores of the Potomac, President Nixon listened to the militant chords of the "1812 Overture." It was Bernstein vs. Ormandy, Haydn vs. Tschaikovsky, "the people" (whatever that meant) vs. Nixon.

Now, almost ten years later, our nation's preoccupation with the Vietnam War had returned to the cathedral. Vietnam veterans, thousands of them, were being drawn to Washington for what was ostensibly the dedication of a memorial to their sacrifice and the final sacrifice of 58,000 U.S. men and women. In reality, every one of us knew that it would be much more. The vets were coming to collect a debt.

The city waited, perhaps a bit anxiously, because almost everyone at one time or another had seen those "crazy Vietnam vets" depicted on some soporific television series as killers or drug addicts. Who knew what might happen when 200,000 of them roamed the streets, mingling with the civilized.

Since there was no immediate evidence of an event in the cathedral, I inquired of one of the purple-robed guides where I might find the Vietnam veterans observance. I was directed to the Bethlehem Chapel, one of several sizable rooms in the cathedral basement.

"It figures," I thought. "They probably thought there would be less damage if the vets started firing rifles and throwing grenades." What I found, however, was something far more dignified and intimate than anything I had expected.

The 20 or so rows of chairs were filled, and people stood against the side and back walls. Subdued golden light washed the room, admitting no hint of the rawness outside.

At the altar, two veterans — one in camouflaged fatigues — knelt facing the chapel, while to their left and forward stood a middle-aged man reciting a litany of names of those who had perished in the Asian conflict. All too quickly, he advanced the alphabetical list to the name that gave purpose to his presence. A son. Twenty years of age.

He haltingly delivered an homage that had been written in his heart years ago, so profoundly filled with love and remorse that when at last his voice broke, not an individual present would have been able to continue for him. Some heads were thrown back to battle tear-filled eyes. Some people sniffled self-consciously. Some simply fixed a stricken gaze. One of the veterans rose, advanced, and, silently standing beside him, laid a hand on the father's shoulder.

In that moment, and in the days immediately following, was fulfilled a need of all Vietnam veterans to speak to the parents or relatives of those who had died, to finally express to them the grief that they have carried, the appreciation that they have felt, to relieve some of the guilt of survival.

In 1968, while awaiting reassignment at Fort Wolters, near Mineral Wells, Texas, I was assigned to a funeral honor guard conscripted to bury Vietnam's dead in North Central Texas.

One morning, while acting as a pallbearer for a black infantry corporal, I moved forward to steady the grieving mother, who I felt was in some danger near the open grave. With furious disconsolateness, she pulled her arm away, wheeled, and shouted, "Why couldn't it have been you, white boy?" Everything stopped. Sound, movement, everything. I moved away, stunned. The weeping father later approached me to offer an unnecessary apology. I have often thought of that moment. It has stayed with me through Vietnam and the years that followed. I still have no answer to her question, and I have asked it myself many times.

But I have always known, since that day, that some catharsis would be necessary, not only for the veterans who had served but also for the loved ones left behind. The scene depicted in that chapel and reenacted in the following days was the fulfillment of that personal hope. As various readers rose to recite names, they began with homemade prayers composed with the roughness and embarrassing sincerity of those not accustomed to such art.

As the week went on, it became apparent that the whole salute was being crafted primarily by veterans of the enlisted ranks. Not the officer corps, not the cabinet officers, not a government agency, not the Congress, but the extraordinary combatants themselves — and the ordinary people were responding.

Veterans were saying "screw you" to a government that had for too long said the same to them. They were doing it themselves.

Certainly, they were aided by those institutions that had helped to pent up their feelings for years. The veterans organizations had contributed part of the money. The Congress had contributed the land. The media, finally finding a Vietnam veterans' event that they could market as "show biz", gave extensive coverage. President Ronald Reagan even made passing reference to the observance in a press conference.

However, the salute was conceived, organized, and structured by the people who years before were left to support each other in a war incompetently managed and then disavowed at the government's highest levels. U.S. institutions, for the most part, neglected Vietnam veterans until it was politically acceptable or necessary to do otherwise.

And as the week wore on, as the drama was revisited nightly in the cathedral, as seminars on lingering problems were held, as sometimes raucous, sometimes tearful, receptions were attended, as veterans extemporized a parade down Pennsylvania Avenue, it was clear that veterans welcomed lay spectators and their participation but that they would have exultantly proceeded even if they had met empty streets.

It was a demonstration of solidarity, and at various times it seemed to me that veterans were actually surprised when they were cheered or questioned by curious nonveterans. It was a logical reaction inculcated by almost two decades virtually devoid of benevolent interest.

Make no mistake about it. These veterans came with at least some degree of bitterness and anger to face a nation curiously awkward and anxious with their presence. Both groups departed better for having made each other's acquaintance.

The above words are coauthor Tim Kolly's. The events are drawn from his life, yet with variations that would reflect the differing circumstances of each author, the story could be repeated. This is a book by participants, not neutral observers.

Our involvement with Vietnam veterans issues, however, is not reflected in eyewitness accounts. This book is not a group autobiography. We have cared about the facts of our nation's neglect of its Vietnam veterans and have sought to tell those facts here. That care is the real reflection of our concern.

We are insiders of a sort, but this book is not full of insiders' stories. We have some personal knowledge, included in the book, but more importantly, we have convictions about how our government actually makes decisions. Those convictions have guided our research and interpretation.

This book is intended as a study of how Vietnam veterans came to be an entity apart from the nation they sought to serve. It is our feeling that this occurred because institutions that had in the past helped to integrate veterans into society failed in this instance.

The Veterans Administration failed to act on behalf of Vietnam veterans, but that failure merely poses a second question. Why was the VA allowed to do nothing? Why did the Congress fail to intervene and mandate action on behalf of Vietnam veterans?

If Congress, in turn, proved hesitant to act, that merely advances the question. The interest groups normally function as a spur to Congressional action, advancing the cause of those they represent. Why did the veterans groups fail to intervene and mandate action on behalf of Vietnam veterans?

The president often acts to set the national agenda, calling the nation to focus on new issues. Even if the president was unwilling to exercise such leadership, the president also serves as a daily check on Congress and has authority to change agency policy. Why did the White House fail to intervene and mandate action on behalf of Vietnam veterans?

The failure to act on behalf of Vietnam veterans required indifference from each segment of our government. Why did the nation accept such a systematic failure? Where was the public call to action that pierced government indifference on behalf of Vietnam veterans?

It would be nice to blame our nation's failure to serve its Vietnam veterans on a small group of indifferent bureaucrats or arrogant Congressmen. The facts, however, will not allow such an easy excuse.

Our government is what it claims to be: a system of checks and balances that disperses power. Dispersed power creates shared accountability.

The media, the Congress, the executive branch, the veterans organizations, almost without exception, concentrated their energies on the struggle for the ideology of the war, on the competence or intentions of its policy makers, or on the struggle of those who opposed the war while it was being fought.

None acted as an advocate for Vietnam veterans while the war was underway, so it is not surprising that new advocacy was not forthcoming at the war's close. When the war ended, quarreling U.S. institutions did not carry their dead from the battlefield, offered no dignity to their wounded, but simply withdrew, leaving those whom they implicitly regarded as irrelevant to make their own way home.

The scope and order of this book are set by the pattern of dispersed power in our nation. Organized into three parts, the book begins with a history of the coverage of the Vietnam soldiers and veterans by the nation's television networks and newspapers, as well as the films that have addressed (or failed to address) their story. The details of the media history help to introduce — with precision, not with vague assertion — the public attitudes that set the climate for Vietnam veterans issues.

The second part of this book explores the role of our presidents and the national veterans organizations in shaping the basic national agenda on Vietnam veterans issues. The final part follows the Congress and the Veterans Administration as they address (or fail to address) specific Vietnam veterans issues.

Acknowledgments

Our greatest debt in writing this book is to the many people who have generously granted us interviews. They did so knowing that this book did not promise flattering portrayals.

We owe a special debt to former presidents Gerald R. Ford and Jimmy Carter, who gave us a look inside the Oval Office.

Colleagues in Congress have answered repeated questions. Four have given us extended formal interviews: the Honorable Melvin Price (D-Illinois), Peter Rodino (D-New Jersey), Thomas Daschle (D-South Dakota), and Senator Alan Cranston (D-California).

The Honorable William Driver, the first administrator of the Veterans Administration during the Vietnam era, also gave us an interview, as did the Honorable Max Cleland, the first Vietnam veteran to head the agency. Cleland is presently secretary of state in Georgia.

Fay Kanin, who wrote the screenplay for *Friendly Fire* and is now president of the Academy of Motion Picture Arts and Sciences, granted us a long interview in her California home. Michael Wayne gave us an inside look at the one film made about the Vietnam War during the war years, *The Green Berets*.

Jack Valenti, an adviser to Lyndon Johnson, who is now president of the Motion Picture Association of America, talked to us about the Johnson White House and about the film industry. He kindly helped us find several films that are no longer easily accessible.

Charles Champlin and Sheila Benson, from the *Los Angeles Times*, provided extensive background information on war films in general and Vietnam films in particular.

Charles Mohr and Bernard Weinraub, both from the *New York Times*, and Peter Braestrup, now with the *Wilson Quarterly*, joined us in an extensive round-table discussion on the coverage of the Vietnam War and Vietnam veterans. Kirk Scharfenberg, of the *Boston Globe*, talked with us about the *Globe*'s editorials on Vietnam veterans issues.

Jed Duvall, now with ABC but then with CBS; Kelly Burke, with WRC in Washington, D.C.; and Professor Larry Lichty, of the University of Maryland, joined in a second discussion focused on television coverage. Morton Dean, with CBS, talked with us about his news pieces.

Although TV fact books abound, detailed information on individual shows is very difficult to find. The networks tend to refer researchers to the producers, who are usually burdened with present production schedules and have little time for history.

Nevertheless, Gene Reynolds, the executive producer and co-creator of *Lou Grant*, talked with us about "Vets," a show from his series, as did Ed Asner. Edana R. McCaffery, at the Television Information Office of the National Association of Broadcasters, used her own time to collect important information for us.

Interviews were granted by several leaders in the veterans organizations: Robert Spanogle, national adjutant of the American Legion; Cooper T. Holt, executive director of the Veterans of Foreign Wars; Norman B. Hartnett, John Heilman, and Ronald W. Drach of the Disabled American Veterans; John Terzano, vice president, and Robert O. Muller, president, of the Vietnam Veterans of America; and Jan C. Scruggs, president of the Vietnam Veterans Memorial Fund.

Mack Fleming, the chief counsel and staff director of the House Committee on Veterans' Affairs, gave us an extended interview. Jon Steinberg, now minority chief counsel, but formerly chief counsel to the Senate Committee, joined in the interview with Senator Cranston.

Stuart Feldman provided extensive information on press and legislative events from the early 1970s and on the early days of the Vietnam Veterans of America. Ken Harbert PA-C talked with us about "Back in the World."

Several years ago, Congressman David E. Bonior had the opportunity to meet with some groups of Vietnam veterans in the federal penitentiary in Atlanta, Georgia. Extracts from these extraordinary discussions are included in the chapter on the Veterans Administration.

Segments from these different interviews appear throughout the book. They can be easily identified because they are the only quotations that are not footnoted.

In fact, during the entire process of writing this book, only four individuals categorically refused interviews: Jim Webb declined repeated requests for an interview, as did Jane Fonda. Former President Richard Nixon declined an interview and never answered questions provided in writing. The Honorable Ray Roberts, former chairman of the House Committee on Veterans' Affairs, also declined an interview.

Our thanks to Sarah Dufendach, who read almost the entire manuscript, providing editorial comments, detailed criticism, and additional research. Alan Kadrofske read large sections of the manuscript. He also provided critical suggestions and helped guide us to additional research material.

Martha Pope and Deborah Woitte both gave their time to read nearly the entire manuscript and provide a final editorial review. Our editor, Dottie Breitbart, was more than patient with her fledgling writers, and our project editor, Rachel Burd, eased countless production problems.

Marci Cox helped type and prepare the chapter on the White House. Christine Metzger typed many drafts of the entire manuscript, a taxing job, but perhaps not nearly as taxing as transcribing the interviews. We thank her for both.

Contents

I The Rush to Forget

1 Television

No story so dominated the television news as the Indo-China War. On the first *Today* newscast with Frank Blair on January 14, 1952, he read of the fighting in Vietnam. And he read of the continued fighting on his last appearance on the show twenty-three years later.

Larry Lichty
"The Night at the End
of the Tunnel"[1]

Without question, the war was the longest running story in the history of television news. From 1960 through 1975, the war was covered on newscasts, regularly scheduled interview and magazine programs, plus news specials and documentaries.[2]

As the number of U.S. troops increased in Vietnam, so did the bureaus of the major television networks. By the fall of 1965, the networks had full-time bureaus in Saigon that grew in size to about 25-30 people each. From 1965 through 1975, there were more than 4,000 individual film reports of Vietnam by more than 300 different network correspondents. From Vietnam, between 1966 and 1972, two to five stories went back to the states every day.[3]

Almost nightly for more than a decade, news of the war's progress reached into U.S. living rooms, bedrooms, and dens, on first and second television sets during summer vacations, or between football games before Thanksgiving dinner. In U.S. living rooms, TV gave casualties human forms: American brothers, husbands, and fathers waded waist deep in mud, crawled through withering fire, and dragged enemy dead from the field.

In addition to the nightly news, the networks ran regularly scheduled special weekly programs on the war. ABC did over 100 weekly half-hour episodes of *Scope* — a synopsis of Vietnam War news and analysis. NBC had its own shows: *Vietnam Report* and *Vietnam: The War, The Week*. CBS offered a smorgasbord of Vietnam War shows ranging from instant specials to documentaries.

In all, there were more than 2,000 specials, documentaries, and interview programs during the war, but the unfavorable time slots for the weekly specials and the unwillingness of many local stations to air the shows kept them from receiving large audiences. There were no such barriers for the nightly news.

On the average day during the war period, 25 percent of the adult population watched one of the evening news programs. At the height of the war, during the Tet Offensive, approximately 20 million people watched *The Huntley-Brinkley Report*. Walter Cronkite at CBS drew a shade below 20 million, with Bob Young at ABC holding an audience of about half that size. Roughly 50 million people watched the television news each night.[4]

Television coverage of the U.S. soldier spanned three rather distinct periods. During the early period, from the beginning of the war through around the fall of 1967, the networks' attentions were riveted on combat action. From late 1967 through the Tet Offensive, which began in January 1968, the coverage reflected increasing uncertainty about the ability of the United States to win the war. With the end of the 1968 presidential campaign, a final period began. The networks turned away from combat scenes to cover dissent at home and the negotiations seeking an end to the war.

From 1965 through the Tet Offensive, the war was covered on about 86 percent of the CBS and NBC nightly news shows. The majority of the pieces centered on ground and air combat. Combat was dramatic and visual. Producers seemed to believe that combat action would attract viewers.[5]

Most importantly, scenes of American men in battle were major stories all by themselves, especially as the casualties mounted. No newsman could safely ignore one-half million American men fighting and dying.

The air and ground wars were covered differently. Correspondents joined the soldiers on the ground, following them as they advanced. The air war was reported from Washington, the Pentagon, or another military center, but not from the air itself.

When correspondents did cover the Air Force in combat, the reporting seemed short on insight. Bruce Morton, aboard a helicopter, described "the most exciting roller coaster ride in the world." In 1965, Walter Cronkite reported from a bomber: "One, two, three, four, we dropped our bombs, and now a tremendous G load as we come out of that dive. Oh, I know something of what those astronauts must go through. WOW!"[6]

Absent were interviews with those who braved the new air warfare as helicopter pilots and tail gunners, or those who dropped bombs and napalm. Because the networks relied on the military, the public received cold reports rather than independent eyewitness accounts. Even the network efforts to add action were often dependent on the use of official military film.

Throughout this early phase of U.S. involvement, which included the first period of massive escalation, there was strong support for the war in Congress and among the public. The networks defined the Vietnam War primarily from the perspective of the U.S. soldier.

The amount of coverage continued to rise. During the fall of 1967, 90 percent of the evening news shows covered the war. Beginning with the North Vietnamese offensive during the Tet holy days at the end of January 1968, the war was on the air nearly every night.[7]

The fall of 1967 brought a subtle shift in the war coverage. Two major battles, for Hills 875 and 882, were savage, and for what seemed the first time, correspondents like Murray Fromson found disturbing questions hidden in the fury. " 'Was it all worth it?' is the question every GI is asking," he reported.[8]

The horror of the war was beginning to come home. During the battle for Hill 882, TV correspondent Dean Brelis filmed a U.S. soldier saying, "Look at my legs. There's nothing left." With the horror came a mounting sense of panic. In the fight for Hill 882, Brelis reported that U.S. soldiers were fighting for their lives, not for a strategic victory leading to the war's end.[9]

In January 1968, the North Vietnamese launched the Tet Offensive, the largest campaign during the U.S. war years. The North won an impressive, if temporary, victory. Their soldiers swept through the South, even besieging the capital of South Vietnam, Saigon. U.S. soldiers were caught in long and bloody battles at Khe Sanh and Hue.

Coverage of the Tet Offensive brought the rising sense of uncertainty about the war into stark relief. The message became increasingly clear. Not merely battles, but the whole war itself might be lost. During the siege of Saigon, NBC anchor David Brinkley reported that "the Viet Cong appear in every alleyway." TV correspondent Howard Tuckner, in a revealing comment, reported that U.S. troops were brought to Saigon to wipe out the Viet Cong but that they were "not doing much good."[10]

Television correspondent Ron Nessen, reporting from Khe Sanh, expressed the emerging consensus. "The North Vietnamese think they will win another Dien Bien Phu [the battle that drove the French from Vietnam]," he reported. "Whatever result is written into history, it will be written in blood." Ten years later, Nessen, to his great credit, would say, "The fact is that we had no idea whether or not it was Dien Bien Phu or not."[11]

With time, scholars of both military history and journalism would conclude that, in fact, Tet was a U.S. victory, not a defeat. The North Vietnamese had hoped that their military sweep would prompt popular uprisings against the South Vietnamese government. None occurred. Ground was won at great cost, but the North Vietnamese were soon driven back. It would take the North years to replace the resources lost in the offensive.[12]

Despite the U.S. military victory, the television coverage had made real to Americans not merely the human cost of the war, but the awful possibility of defeat. The North Vietnamese had won a major psychological victory. In retrospect, it is clear that the countdown on U.S. involvement in Vietnam had already begun.

The coverage of Tet helped advance a swing in public attitudes. As reflected in the 1968 presidential campaign, doubt was sweeping the nation. George Romney, Michigan's Republican governor, suggested that he and the nation had been "brainwashed." Democratic candidates for the presidency declared their opposition to a war waged by presidents of their own party.

Coverage of the war remained heavy throughout the summer of 1968, but inevitably the war began to compete with a variety of other news stories that preempted combat coverage. On April 4, Martin Luther King, Jr., was assassinated. Robert Kennedy was shot on June 5 and died on June 6.

Life in the United States seemed to be unraveling. The chaos created by the sheer frequency of important events propelled the nation into a period of confusion. A whole generation of draft-age men and their families shaped their future in response to the war.

Some left sweethearts behind to take up arms as their fathers and uncles had done in earlier wars. Others married and had children before they otherwise might have. Some interrupted school or career with military service. Others stayed in school longer than they wished or needed.

The inability of Americans to reconcile the national sacrifice that is needed in time of war with the facts of the Vietnam conflict caused anxiety and produced a clash of symbols. Long hair, flag and draft-card burning, and sexual freedom bumped up against values nurtured during the cold war years. Short hair, religion, "God Bless America," and Saturday afternoon football now shared the television screen with a new culture.

Television had a choice of two wars to cover: one in Southeast Asia or one in the streets of the United States. War demonstrations, race riots, and campus unrest were as visual as combat in Vietnam was and became a kind of equivalent to war footage.

From Richard Nixon's election through February 1969, Vietnam War coverage declined from 90 percent of all newscasts to 61 percent. Combat footage continued to arrive in New York but was aired only three times on the NBC evening news in November and December of that year. The story of the U.S. soldier in Vietnam was beginning to fade.[13]

In May 1968, the Paris Peace Talks began. On October 31, 1968, President Lyndon Johnson announced that the bombing of North Vietnam would stop and that negotiations would be more seriously pursued by both sides. Television journalists rushed to Paris to cover the talks.

Robert Northshield, producer of the nightly news at NBC, declared that the real war story was now the negotiations and not the fighting in Vietnam. Northshield explained that "combat stories seemed like a contradiction and would confuse the audience."[14]

When Richard Nixon became president in January 1969, "Vietnamization" (Melvin Laird coined the term) became the new U.S. policy. It sought to reduce the U.S. combat role by strengthening the South Vietnamese army and turning the battle over to them. Vietnamization could only reinforce the sense that combat footage was a paradox.

At ABC in March 1969, Av Westin, executive producer of the evening news, wrote to his correspondents, "I have asked our Vietnam staff to alter the focus of their coverage from combat pieces to interpretive ones, pegged to the eventual pullout of American forces. This point should be stressed for all hands."[15]

By the end of 1969, both CBS and NBC focused their coverage on Vietnamization. From 1970 until the end of the U.S. involvement, the so-called "bang-bang" stories involving U.S. soldiers in combat amounted to only 13 percent of the stories that were run on the war by the networks. From 1965 through 1969, the percentage had been 48 percent.[16]

The U.S. soldier was no longer a story. His place was not taken by the new Vietnam veteran. As Jed Duvall, who covered the war in Vietnam for CBS, recalled in 1982:

> I had to go to a conference a couple of years ago, a veteran conference, and . . . I figured I'd arm myself with what we've done and I took this big, fat book which is the CBS news index, for stuff they've run on veterans, and it was hard to find any entries, a couple of documentaries and things, but there hasn't been much coverage.

As Duvall noted, there were exceptions. Howard K. Smith, at ABC, did an early and important editorial in 1974 on the GI Bill. At CBS, Morton Dean, who had covered the war in Vietnam, tracked down soldiers from the pieces filmed as he followed a medivac crew. The result was a series of extraordinary stories on the veterans' lives and the subtle but pervasive impact of their wartime service.

Whatever the trends in the industry as a whole, Dean would not forget the soldiers he had come to know in Vietnam. Even in 1983, he recalled his profound encounter with a particular veteran:

> One was a medic. . . . He told a story of when he got off the plane, when he first returned from Vietnam. There was a crowd of war protestors shouting at him. When he reached the tarmac, someone spit in his face. He walked to the men's room, took a change of clothes out of his suitcase and put them on, stuffed his uniform into his suitcase and never wore it again. . . . He tried to get into medical school with all his experience in Vietnam, but the schools wouldn't consider it, and he couldn't get in anywhere. . . . I went with him to a party and found that none of his friends even knew he had been in the war except a

girl he used to date, who only knew he had been in Vietnam. I told them the guy was a hero — had saved many lives. Everyone was flabbergasted. . . . I spoke to the medic's parents and found they didn't know anything about their son's experiences either. He had never said anything about the war.

In 1975, when Saigon fell, each network aired a long special that recapped its war coverage.[17] It was one thing, however, to look back, but another to face the present. The networks would not report the struggle of Vietnam veterans for benefits, recognition, and readjustment until late 1977.

When television news finally discovered the Vietnam veteran, there was an explosion of activity. At ABC's *20/20*, both Geraldo Rivera and Sylvia Chase did a number of pieces on Vietnam veterans, including an important series on Agent Orange. At CBS, Mike Wallace did several pieces for *60 Minutes*, and *Sunday Morning* provided additional coverage.[18]

In 1970, John Laurence did an important documentary on the American soldier in Vietnam entitled *The World of Charlie Company*. In 1977, Bruce Morton sought out eight of the soldiers who had served in Charlie Company, portraying their lives since the war in a documentary entitled *Charlie Company at Home: The Veterans of Vietnam* (January 17, 1978).

In 1981, CBS did a third documentary on Charlie Company with their new correspondent Bill Moyers, completing a Charlie Company trilogy that spanned nearly the entire war era and the range of emotions it evoked. Entitled *Bittersweet Memories: A Vietnam Reunion* (December 12, 1981), the documentary was an unprecedented joint CBS/*Newsweek* effort that would also produce a *Newsweek* cover story.[19]

ABC aired *The Class That Went to War* (December 1, 1977), which followed the 1964 graduating class of the Chatham, New Jersey High School through the war and beyond. On July 15, 1982, ABC aired a rare and powerful look at incarcerated veterans. *Vietnam Requiem* focused on five highly decorated Vietnam veterans who had committed violent crimes.

In 1983, PBS aired a moving documentary in the Jessica Savitch series *Frontline*. Entitled *Vietnam Memorial* (May 30, 1983), it chronicled the dedication of the Vietnam Veterans Memorial and looked at several Vietnam veteran issues.[20]

Local television stations followed the pattern set by the national networks. A special survey was done of each network affiliate in five major media markets: New York, Washington, D.C., Atlanta, Detroit, and San Francisco. No Vietnam series was discovered before 1979.[21]

Among the stations surveyed, Nancy McCaulley at the CBS affiliate in Detroit, WJBK, did the first series, on Agent Orange, in 1979. The other stations were not far behind. Of the 15 affiliates surveyed, seven produced a local series on Vietnam veterans. Two of those stations did two series, and one, WXYZ – the ABC affiliate in Detroit – did three.

The local stations recognized the importance of the subject and sought to ensure a quality product. Of the 11 series done, at least two were nominated for Emmys. *The War Within* – a series produced by Jonathan Den for KRON, the NBC affiliate in San Francisco – won six local Emmys, the Robert F. Kennedy Award for Journalism (beating out ABC's distinguished *Vietnam Requiem*), and the San Francisco Film Festival Award.[22]

Of special importance were the three documentaries on Agent Orange done by Bill Kurtis at the CBS Affiliate in Chicago, WDVM. The first, *Agent Orange: Vietnam's Deadly Fog*, aired on March 23, 1978. The second, *Agent Orange: The Human Harvest*, aired on March 28, 1979. The last, *Agent Orange III: A View from Vietnam*, aired on April 21, 1980.

Along with ABC's *20/20*, which aired Agent Orange documentaries beginning in 1978, the Bill Kurtis series gave the Agent Orange issue its first major exposure. The two sets of documentaries played a historic role in the development of the issue.

In 1980, Kurtis was named the Illinois Journalist of the Year. The documentary series was a milestone in an already distinguished career that would lead to his selection as the new anchor for CBS's two-hour morning news show.

The 1979 documentary *Agent Orange: The Human Harvest* won a national Emmy in 1980, as well as the Community Service Award, the Illinois UPI Award, and the Illinois AP Award. The 1980 film *Agent Orange III: A View from Vietnam* won the Ohio State University best Documentary Award in 1981.

In 1983, PBS began a 13-part series that charted the history of the Vietnam War. The huge production was a rare joint effort between PBS and ABC. Canadian journalist Michael Maclear had done an earlier documentary, *Vietnam: The Ten Thousand Day War*, also in 13 parts. The extraordinary Canadian series has received little exposure in the United States, although it did air on the independent Channel 5 in Washington, D.C., during 1982.

With these two comprehensive documentary series, television coverage had come full circle from the extensive coverage when the war was new and novel, between 1965 and 1967, through the near silence that followed Tet, to a second era of intense preoccupation with the Vietnam War, its soldiers and veterans.

THE SOLDIER'S STORY

For a few years, before Vietnamization and the Paris Peace Talks became the"real"war story, the television networks concentrated on the U.S. soldier in the field. Those stories set an image of the young Americans fighting in Vietnam. Shaping that image were the TV correspondents who went into the field, seeking to capture the battle on film.

Prior to 1965, nearly all the reporting in Vietnam was done by correspondents who were stationed in Hong Kong, Tokyo, and Bangkok. Most of the soundmen and cameramen were Vietnamese stringers. As the U.S. commitment to the war increased, the networks each established permanent bureaus in Saigon.

During the course of the war, hundreds of network correspondents went to Vietnam. Most of the correspondents were assigned to Vietnam for short tours, averaging six months. Some, however, like Don Webster, John Laurence, and Richard Threlkeld spent years covering the war.

Like the military, those in television who desired promotions sought assignments in Vietnam. They did so at great risk. From 1964 through the summer of 1973, 45 journalists died covering the Indochina War. Eighteen are still listed as missing in action.[23]

A majority of the television correspondents had had previous military experience. Some, like Phil Bradley and Frank Marina, had done several tours in Vietnam with the military.[24] Not surprisingly, many of today's top network news personalities spent a tour covering the war.

John Laurence, now with ABC but then with CBS, was "the best . . . sensational, a shooting star, the Edward R. Murrow of Vietnam," according to Professor Larry Lichty of the University of Maryland, the leading scholar of TV coverage of the Vietnam War.

In the fall of 1967, at the battle of Con Thien, Laurence interviewed Corporal Edward Broderick, who read a poem written on the back of his jacket:

> When youth was a soldier
> and I fought across the seas
> we were young and cold hearts
> of bloody savagery.
> Born of indignation
> children of our time
> we are orphans of creation
> dying in our prime.

After Broderick completed reciting the poem, Laurence asked him, "What made you write the poem?" The corporal responded simply, "Just the way things are."[25]

Laurence described his objective as simply showing "the price that was being paid in blood and lives by American and Vietnamese soldiers. That was the basic purpose of our reporting. . . . I just considered myself one who tried to stay with the troops as much as possible and report on what they saw."[26]

Reporting in the field did not require nuanced commentary or scoops carefully engineered through leaks and intuition. Yet it was not easy. It required a studied simplicity and measured the reporter's personal integrity.

Jed Duvall, who covered the war for CBS and is now with ABC, reported on a volunteer helicopter unit with a high casualty rate, Charlie Horse. At the rear of the company's base camp, there was a chapel where the fallen men of Charlie Horse were remembered. In the story, taps play and prayers are offered in the chapel as Jed Duvall evokes the unit's courage and quiet dignity.[27]

The men of Charlie Horse had a deep suspicion of reporters. By staying with them, Jed Duvall and his cameraman Norman Floyd earned a measure of their trust. As Laurence put it, commenting on his own work, "Very much depended on how long you were with the unit and whether you melded with them, meshed with them."[28]

Laurence, his cameraman Keith Kay, and his soundman James Clevenger spent long periods in the field, but "melding" required more than time. A correspondent only stayed in the field because he was truly interested in the soldier's side of the war. It was the attitude that was dominant.

Laurence's and Duvall's stories were not unique. The image portrayed of the U.S. soldier was very positive, one of determination and courage. There were, of course, negative stories, but even the negative ones were carefully balanced.

In 1965, at the village of Cam Ne, Morley Safer's cameraman, Ha Thuc Can, photographed a marine setting the roof of a hooch on fire with a cigarette lighter and then with a flame thrower. Eventually 150 dwellings were destroyed.

"There is little doubt," Safer commented, "that American firepower can win a military victory. But to a Vietnamese peasant — whose home means a lifetime of backbreaking labor — it will take more than presidential promises to convince him that we are on his side."

Two weeks later, Safer filed another story from the same village when a second sweep was handled differently. Civilians were notified that the Marines were coming. Women and children were protected. Food and medical treatment were provided.

Safer had carefully returned to document that his first story was not the entire story and that the military was capable of learning. His commentary noted, "This is the type of action that could win them over."[29]

In September 1967, Don Webster filed a report on U.S. soldiers who were cutting the ears off the dead enemy. "This is not a pretty story," Webster stated. "In fact, it is an appalling one. What men will do under strain." Webster did not rush to condemn, but instead asked the viewer to understand the emotions of U.S. soldiers who had survived a bloody battle and seen their comrades slain. The soldiers were not the villain. The war was.[30]

Extraordinary heroism was the dominant image. Dean Brelis reported on the amputation of the leg of Marine colonel Michael Yunck. From the operating table, the colonel said:

I said hell, they can't be right around in there. So I didn't call bombs and napalm on these people. But that's where they were. I'm sure that's where they were. God damn it. I hate to put napalm on these women and children. I just didn't do it. I said, they can't be there.[31]

The year 1968 brought the Tet Offensive and the overwhelming image of a U.S. defeat in Vietnam. Despite the increasing doubts about the United States's overall strategic position in Vietnam, the picture of the individual U.S. soldier remained positive, even heroic.

Chet Huntley, reporting on the battle for the U.S. embassy in Saigon, was careful to note that "not a single guerrilla had actually penetrated the building." The film clips from Hue, on all three networks, showed marines risking death to help the wounded.[32]

Isolated acts of heroism, however, were hard to remember as Americans watched the North Vietnamese swing through the south in apparent victory. Network executives were aware that victory was elusive, but that awareness never made the nightly news.

Howard K. Smith of ABC, a hawk to the end of the war, once complained bitterly about the networks' coverage of the battle of Khe Sanh: "The Viet Cong casualties were one hundred times ours. But we never told [the public] that. We just showed pictures day after day of Americans getting the hell kicked out of them."[33]

Edward Jay Epstein, a leading scholar of television journalism, explained:

In late 1968, Jack Fem, a field producer for NBC, suggested to Robert T. Northshield [overall producer of the nightly news] a three-part series showing that Tet had indeed been a decisive military victory for America and that the media had exaggerated greatly the view that it was a defeat for South Vietnam. After some consideration the idea was rejected because, Northshield said later, Tet was already "established in the public's mind as a defeat, and therefore was an American defeat."[34]

There would be no looking back to sort out errors and to re-sharpen perceptions. The networks shaped defeat into a public perception. Having done that, they used the resulting opinions to justify the futility of taking a second look.

Television documentaries followed the same pattern. From 1966 through 1968, there would be several powerful studies of the U.S. soldier in Vietnam. A precursor was *Christmas in Vietnam*, a CBS film narrated by Charles Kuralt, which aired in December 1965.

The documentary was inspired by Edward R. Murrow's documentary on the Korean War, *Christmas in Korea*.

CBS led the networks. John Laurence chronicled the battle for *Hill 943* (June 4, 1968). In a rare example of international cooperation, CBS aired the French documentary *Anderson Platoon* in 1967.[35]

NBC aired *Vietnam: The Home Front* (April 1, 1966), which surveyed reaction to the war at home and its effect on the soldiers in Vietnam. On December 1, 1967, *Same Mud, Same Blood*, a documentary narrated by Frank McGee, looked at the black soldier in Vietnam fighting side by side with white soldiers.[36]

In 1970 Laurence completed his classic documentary, *The World of Charlie Company* (July 4, 1970). For four months, Laurence and his crew lived with the 100 Army riflemen of Company C, Charlie Company, filming them on maneuvers through Cambodia and Vietnam.

The film, however, did not initiate a new look at the war, then in its peak years. Instead, it was the coda, nearly the final network documentary word on the U.S. soldier in Vietnam.

In the early 1970s, several documentaries focused on the separate but important issues of the POWs and those missing in action. There were no companion documentaries on the life of the U.S. soldier in Vietnam fighting the final days of a war where victory was no longer the goal.[37]

The failure to address the U.S. soldier after 1968 was part of a larger trend in network documentaries. As Charles Montgomery Hammond, Jr., of the State University of New York at Morrisville, noted in his study of television documentaries, in 1968 the networks turned away from controversy — the so-called hard subjects — toward soft documentaries in general.

As Hammond noted, "Vietnam had something to do with this." A half-decade of strain had taken its toll:

> When hard news documentaries became too hard to take, they often were replaced by so-called soft subjects. The horrors of Vietnam and the excesses of Watergate were diminished by dramatic reenactments of the critical days in the careers of Presidents Truman and Kennedy, as if the tragic aftermath of Vietnam and the chaos of Watergate somehow could be overcome by showcasing appropriate national icons who could demonstrate more positive national leadership qualities than those manifested during the Johnson and Nixon years.[38]

There was one great exception to the nightly news and documentary decision to abandon stories about the U.S. soldier in Vietnam. On March 16, 1968, in a small skirmish practically unnoticed during the Tet Offensive, a task force, including a Lieutenant William L. Calley, stormed a distant village.

According to official reports, the operation was a success, killing more than 100 enemy soldiers. One year later, the truth would begin to emerge about the horrible massacre at My Lai. The massacre and Lieutenant Calley's trial became one of the war's leading stories. As late as March 17, 1973, two years after the verdict, ABC's *Reasoner Report* devoted an entire show to My Lai.[39]

In the rush to declare the Vietnam War over through stories on Vietnamization and the Paris Peace Talks, in the rush to judgment without second thought on Tet, in the rush to avoid controversy at any cost, the U.S. public was left with one climactic image of their soldiers in Vietnam — losing the Tet Offensive while massacring civilians at My Lai.

BLAMING THE MESSENGER

The United States saw two Vietnam Wars on the evening news. The first war ran through the end of 1967. It emphasized the U.S. soldier's courage. The second war began in late 1967. It emphasized diplomacy and politics. Forgetting the soldier in battle, the networks let Tet and My Lai shape the U.S. soldier's image.

Yet if there were two wars on television, the veterans themselves would return in time to catch just one, the second war. Although 3 million veterans served in Vietnam during the war years, only 200,000 had been discharged by the end of 1967. The overwhelming majority served after 1968.[40]

If the early coverage of the war, with its emphasis on the heroism of the U.S. soldier, encouraged any men to enlist, the stories they saw on the evening news when the soldiers returned from Vietnam were decidedly different. Nearly 60 percent of those who served in Vietnam, according to a Louis Harris poll done in 1979, felt that the television coverage was not positive. More than two-thirds, according to a special study done by Professor Anthony Adams, of California State University at Los Angeles, felt that the stories on My Lai helped shape the public's image of the U.S. soldier fighting in Vietnam.[41]

The conclusions of Vietnam veterans are not, perhaps, surprising. More surprising is the opinion of the majority of the general U.S. public. Despite Tet, despite My Lai, the Harris poll found that most Americans felt that television presented a positive picture of the U.S. soldier.[42]

Whatever the actual role of television coverage, Vietnam veterans know the final outcome. They were forgotten for a decade. The veterans are thus prepared to lay some of the blame on the nightly news broadcasts.

Whatever the actual role of television coverage, the people in the United States know what they would like to feel. They would like fond memories of their veterans, would like to thank them for their service, and would like to help them adjust. The public is prepared to assume that television is serving their finest aspirations.

By overwhelming margins, both the American people and the veterans themselves agree that television was important in shaping the public image of Vietnam veterans. They disagree completely on the image that the networks presented. The role of television in forming public opinion thus is clearly complex.[43]

On March 31, 1968, President Lyndon Johnson gave a major address on the Vietnam War. The horror of the Tet Offensive was sweeping the country. Eugene McCarthy had made a strong showing in the New Hampshire primary on March 12, and Robert Kennedy had announced his candidacy for the Democratic presidential nomination on March 16.

"There is a division in the American house now," the president noted at the close of his address. "There is divisiveness among us all tonight." The dispute over the war was threatening not merely the conduct of the war, the president suggested, but the nation itself. To meet that threat, he announced that he would not seek another term.[44]

It was an extraordinary statement, nearly unprecedented in U.S. history. In a press conference following the speech, the president repeatedly declined to elaborate on his decision. The next day, however, he gave a speech before the National Association of Broadcasters, which gave a glimpse into his mind:

> As I sat in my office last evening, waiting to speak, I thought of the many times each week when television brings the war into the American home.

No one can say exactly what effect those vivid scenes have on American opinion. Historians must only guess at the effect that television would have had during earlier conflicts on the future of this Nation:

— during the Korean War, for example, at that time when our forces were pushed back there to Pusan;

— or World War II, the Battle of the Bulge, or when our men were slugging it out in Europe, or when most of our Air Force was shot down in June 1942 off Australia.[45]

Vietnam was television's first war. The closest that Americans came to the battles of World War II was the weekly newsreels shown in movie theaters. During the Korean War, television was still a fledgling industry with a small audience. In 1950, there were television sets in just 9 percent of U.S. homes. In 1966, the figure was 93 percent.[46]

By the time of President Johnson's speech in April 1968, the nation was already divided over the war. By the end of 1968, the war policy makers themselves became committed to limiting the direct involvement of the United States. Intense controversy continued, but it swirled around the "how" and the "when" of withdrawal.

Had television helped to create the division President Johnson faced in 1968? Had the nature of this new medium biased coverage and helped turn the nation against the war during its crucial first years, before the policy became locked in public controversy? Apart from the issue of television's actual impact on the public image of Vietnam veterans lies the question of its impact on attitudes toward the war itself.

The World War II newsreels had been summaries of events. There was time for careful editing. Television covered the individual events of a single day, almost as they happened. However graphic the film footage, the format of the newsreels kept events of World War II at a distance. Television's sharper focus brought events up close.

The question of how graphic stories should be was known as the "taste issue." During most of the Vietnam War, the networks adopted a policy of restricted coverage. In the words of Fred Friendly, former president of CBS News, the networks would "shield the audience from the true horror of war."[47]

The policy of restricted coverage, however, changed over time. The Vietnam War forced an evolution in network attitudes. What was acceptable at the beginning of the war was much milder than what was accepted at the end.

Robert MacNeil recalled his experiences as an editor for NBC during the earlier war years:

> We had a producer who said one particular night, when we decided not to show American soldiers cutting the ears off dead Vietnamese and taking them as trophies — which was a thing that CBS six months later did, in fact, show — but we decided not to that evening because the producer said, "After all, we go on the air at supper time, and there are things we can't show."[48]

Looking back over the war, David Brinkley concluded that Vietnam was "the first uncensored war we ever had. . . . People have grown up thinking of wars — and those who have not been in them have grown up thinking of them in terms of Gary Cooper in uniform and handsome military units charging forward, and a bugle blowing, all very gallant and very grand." Television brought home a different war: muddy, bloody, and brutal.[49]

Michael Arlen, television critic for *The New Yorker*, wondered nevertheless if the television coverage was actually as real or as intense as is commonly assumed:

> They are also made less "real" — diminished, in part, by the physical size of the television screen, which, for all the industry's advances, still shows one a picture of men three inches tall shooting at other men three inches tall, and trivialized, or at least tamed, by the enveloping cozy alarums of the household.[50]

Assuming television did bring home the horror of the war, that was not the only implication of the new medium. Newspapers can cover the details of events on the back pages, seeking depth and balance, but television had to fit all of the world's events into no more than 30 minutes.

That simply cannot be done, forcing television news to function as a kind of headline service. The constant drive for compression, noted critic Michael Arlen, required a constant distortion of the facts that lent support to the war effort:

> The cumulative effect of all these three- and five-minute film clips, with their almost unvarying implicit deference to the importance of purely military solutions (despite a few commentators' disclaimers to the contrary) and with their catering (in part unavoidably) to a popular democracy's insistent desire to view even as unbelievably complicated

a war as this one in emotional terms (our guys against their guys), is surely wide of the mark, and is bound to provide these millions of people with an excessively simple, emotional and military-oriented view of what is, at best, a mightily unsimple situation.[51]

Nor were the television reporters themselves opposed to the war. Walter Cronkite at CBS, who had the second largest share of the market, strongly supported the war up until the Tet Offensive. The market leader Chet Huntley at NBC was a hawk throughout, as was Howard K. Smith at ABC. Huntley even narrated an official Navy film, *American Navy in Vietnam 1967.*[52]

Professors Raymond Carroll of the University of Alabama and Lawrence Lichty of the University of Maryland have studied the attitude toward the war of the guests on network news-interview programs. There was no evidence of an antiwar bias here either. "Until 1969," Carroll and Lichty conclude, "the overall tone of network news-interviews programs was neutral-to-positive."[53]

Newsweek found in 1967 that 64 percent of the Americans surveyed felt that the television coverage of the war had made them *more* supportive of the war effort. Those results led *Newsweek* to conclude: "TV has encouraged a decisive majority of viewers to support the war." [54]

If the impact of television on the public image of Vietnam veterans is unclear, the impact of television on the public's attitude toward the war itself is doubly so.

Vietnam was television's first war. It may be its last. The Reagan administration successfully barred the press from the invasion of Grenada. Americans learned the battle details of that war only later, through catch-up journalism when the war was over and television crews were allowed on the island.

Asked to explain the decision, Secretary of State George P. Schultz, one of the administration's most respected figures, suggested, "It seems as though the reporters are always against us and so they're always seeking to report something that's going to screw things up." Grenada, the secretary suggested, might not be the last time reporters were excluded from the battlefield.[55]

Whatever the facts of the complex story of television's influence on Vietnam War policy, Secretary Schultz probably overstated his case. Nevertheless, the Reagan administration's decision was not unique. The Begin government of Israel successfully barred the press from Israel's invasion of Lebanon. The Thatcher government of Great Britain barred the press from the invasion of the Falkland Islands.

Television's impact on public attitudes toward the Vietnam War is decidedly unclear, but its political legacy is not. It is hard to blame television for reporting the doubts about the war that swept the country after 1968, but the messenger has nevertheless been blamed. Whatever the facts, the war's history is now the implicit justification for a new censorship.

PRIME TIME

While Vietnam veterans were waiting to recapture the attention of network news executives, they were discovered by television producers seeking to fill out the plots of action dramas. It would be some time, however, before their new stardom would return any benefits.

As Larry Lichty noted: "Television drama depicted, it did for a time depict, the Vietnam vet as a bad guy, a crazy guy. He took the place of the Mafia. . . . The guy, you know, who held people hostage because he couldn't get a job, got fired by the railroad company, was a Vietnam vet."

In a 1976 *S.W.A.T.* episode, "Soldier on the Hill," for example, a deranged Vietnam veteran suffers a violent flashback while on a tour of a movie studio. The Vietnam cliché did not die easily. It continued for years.

CHiPs had a 1981 episode, "Hawk and the Hunter," which featured another troubled Vietnam veteran who resorts to violence to halt the spraying of pesticides. A heavily armed Vietnam veteran captured Jim McClain in "The Last Hero," a 1981 episode of the series *McClain's Law*.

One industry source explained the cliché. There is a saying, he noted, that there are only 100 plots in TV, and producers just keep using them over and over. The psychotic Vietnam veteran meant that writers did not have to develop a motive for bizarre behavior. Without "wasting" time on character development, the executive said, they could go directly to the "shoot-em-ups." All the action shows, he continued, "had at least one character in at least one episode like that."

The material was at hand for a serious look at Vietnam veterans, but the networks were hesitant to seize the opportunity. In 1973, CBS was scheduled to air a special produced by Joseph Papp. Entitled "Sticks and Bones," it was a classic drama of one Vietnam veteran's bitter homecoming, written by David Rabe. Fred Zimmerman reportedly told Papp that the show was headed for an Emmy.

Network affiliates, however, feared the show's potential for controversy, and CBS pushed the show out of a prime time slot. Joseph Papp, in an act of protest rare to the Vietnam era, broke with CBS over the incident.[56]

In 1974, ABC rejected a script written by a Canadian correspondent who had covered Vietnam, *P.O.W.* by David Wolper. The script was considered too graphic in its portrayal of the psychological torture of Air Force prisoners.[57]

Only in 1979 would the use of Vietnam veterans as an excuse for violence begin to be replaced with a deeper characterization that sought to be neither exploitative nor cheaply flattering. Two shows played a particularly important role. Both CBS's *Lou Grant* and ABC's *Barney Miller* broke important ground by including a Vietnam veteran as a regular character: Wojo in *Barney Miller* (played by Max Gail), and Adam Wilson, the business editor, in *Lou Grant* (played by Alan Williams).

In "Agent Orange," a *Barney Miller* show that aired originally in December 1980, a Vietnam veteran is arrested for holding up a liquor store. The show portrays the veteran as one who uses problems caused by the war as facile excuses for his own failures.

While Wojo is disdainful of the veteran's deadbeat attitude, he is also puzzled by the issue of Agent Orange, which Wojo learns of for the first time from the veteran. Wojo seeks answers from the VA, the Air Force, and a chemical company.

Instead of receiving honest information, Wojo finds that officials are preoccupied with protecting themselves at each other's expense. Even stoical, never-get-upset-about-anything Wojo finally reacts, capturing the frustration of Vietnam veterans across the country: "When you think about this, it could make you angry."

The producers of "Agent Orange" had done careful research, including interviews with Vietnam veterans and veteran groups. "Vet," the *Lou Grant* show that aired originally on January 15, 1979, was written with equal care. Gene Reynolds, its executive producer and co-creator, explained that the script was based on extensive interviews with Vietnam veterans, government personnel, and private counselors.

The episode carefully captured the slow reaction of the nation's media to Vietnam veterans. In a key early scene, the editors of the show's *Los Angeles Tribune* explore the idea of a story on Vietnam veterans:

> Lou Grant: You ever think of Vietnam?
>
> Charlie Hume (a senior editor): You mean the war? Not if I can help it.
>
> Lou: I think there's a story there.
>
> Charlie: Lou, we had the Vietnam War on the front page for over seven years. You think there's really something more to be said that hasn't already been chewed over?
>
> Lou: Well, yeah. We had the war on the front page, but I'm not talking about the war. I'm talking about the veteran. And I don't think their story's been told.
>
> Charlie (reflectively): The question occurs to me — is anyone interested anymore?
>
> Lou: Is that the question, or is that the problem? Either way it's a hell of a story.

The paper does do a story. In a final scene, the editors are again discussing the now completed Vietnam veteran story. For the first time, they learn that Adam, their colleague, is a Vietnam veteran:

> National Editor: Yeah, that's what I don't understand. A war's a war. It's these vets who are acting so different.
>
> Adam: Vietnam was different.
>
> (A beat. Something in his tone makes them pause.)
>
> Charlie: Adam, you were in Vietnam?
>
> Adam: Yeah.
>
> Charlie: You never told me.
>
> Adam: Nothing to tell.
>
> Lou: A reporter or in combat?
>
> Adam: Combat.
>
> Foreign Editor: Well, doesn't your being here belie everything in Lou's series? I mean, here you are, successful at a young age, an editor for a good newspaper?

Adam: Yeah, I'm here. Maybe someday I'll tell you how close I came to being one of those guys. I feel like I know all of them. It's a good series, Lou. Thanks.

Friendly Fire, an ABC made-for-TV movie, aired in April 1979. It is the story of the Mullin family, whose eldest son was killed by a U.S. artillery shell (friendly fire) in Vietnam. The Pentagon's failure to give the Mullins an honest explanation for their son's death starts a family odyssey of personal anguish and antiwar protest.

The movie resists romanticizing either the war or those who opposed the war. It sticks instead to a direct narration of one family's private struggle to separate personal grief from outrage over public policy, one family's discovery that their convictions separate them from their neighbors.

Even today, the anguish of the war continues. Fay Kanin, the acclaimed author of the screenplay, described visiting the Mullin family:

> About seven or eight of us sat down in a lunch place with John [Mullin], and our assistant director said he was paying the bill. The men at the bar said to him, "Who are all of these folks with John?" And he said, "We're movie people. We're going to do a movie." And he said, "Oh, you don't make a movie about that. Those Mullins, you know, half of that stuff wasn't true." . . . They felt that the Mullins had in some way, I guess, even disgraced the town.

Friendly Fire won four Emmys, including the award for Outstanding Drama or Comedy Special and the award for Outstanding Directing in a Limited Series or a Special. "Vet," the Lou Grant episode, won the coveted Humanitas Award and received an award from the Department of Labor.

By 1979, TV was beginning to rediscover the war and its veteran. In 1979, NBC aired *When Hell Was in Session*, a made-for-TV movie based on Admiral Jeremiah Denton's harrowing years in a Vietnam prison camp. In 1980, CBS broadcast *Children of An Lac* and *A Rumor of War*, a two-part, four-hour miniseries based on Philip Caputo's book. In 1981, ABC broadcast *Fly Away Home*, a made-for-TV movie about a combat cameraman.

In time, even the prime-time action shows would abandon the old cliché and use Vietnam veterans as positive characters. Both

Magnum, P.I. and *The A-Team* are built around a squad of Vietnam veterans. *Trapper John, M.D.*, *Riptide, Simon and Simon*, and *Manimal*, among others, all feature Vietnam veterans in positive leading roles. Characteristically, in the first regular episode of *Hardcastle and McCormick*, we are carefully told that Judge Hardcastle's son had died in Vietnam.

The network failure to give Vietnam veterans positive attention until 1979 came at a heavy price. The negative cliché of Vietnam veterans as disturbed killers operated in a vacuum left by the nightly news decision to turn away from combat stories and the heroism of the U.S. soldier in Vietnam. It reinforced the final image of U.S. men in combat left by the coverage of My Lai and the Tet offensive.

Prime time shows and the nightly news were acting in tandem. Television dramas featuring berserk Vietnam veterans implicitly proclaimed that My Lai was the norm and that Lieutenant Calley was indeed the characteristic Vietnam veteran. The image of lost veterans, unable to win in civilian life, seemed to suggest that Vietnam veterans were indeed responsible for the U.S. defeat in Vietnam. The action dramas brought to life the assumptions seemingly implicit in the nightly news broadcast while the nightly news gave credibility to the action dramas.

NOTES

1. Larry Lichty, "The Night at the End of the Tunnel," *Film Comment*, July- August 1975, pp. 32-35, at p. 32.

2. George Bailey, "Television War: Trends in Network Coverage of Vietnam 1965-1970," *Journal of Broadcasting*, 20:2, Spring 1976, pp. 147-158.

3. See Lawrence Lichty's comments in the symposium *Vietnam War on TV*, April 5, 12, and 18, 1978, sponsored by the National Archives, on April 5, and Larry Lichty, "The War We Watched on TV: A Study in Progress," *AFI Quarterly*, Volume 4, Number 4, Winter 1973, pp. 29-37, at p. 30.

4. Lawrence W. Lichty and George A. Bailey, "Violence in Television News: A Case Study of Audience Response," *Central State Speech Journal*, Volume 23, Number 4, Winter 1972, pp. 225-229, at p. 226.

5. George Bailey, "Television War: Trends in Network Coverage of Vietnam 1965-1970," op. cit., especially p. 150.

6. From approximately August 1965 through August 1970, the Pentagon filmed television sets tuned to the nightly network news shows. The tapes were then edited to contain only the war coverage. Although it is generally

believed that the Pentagon editing produced a series that emphasized the coverage of the war in Vietnam as opposed to the domestic events surrounding the war, the resulting reels, called Kinescopes, are our *only* record of the TV news coverage of the war until 1968, when the Vanderbilt archives were begun, and the 1970s when the networks began to record their news shows. Although a sense of relative chronology is maintained through the reels, the Kinescopes do not provide dates for the shows taped. Many of the stories referenced in this chapter were viewed on the Kinescopes and transcribed, as were these two stories by Bruce Morton and Walter Cronkite. They are footnoted with "Kinescopes."

7. George Bailey, "Television War: Trends in Network Coverage of Vietnam 1965-1970," op. cit., especially p. 150.

8. Kinescopes.

9. Ibid.

10. Ibid.

11. Nessen's story is from the Kinescopes. For his later comment, see *Vietnam War on TV*, op. cit., April 12, 1978.

12. Don Oberdorfer, *Tet!* (Doubleday & Co.: New York, 1971), and Peter Braestrup, *Big Story: How the American Press and Television Reported and Interpreted the Crisis of Tet 1968 in Vietnam and Washington* (Anchor Books: Garden City, New York, 1968).

13. George Bailey, "Television War: Trends in Network Coverage of Vietnam 1965-1970," op. cit., p. 162.

14. Edward Jay Epstein, "Vietnam: What Happened vs. What We Saw," *TV Guide*, (three parts), September 29, 1973, pp. 7-10; October 6, 1973, pp. 20-23; October 13, 1973, pp. 49-54; at p. 51 in the October 13 article.

15. Edward Jay Epstein, *News from Nowhere: Television and the News* (Random House: New York, 1973), p. 17.

16. The comparison is between the figures given by Lawrence Lichty for the later period, *Vietnam War on TV*, op. cit., April 18, 1978, and the early period figures of George Bailey, "Television War: Trends in Network Coverage of Vietnam 1965-1970," op. cit., p. 155.

17. See Larry Lichty, "The Night at the End of the Tunnel," op. cit.

18. *20/20* aired Vietnam veterans pieces on July 25, 1978, (Geraldo Rivera, Agent Orange), August 1, 1978, (Geraldo Rivera, Agent Orange), December 18, 1978, (Sylvia Chase, VA hospital care), January 8, 1979, (Geraldo Rivera, Agent Orange), July 15, 1980, (Geraldo Rivera, Agent Orange), November 13, 1980, (Sylvia Chase, delayed stress), and May 28, 1981, (Sylvia Chase). *60 Minutes* did "Looking Back," November 11, 1979, Mike Wallace; "Memory of Vietnam," May 25, 1980, Mike Wallace; "Soldier of Misfortune," February 13, 1983, Mike Wallace; "Lest We Forget," October 10, 1982, Morley Safer; "Vietnam '82," November 14, 1982, Mike Wallace.

19. CBS documentaries, in chronological order, included: *Charlie Company at Home: The Veterans of Vietnam*, January 17, 1978, Bruce Morton; *Look Up and Live*, May 28, 1978, Alan Harper; *Vietnam Today: The Problem of Peace*, June 30, 1981, Dan Rather; *Bittersweet Memories: A Vietnam*

Reunion, December 12, 1981, Bill Moyers; *The Uncounted Enemy: A Vietnam Deception*, January 23, 1982, Mike Wallace and Walter Cronkite.

20. NBC, apparently, did almost nothing. *Tomorrow: Coast to Coast* did a series entitled *Vietnam: America's Broken Promise* on July 6, 7, 8, and 9, 1981. *NBC Nightly News*, like the other nightly news shows, did a series on one Vietnam veterans-issue, delayed stress, which aired January 29, 30 and 31, 1979. In addition to *Vietnam Memorial*, PBS also aired *The Vietnam Veteran: A Matter of Life and Death*, November 11, 1981, which included the controversial documentary *Frank: A Portrait of a Vietnam Veteran*. Regular news shows, like *The Lawmakers*, also focused on Vietnam veterans issues.

21. With the help of the Television Information Center of the National Association of Broadcasters in New York, a geographically representative sample of the major U.S. TV markets was selected. In each market, the news director or program director of the three major networks was asked if the station had produced and aired, since the early 1960s, a series dealing with Vietnam veterans. It was assumed that local documentaries would be rare and that a series was, accordingly, a more appropriate form to study. There was no avoiding the fact that television stations, on the whole, do not keep adequate records. Some stations had no programming records prior to 1975, for example. Others were just then beginning to keep any sort of programming records. In other cases, what records did exist traveled with the producer-reporter who did the series. Therefore, in a few cases, information received was basically the product of the newsrooms' collective memory rather than of more reassuring documents.

22. In New York, the NBC affiliate, WNBC, had done no series. The ABC affiliate, WABC, had done one, a five-part series on VA hospital care, *VA: Hell for Heroes*. The CBS affiliate, WCBS, had done none. In Washington, D.C., both the NBC affiliate, WRC, and the ABC affiliate, WJLA, reported no series. The CBS affiliate, WDVM, had done a five-part series called *Viet Vets* on how veterans coped with coming home. In Atlanta, the CBS affiliate, WAGA, reported no series. The NBC affiliate, WXIA, reported two series: *Forgotten Vet*, a five-part series; and *Vetathon*, a special two-day call-in program. The ABC affiliate, WSB, reported two series: a five-part series on the VA hospital in Atlanta, and a five-part series called *Vets*. In Detroit, the NBC affiliate, WDIV, reported no series, but "Sonya," a daytime talk show produced locally, had done several shows on Vietnam veterans issues. The ABC affiliate, WXYZ, has done three series, an initial five-part series on the problems facing veterans on their return home and two follow-up series. The CBS affiliate, WJBK, did an Agent Orange series. In San Francisco, the ABC affiliate, KGO, and the CBS affiliate, KPIX, did not do a series, although KPIX ran a public service announcement on jobs for veterans for more than a year. The NBC affiliate, KRON, ran the award-winning series, *The War Within*.

23. Larry Lichty, "The War We Watched on TV: A Study in Progress," op. cit., p. 36.

24. See Lawrence Lichty's comment in the symposium, *Vietnam War on TV*, op. cit., April 12, 1978.

25. Kinescopes.

26. *Vietnam War on TV*, op. cit., April 5, 1978.

27. Kinescopes.

28. *Vietnam War on TV*, op. cit., April 5, 1978.

29. Both stories are reported from the Kinescopes.

30. Ibid.

31. Ibid.

32. Ibid.

33. Edward Jay Epstein, "Vietnam: What Happened vs. What We Saw," op. cit., October 6, 1973, p. 23.

34. Ibid.

35. The CBS documentaries included *Christmas in Vietnam*, December 1965, Charles Kuralt; *The Battle for the Ia Drang Valley*, December 1965, Walter Cronkite and Morley Safer; *The Anti-Americans*, June 7, 1966, Harry Morgan and John Sharnick; *Westmoreland on Vietnam*, December 27, 1966, Morley Safer and Charles Collingwood; *Saigon*, March 14, 1967, produced by Beryl Fox; *The People of South Vietnam*, March 21, 1967; *Morley Safer's Vietnam: A Personal Report*, April 4, 1967; *Anderson Platoon*, July 1967, French production; *Viet Cong*, February 20, 1968, Bernard Kalb; *Report from Hanoi*, April 6, 1968, Charles Collingwood; *Hill 943*, June 4, 1968, John Laurence; *A Timetable for Vietnam*, December 2, 1969, Charles Collingwood; *The World of Charlie Company*, July 14, 1970, John Laurence.

36. NBC documentaries include *Vietnam: It's a Mad War*, December 1, 1964, Chet Huntley; *Vietnam: December 1965*, December 20, 1965, Chet Huntley and Frank McGee; *Vietnam: The Home Front*, April 1, 1966, Frank McGee; *Vietnam Report: A New Phase*, June 30, 1966; *Raymond Burr Visits Vietnam*, October 6, 1967; *Same Mud, Same Blood*, December 1, 1967, Frank McGee; *Vietnam and After: What Should We Do?* February 1, 1968; *The Road to Vietnam: Why and How We Got There*, December 21, 1971, produced by Fred Freed. ABC did few documentaries, except for the *Reasoner Report* listed below. ABC's *Scope* (later, *ABC Scope: The War in Vietnam*) ran from 1966 through 1968. There were two *ABC Special Reports* about the POW issue, listed below.

37. *The Prisoners of War Return*, February 12, 1973, *ABC Special Reports*; *POWs Arrive in San Diego*, February 13, 1973, *ABC Special Reports*; *Staying Sane in the Hanoi Hilton*, April 7, 1973, *Reasoner Report*; *The Men We've Left Behind*, June 2, 1973, *Reasoner Report*; *POWs: The Black Homecoming*, July 27, 1973, Gregory Jackson, an ABC documentary. *The Reasoner Report* also did a documentary entitled *She's Still My Sister*, July 14, 1973, on a war protester and her veteran brother, and another entitled *The Land We Left Behind*, March 17, 1973.

38. Charles Montgomery Hammond, Jr., *The Image Decade: Television Documentary, 1965-1976* (Hasting House: New York, 1981), pp. 70 and 251.

39. See Peter Braestrup, *The Big Story*, op. cit., pp. 249-253, and Seymour M. Hersh's two books, *My Lai 4: A Report on the Massacre and its Aftermath* (Random House: Clinton, Mass., 1970) and *Cover-Up* (Random House: Clinton, Mass., 1972).

40. *Data on Vietnam Era Veterans*, Veterans Administration, Office of Reports and Statistics, September 1981, p. 18.

41. *Myths and Realities: A Study of Attitudes Toward Vietnam Veterans*, conducted by Louis Harris and Associates, Inc., for the Veterans Administration, July 1980, reprinted by the Veterans Administration, p. 163; and Anthony A. Adams, "A Study of Veteran Viewpoints on TV Coverage of the Vietnam War," *Journalism Quarterly*, Volume 54, Summer 1977, pp. 248-253.

42. *Myths and Realities: A Study of Attitudes Toward Vietnam Veterans*, op. cit., p. 163.

43. Ibid., p. 162.

44. *Public Papers of the Presidents of the United States, Lyndon B. Johnson, 1968-1969* (in two books), (United States Government Printing Office: Washington, 1970), entry 170, March 31, 1968, p. 475.

45. Ibid., entry 172, April 1, 1968, p. 484.

46. Cobbett S. Steinberg, *TV Facts* (Facts on File, Inc.: New York), p. 142.

47. Edward Jay Epstein, "Vietnam: What Happened vs. What We Saw," op. cit., September 29, 1973, p. 10. The taste issue was at the heart of the coverage of one of the war's most graphic scenes: the execution in the street with a pistol of a captured Viet Cong officer. The story has been studied in detail by George Bailey and Lawrence W. Lichty, "Rough Justice on a Saigon Street: A Gatekeeper's Study of NBC's Tet Execution Film," *Journalism Quarterly*, Summer 1972, pp. 221-238.

48. The story was told during Dick Cavett's three-part series on TV reporting. Show numbers 5011 through 5013, originally broadcast on November 2, 1981 through November 4, 1981. The shows were rebroadcast on September 20, 1982 through September 22, 1982 and on June 27, 1982 through June 29, 1982. The show was broadcast by PBS.

49. Ibid.

50. Michael H. Arlen, *Living Room War* (The Viking Press, Inc.: New York, 1969), p. 8.

51. Ibid., pp. 7-8. See also Tom Shales, "Reliving 'The Living Room War,'" *Washington Post*, October 4, 1979; and George Bailey, "Interpretive Reporting of the Vietnam War by Anchormen," *Journalism Quarterly*, Summer 1976, pp. 319-324.

52. See Peter Braestrup, *Big Story*, op. cit. Braestrup documents the evolution of Cronkite's views at length. See especially, p. 493. See also Edward Jay Epstein, "Vietnam: What Happened vs. What We Saw," op. cit., September 22, 1973, p. 6.

53. Raymond Carroll and Lawrence Lichty, "Network News-Interview Programs and the 'Television War,'" presented at the Annual Convention of the Association for Education in Journalism, Radio-TV Journalism Division, East Lansing, Mich., August 10, 1981, p. 5.

54. Edward Jay Epstein, "Vietnam: What Happened vs. What We Saw," op. cit., September 29, 1973, p. 7.

55. Margaret Shapiro, "Schultz Defends Press Ban: Hints at Future News Blackouts," *Washington Post*, December 16, 1983.

56. Tom Shales, "Reliving 'The Living Room War,'" op. cit.

57. Andrew Laskos, "Why Are We in Vietnam Again?" *Emmy: The Magazine of the Academy of Television Arts and Sciences*, Spring 1979, pp. 22-25, 51-52, at p. 24.

2   Newspapers

REPORTERS IN THE FIELD

In 1964, Jim Lucas, a reporter for the Scripps-Howard newspaper chain, noted that he "was the only correspondent regularly assigned to working and living with combat troops . . . this is the only war of recent memory which has not been covered to saturation."[1] In mid-1964, there were only around 20 U.S. and foreign correspondents in Saigon.

Perhaps it is not surprising that during the early period of U.S. involvement, most local newspaper coverage of the war came from the major wire services and the leading national papers. Yet even with the commitment of U.S. ground troops in March 1965, many large U.S. newspapers and chains did not have reporters in Vietnam, including the huge Gannett and Newhouse chains and both Chicago papers.[2]

If Vietnam was television's first war, posing a host of new problems, newspapers had a longer tradition. Nonetheless, the papers were hesitant in committing resources to cover the war. Peter Braestrup, who covered the war for the *New York Times* and the *Washington Post*, explained:

> Then, as now, cable charges and other costs made foreign coverage expensive and — it was widely felt — not worth it in terms of selling papers. Moreover, service abroad was not part of the professional experience of most American news executives — those who allocate

budgets — or of many of the harried telegraph editors forced to choose among wire traffic from abroad, Washington, and nearby states. American newspapers are primarily locally oriented businesses, and resources are allocated accordingly.[3]

As the number of U.S. soldiers in Vietnam grew, reaching 500,000 in 1967, the U.S. press corps expanded proportionately. Yet few correspondents covered the soldier in the field. Peter Braestrup added:

> One of the striking things about the coverage of the war was — it was kind of like the Army itself — it was a small group that was actually out in the field. . . . The number of correspondents who actually saw, lived with, understood the life of an American GI over there was very small.

The problem was not the danger or difficulty of covering action in the field. The Vietnam War, in many ways, was easier to cover than were earlier wars. As Charles Mohr, a reporter who covered the war first for *Time* and then for the *New York Times*, noted: "It was very convenient for correspondents to cover because of the transport and because of communications on the so-called 'tiger telephone' network. You could phone stories in."

The real difficulty was the huge gap between the soldier and the reporter, a gap measured in age, education, and background. Peter Braestrup concluded:

> I think there was a class problem for a number of people who came over there, particularly people who had gone to fairly good schools, and they felt more comfortable talking to State Department people. . . . They didn't feel comfortable around the military. There was a whole different culture — a whole different world — and many of them did not bother to understand it.

There were differences, but the differences could be overcome by a sense of humor, if nothing else. Charles Mohr recalled:

> I remember getting off a helicopter with Jack Laurence of CBS in a Marine camp called Cantienne, which was under siege in 1967 and being shelled, and the first thing we did after we got off the helicopter was jump in a hole, and there were a couple of Marines in there and they said, "Jesus, a couple of these reporters," and they said, "Do you

want some beer or something better?" And I was so square, I said, "Well, what's better?" And Laurence just rolled his eyes upward, and then pretty soon that odor of marijuana began to waft up. That was 1967, and you know I wasn't all that square. But there was to some extent that generation gap.

Reporting from the field, however, caught the papers' attention for only a few short years. At the newspapers, like at the television networks, the novelty of the U.S. soldier fighting in a foreign jungle wore thin. By late 1968, Peter Braestrup noted, "Hero stories were off the menu." He explained:

People didn't really care about the war or understand it. When I say people, we mean our peers, our editors, because their sons weren't in the war. . . . By and large, the people who were in the war were that strata of society whose fathers were not in government, or newspaper editors, or publishers, or magazine editors, and if their sons were in the war there would be intense interest, intense involvement, and because their sons weren't, you could easily separate yourself from the whole thing. It was very significant.

Along with Vietnam veterans, those reporters who had struggled to cover the Vietnam battlefield were left alone with a story no one wanted to hear. Bernard Weinraub covered the war for the *New York Times*. He recalled:

In terms of readjustment problems, I think everybody went through readjustment problems, like veterans, in terms of coming back and being stunned at how little everybody knew and basically how little everybody – unless they had family there or had sons involved – cared. I mean, this didn't just stretch to people on the streets, it stretched to newspaper editors – people who were your bosses – people who should know.

At the war's beginning, the locally dominated newspaper community had been uncertain of their readers' interest in distant Vietnam. Once they had been convinced to give the war serious attention, only a handful of reporters would ever actually write about the Vietnam battlefield. In just a few years, even those stories declined.

There would continue, of course, to be some stories. The most graphic exception was a *Life* piece for June 1969. In a powerful,

16-page portfolio, the story ran the faces, the names, and the hometowns of the 242 American men killed in Vietnam during one week of fighting.

The pictures were accompanied by an essay that suggested something of the war's impact on its soldiers:

> Writing his family just before the time he was scheduled to return to the U.S., a California man said, "I could be standing on the doorstep on the 8th [of June]. . . . As you can see from my shaky printing, the strain of getting 'short' is getting to me, so I'll close now." The ironies and sad coincidences of time hang everywhere. One Pfc. from the 101st Airborne was killed on his 21st birthday. A waiting bride had just bought her own wedding ring. A mother got flowers ordered by her son and then learned he had died the day before they arrived. A Texan had just signed up for a second two-year tour of duty when he was killed, and his ROTC instructor back home remembered with great affection that the boy, a flag-bearer, had stumbled a lot. In the state of Oregon a soldier was buried in a grave shared by the body of his brother, who had died in Vietnam two years earlier. A lieutenant was killed serving the battalion his father had commanded two years ago. A man from Colorado noted in his last letter that the Marines preferred captured North Vietnamese mortars to their own because they were lighter and much more accurate. At four that afternoon he was killed by enemy mortar fire.[4]

Fighting in Vietnam, Charles Mohr remembered, was "an extremely traumatic and weird experience. You know, people were coming back [to their base camps] and seeing movies and then going out and fight." True enough, but the nation would not understand, for the Vietnam veteran had already begun to disappear while the war was still under way.

Charles Mohr concluded: "A big failure of journalism, I think in retrospect now — and I'm not just polishing apples for you — is probably a lot more should have been written about what was happening to young men during those 12 month tours of duties."

FORGOTTEN PROMISES

During the 1970s, America was in a rush first to end, and then to forget, the Vietnam War and the turmoil it created. The deep national unease about the war was made clear by the polls. As early as 1972, Louis Harris found that 61 percent of America agreed that Vietnam was a war "we could never win." A full 49 percent went even further. They felt that Vietnam veterans "were made suckers, having to risk their lives in the wrong war, in the wrong place, at the wrong time."[5]

As businessmen in the marketplace of public opinion, the managers of the U.S. media could not directly fight the nation's rush to forget the Vietnam War. Seemingly, people wanted to end the nation's nightmare in Southeast Asia. As the concept of Manifest Destiny stirred national jingoistic feelings at the turn of the century, during the 1970s the national psyche demanded a retreat from international adventurism, a retreat from Vietnam. Unable to separate the Vietnam veteran from the Vietnam War, a retreat from the war brought a retreat from our veterans.

When "hero stories went off the menu" in 1968, they were not replaced by stories about the needs and character of the returning Vietnam veteran. During the early 1970s, two rounds of debate over the GI Bill prompted the normal set of Washington stories, but they focused on the legislative process and its actors, not on the veteran and his needs. Otherwise, there was near silence, broken only by the regular Veterans Day or Memorial Day features.

The great exception was the *Washington Post*. The *Post* gave Vietnam veteran issues both early and broad coverage. Beginning in the late 1960s, coverage of daily events in Washington was reinforced in the *Post* with editorials and columns by the paper's leading journalists.

Because the debate over Vietnam veteran policy was preeminently a Congressional story, the dominance of the *Post* is partly understandable. Yet eyewitness observers felt that there was more at play. The *Post* was sensitive to the concerns of Vietnam veterans because its leadership was unusually close to veteran problems.

Peter Braestrup, who wrote for several papers during this period, including the *Post*, and was himself a Marine Corps veteran of the Korean War, suggested:

> The *Post* was interested because the managing editor had been a veteran – the editor of the editorial page had been a veteran. Some of the other executives had been veterans – Harwood, Bradlee, Geyelin – all combat veterans of one kind or another, and so they were interested in the veteran.

Braestrup's list catches only some of the figures at the *Post* who wrote important early stories. Leading columnists like Haynes Johnson and David S. Broder, staff writers like Tim O'Brien (who is a Vietnam veteran), as well as Braestrup himself, added important pieces. As early as 1969, *Post* writer William Greider wrote one of the first major stories on the inadequacy of the Vietnam GI Bill.[6]

The *Post*'s early coverage was exceptional, but it was not unique. Although the combined efforts of individual reporters at the *New York Times* never produced the almost institutional commitment present in the *Post* newsroom, John Herbers, Drummond Ayres, and John Nordheimer produced a set of important and detailed early articles. At the *Evening Star and Daily News* (later named the *Washington Star*), Mary McGrory wrote striking pieces, as did William Steif for the Scripps-Howard chain.[7]

In 1977, Philip Geyelin, a Marine veteran of the Korean War who had edited the *Post* editorial page since 1968, began a long series of editorials and columns with Coleman McCarthy, an editorial writer and columnist. The first editorial ran the entire length of the editorial page. (It is reprinted in the appendix.) In just over one year, there would be some 30 editorials and columns. (The appendix includes a list.)

Such an extended and persistent commitment is rare in editorial writing. The extraordinary series written by Geyelin and McCarthy raised the level of debate on Vietnam veteran issues and captured the attention of other papers, helping to generate coverage across the country on Vietnam veteran issues.

The *Washington Post* editorial series marked a new era in the coverage of Vietnam veterans. In fact, it marked the beginning of the first era in which Vietnam veterans would receive sustained attention. The *Boston Globe* ran a second important series of editorials under the leadership of editorial writer Kirk Scharfenberg.[8] By 1979, local and regional papers across the country were printing long feature stories and giving Vietnam veteran issues editorial attention.[9]

The support for Vietnam veterans cut across ideological lines. In Michigan, the progressive *Detroit Free Press*, edited by Joseph Stroud, as well as the more conservative *Detroit News*, were both quick to give support to Vietnam veterans. Among smaller papers, both Mitch Kehetian, editor of the conservative *Macomb Daily*, and Bernard P. Lyons, editor of the moderate *Port Huron Times*

Herald, gave Vietnam veterans special attention.

The *Atlantic Monthly* helped focus the nation's attention with a major article in early 1978, "Soldiers of Misfortune," by Tracy Kidder. Marlene Cimons, at the *Los Angeles Times*, wrote a classic series exploring "delayed stress" in 1979. That same year, *Life* sought out soldiers from their combat photos and contrasted the combat scenes with poignant pictures of the veterans now.[10]

These articles painted a disturbing picture of the problems facing Vietnam veterans. As many as 40 to 50 percent of combat veterans faced serious readjustment problems. For too many, readjustment difficulties were compounded by drug addiction and an estimated 1.4 million had serious drinking problems. Unemployment among Vietnam veterans remained a persistent problem, especially for minority veterans. An estimated 30 to 50 percent of the disabled Vietnam veterans could not find jobs. For a disturbing number of veterans, the road home from Vietnam had led to jail instead of proud victory parades.

At the *New York Times*, Bernard Weinraub wrote several pieces, culminating in a long story for the Sunday magazine.[11] Under the direction of Richard Harwood and A. D. Horne, the *Washington Post* invited distinguished men from the Vietnam generation – all but one were Vietnam veterans – to a round-table discussion. A transcript was then edited and printed as the *entire* Sunday "Out-look" section.[12]

In 1981, the Vietnam veteran issue appeared on the cover of both *Time* and *Newsweek*.[13] A public awakening was tracking the expanding interest of reporters, newspapers, and magazines. In 1979, Louis Harris conducted a special survey designed to track any changes since his 1972 poll. He discovered the nation's basic attitudes toward the war had only deepened. Sixty-five percent continued to believe that Vietnam was a war "we could never win." Sixty-four percent by then thought Vietnam veterans were "suckers."[14]

Yet the survey also found a broad recognition of the nation's unpaid debt to Vietnam veterans. A full two-thirds felt "that the federal government should be doing more to help Vietnam veterans." Sixty-three percent felt that the reception extended Vietnam veterans was worse than that extended earlier veterans.[15]

The nation, in a rush to forget the war a decade earlier, was finally prepared to remember the war's veterans.

THE EDITORIAL DILEMMA

Although it seems now almost the paradigm of a good government program, policy makers had been uncertain about the World War II GI Bill. Educators feared that the massive influx of students would dilute standards. University of Chicago president Robert Hutchins speculated that the GI Bill would turn colleges "into educational hobo jungles."[16]

Yet the Great Depression was still a recent memory. Millions of recently discharged soldiers, all seeking jobs at once, might bring back unacceptably high unemployment. The World War I Bonus Army was also a fresh memory, reminding leaders of the price of neglect.

There was a deep conviction that this time, with World War II, the nation should do what was right. Because World War II veterans had been key players in a grand and successful event, the nation was eager to recognize and help them. Their sacrifices had brought the country an exceptionally important and very clear victory. It was time to say thanks.[17]

No newspaper writer found in the Vietnam War a similar argument for generous treatment of its veterans. With each passing year, it also became increasingly difficult to believe that the United States had won the war. The fall of Saigon in 1975 made such a belief all but impossible. Clearly, if the World War II GI Bill had been a hard sell, the Vietnam GI Bill would be nearly impossible.

From the beginning, separating the just claims of Vietnam veterans from the debate over the war was perceived by editorial writers and columnists as the fundamental problem. The nation's ambivalence toward the war threatened to affect the nation's reaction to its veterans.

Washington Post editors caught the point in the title given to an early 1973 column by David S. Broder, "Vietnam Vets: An Unpopular War Rubs Off."[18] The opening lines of a *Post* column by William Raspberry in 1974 urged simply and emphatically: "The American people came to hate the war in Vietnam, all right. But it does not follow that they also hate the men who fought in that war."[19]

Benefits for Vietnam veterans could have been justified on the basis of service and sacrifice alone. Despite the nation's attitudes toward the war, Vietnam veterans should have had a just claim on the nation's affections completely independent of the war's success or failure.

This argument was merely the implication of the repeated call to separate the war from the warrior, but the nation's reaction to the war was too intense. The argument on behalf of Vietnam veterans had to be approached indirectly. Vietnam veterans deserved attention because of the generous help given to World War II veterans. Equity must be served.[20]

The demands of equity, however, would not be met. As the war's end merged with Watergate, reporters who were increasingly preoccupied with the scandal found in the Vietnam veterans policy a case study of government at its worst. As David S. Broder concluded: "Of all those victimized by the Nixon administration's preoccupation with self-preservation and the Democratic Congress' dawdling do-nothingness, the case of the Vietnam veteran may well be the most outrageous."[21]

To explain the human implication of government policies, reporters are often driven to personal illustrations. Stories on the Vietnam veterans policy were no different. Inadequate benefits were portrayed through the lives of Vietnam veterans forced to postpone college education or left standing in unemployment lines.

An argument based on need, however, required an empirical demonstration. Beginning in the late 1970s, the debate over Vietnam veterans policy increasingly swirled around a series of studies addressing the actual readjustment of Vietnam veterans. The need was real, and in 1981 a major VA-funded study documented the problems at length.[22]

The nation's attitude toward the war reinforced the perception that Vietnam veterans faced problems. These veterans, after all, were "suckers." Their years of service were at least a stigma, and at worst a personal crisis. The Vietnam GI Bill, or special counseling and employment programs, were merely earned compensation.

At last, here was an argument that Vietnam veterans could win, and that the public was prepared to hear. Lost in the social scientists' debate over the exact dimensions of the problem, however, was the issue of the nation's moral obligation — independent of need — to those who had served.

Placed against the backdrop of the exploitative use of veterans in television dramas, the picture of the needy veteran also risked reinforcing the stereotype of Vietnam veterans as social misfits. Long after backers of the civil rights movement prevailed on publishers to discontinue the use of the term "Negro" or "black" in crime headlines, "Vietnam veteran" was still an easy epithet of abuse.

An AP banner, for example, proclaimed, "Crippled Vietnam Vet Arrested in Drug Ring." A UPI story emphasized, "unemployed Vietnam vet charged with killing a Coffee County Sheriff." The problem was not limited to the harried reporting of the wire services. A *Washington Post* story almost offhandedly emphasized that a burglar was a Vietnam veteran.[23]

World War II veterans are both better educated and more successful than their nonveteran peers. Few would use that fact to prove that the World War II GI Bill was unnecessary. Nor would many feel compelled to stop and justify the World War II benefits on the basis of need.

Vietnam veterans, on the other hand, could only win help by first proving they were failures. To win the battle to gain benefits, they would first have to lose the battle for pride against persistent negative stereotypes.

Characteristically, it was a writer who was both a Vietnam veteran and a veteran of the *Washington Post*, Tim O'Brien, who saw the difficulty most clearly:

> The nation seems too comfortable with — even dependent on — the image of a suffering and deeply troubled veteran. Rather than face our own culpabilities, we shove them off onto ex-GI's and let them suffer for us. Rather than relive old tragedies, rather than confront our own frustrations and puzzlements about the war, we take comfort in the image of the bleary-eyed veteran carrying all that emotional baggage for us.[24]

APPENDIX

THE *WASHINGTON POST* EDITORIAL SERIES

"Those Who Served," [Editorial], January 9, 1977.

"Those Who Served (Cont.)," [Editorial], April 11, 1977.

Jan Craig Scruggs, "Forgotten Veterans of 'That Peculiar War,'" [Column], May 25, 1977.

"Those Who Served [Cont.]," [Editorial], May 30, 1977.

Don Winter, "Upgraded Discharges: Will a Double Standard Apply?" [Column], June 14, 1977.

" 'Bad Paper' Discharges [Cont.]," [Editorial], June 14, 1977.

"The Role of the VA Hospitals," [Editorial], June 18, 1977.

"Vietnam: An Instant Editorial," [Editorial], June 21, 1977.

Colman McCarthy, "Veterans of a Lost War," [Column], June 28, 1977.

"Vietnam Veterans and the GI Bill," [Editorial], July 19, 1977.

"The House and the GI Bill," [Editorial], July 25, 1977.

"Renewing the GI Bill Debate," [Editorial], September 15, 1977.

Colman McCarthy, "Vietnam Vet: Who Listens to Them in Washington," [Column], September 27, 1977.

"Benefits for Vietnam Veterans," [Editorial], October 6, 1977.

"A Setback for Ex-Servicemen," [Editorial], October 11, 1977.

"Equalizing Veterans Education," [Editorial], October 11, 1977.

Colman McCarthy, "The Continuing Neglect of Our Newest Veterans," [Editorial], October 24, 1977.

"A Special Debt," [Editorial], October 30, 1977.

"A Full Debate for the GI Bill," [Editorial], November 2, 1977.

"The President and the GI Bill," [Editorial], November 12, 1977.

Frank Greve, "A Legacy of 'Lost' Veterans," [Column], November 18, 1977.

Colman McCarthy, " 'Tiger Teague' and the Veterans Compromise," [Column], November 21, 1977.

" 'The Class That Went to War,' " [Editorial], December 2, 1977.

"Slighting the Veterans," [Editorial], December 19, 1977.

"The Bad Paper Regulations," [Editorial], December 29, 1977.

Colman McCarthy, "An Advocate for Vietnam Veterans," [Column], February 10, 1978.

"Veterans' Unemployment," [Editorial], March 6, 1978.

"HIRE, Promises and Jobs," [Editorial], March 25, 1978.

Ray Marshall, "HIRE Is Helping the Jobless Vietnam Vet," [Column], March 25, 1978.

"Vietnam Veterans in Congress," [Editorial], May 8, 1978.

Note: This listing is not necessarily complete, and the ending point is slightly arbitrary. Additional editorials continued to appear.

THE FIRST EDITORIAL

Those Who Served

In the area of the country where I live, defecting from military service is almost unheard of. Most of the young people in my section of Georgia are quite poor. They didn't know where Sweden was, they didn't know how to get to Canada, they didn't have enough money to hide in college. They thought the war was wrong. They preferred to stay at home, but still they went to Vietnam. A substantial disproportion of them were black. They had never been recognized for their service to the country. They had often been despised, characterized as criminals, they were never heroes and I feel a very great appreciation to them. They were extraordinarily heroic, serving their country in great danger even if they didn't have the appreciation of their fellow citizens and even if they felt the war was wrong. It's very difficult for me to equate what they did with what the young people did who left the country. . . .

But I think it is time to get the Vietnamese war over with. I don't have any desire to punish anyone. I'd just like to tell the young folks who did defect to come back home with no requirement that you be punished or that you serve in some humanitarian capacity or anything. Just come back home, the whole thing's over.

THAT'S HOW JIMMY CARTER explained, in an interview with editors and reporters of this newspaper last March, what he was to describe in a speech to the American Legion in August as "the single hardest decision I have had to make during the campaign" — his decision to grant a blanket pardon to draft evaders in his first week in office as President, and to deal with Vietnam deserters on a case-by-case basis. Performance on this campaign promise is not going to be popular among many Americans. Those who resisted the war and joined the protest against it are not likely to be satisfied unless Mr. Carter does his pardoning in a way that suggests the "defectors" were right and that the war was wrong. And those who engaged in the war or supported it and who care most deeply about its hundreds and thousands of victims — the dead, the wounded, the drug-addicted, the men with bad conduct discharges, the unemployed — are going to resent any suggestion that those who served were wrong.

So it has the look of a no-win proposition for Mr. Carter, when you look at it in the narrow and inflammatory terms of a pardon for "defectors," which is the way most people have been impelled to look at it by the nature of the campaign debate on this issue, by the sharp focus on draft evaders and deserters as the unfinished business of Vietnam, and by Mr. Carter's own emphasis on "the young people who left the country." But it becomes a far more palatable and promising proposition if you approach it in the context of the Vietnam legacy in its totality and of what the new administration can do about those hundreds of thousands of victims of the war who never left the country — or left it to serve the country in Vietnam.

We have no clear indication of how Mr. Carter is looking at it right now. But the deadline for the President elect's decision is drawing closer. So we would like to draw attention today to that larger problem — to the totality of the wreckage — and to suggest some ways to deal with *that*. And we would take as our text some other things that Jimmy Carter said in his American Legion speech that did not receive quite as much attention as his controversial commitment to a "blanket pardon" for the draft evaders now in exile in Sweden and Canada:

We must recognize that, in far too many cases, the Vietnam veterans have been a victim of governmental insensitivity and neglect. Large bureaucracies of the federal government have often been incompetent, inefficient, and unresponsive in their fulfillment of responsibilities to veterans. . . . Each month, thousands of veterans are plagued with later delivery of badly needed benefit checks. Hundreds of millions of dollars of benefit payments have been improperly computed. . . . In 1973 and 1974 Congress passed legislation requiring special consideration of veterans in public service jobs, in training programs, for jobs with federal contractors, and for jobs in the federal government. None of these requirements has been fully or effectively carried out. . . . The record of placement in private sector jobs and training is no better. . . . Last month [July 1976] *there were still 531,000 Vietnam veterans who had no jobs. . . .*

The Vietnam veterans are our nation's greatest unsung heroes. . . . a lot of them came back with scarred minds or bodies, or with missing limbs. Some didn't come back at all. They suffered under the threat of death, and they still suffer from the indifference of fellow Americans.

We recite these campaign statements by Mr. Carter not to suggest any lack of support for his pledge to pardon the draft evaders and deal with the deserters case by case, but simply to put that pledge in its proper perspective as a part of the unfinished business of Vietnam — but only a very small part, and to our mind, by no means the most important part. To put it in its simplest terms, the Vietnam war was a *generational* calamity. Leaving aside for the moment the private citizens who agonized over it and the taxpayers who paid for it and the next of kin of those who served or resisted, it has been calculated that there was a "Vietnam generation" of draft-age men numbering 26,800,000, and it is probably fair to say that, one way or another, the war touched the lives of most of them. Some of the brightest and best educated took refuge in higher education, or found other grounds for avoiding the draft. Roughly 570,000 were draft offenders. Nearly 9,000 draft offenders were convicted. Three thousand more draft offenders are thought to be still at large. From these two groups, it is estimated that about 5,000 are now expatriates, unable to return to the United States.

On the other side of the ledger, almost 11 million draft-age men served in the military, of whom only about 2 million can be classified as Vietnam veterans — those who actually served at one time or another in Indochina. Of these, about 52,000 died, 270,000 were wounded, and 70,000 received "bad paper" discharges under other than honorable circumstances. Another 180,000 young Americans who did not go to Vietnam received bad discharges, a handful for failure to report for Vietnam duty (7,000) and the great majority for other offenses. Astonishingly, of the bad discharges awarded to Vietnam veterans, only 24 were awarded for desertion under fire, 2,000 were awarded for those who went absent without leave in the combat zone and the great majority (68,000) were for other offenses.

Now "other offenses" covers a multitude of things, including such "civilian" crimes as assault, homicide, and theft, as well as violations of military codes and regulations. But when you consider that the overwhelming majority of those who got caught up in the draft were poor, undereducated and the least qualified for military service, do you not have to include them, in a certain sense, among the victims of the war? It is estimated that at least one quarter of the 200,000 Vietnam-era veterans who received "undesirable discharges" or bad conduct discharges got into trouble *after* serving honorably in Vietnam. Yet their "bad paper" discharges severely damage their employability and will dog them the rest of their lives. Once you start talking about pardons, the numbers and the number of categories of potential candidates boggles the mind. What, for example, of those war resisters who stayed home to protest and were convicted of non-violent offenses under federal law? The point is simply that the problem only begins with the estimated 6,000-or-so self-exiled draft evaders and deserters in Sweden, Canada or elsewhere.

There are other measurements, equally devastating, and even more difficult to calculate, of the full legacy of Vietnam: the drug-addicted, the psychiatrically disturbed (some of whom committed crimes of one sort or another after the service), the unemployed. The jobless rate in the 20- to 24-year-old category is almost twice as high for Vietnam veterans whose employability has been marred two ways: directly, by drug addiction, psychiatric problems and service-connected physical disability; and indirectly by the popular image of Vietnam veterans as unstable and violence-prone.

President-elect Carter, we think, is on the right track — and never mind the semantical confusion he has created by his misuse of the strict meaning of "pardon" as opposed to "amnesty." He is proposing to deal with draft evasion and desertion (under some circumstances) as offenses to be forgotten and in a sense forgiven, without respect to the rightness of the act or the wrongness of the war. This is a welcome first step beyond President Ford's clemency program, which demanded a penalty for those who evaded the draft — which said, in effect, that *they* were wrong and that the war, by implication, was right. But if that is all Mr. Carter intends to do, he will not put Vietnam behind us. For he will be picking up only a small piece of the Vietnam wreckage. The rest of it — the biggest part of it — is also the hardest part. But if Jimmy Carter really wants to be able to proclaim that "the whole thing's over" he is going to have to make good on some of those other promises he made to the American Legion. He is going to have to do something about the wreckage of those who served.

NOTES

1. Peter Braestrup, *Big Story: How the American Press and Television Reported and Interpreted the Crisis of Tet 1968 in Vietnam and Washington* (Anchor Books: Garden City, New York, 1968). p. 7.

2. Ibid., p. 8.

3. Ibid., pp. 7-8.

4. "Vietnam: One Week's Dead, May 28-June 3, 1969," *Life*, Volume 66, Number 25, June 27, 1969.

5. *A Study of the Problems Facing Vietnam Era Veterans on Their Readjustment to Civilian Life*, Senate Committee Print No. 7, 92nd Congress, 1st Session, January 31, 1972, pp. 4 and 6.

6. William Greider, "GI Bill Fails to Attract Many Veterans of Vietnam," *Washington Post*, March 30, 1969.

7. John Nordheimer, "Postwar Shock Besets Veterans of Vietnam," *New York Times*, August 28, 1972; B. Drummond Ayres, Jr., "The Vietnam Veteran: Silent, Perplexed, Unnoticed," *New York Times*, November 8, 1970;

B. Drummond Ayres, Jr., "Job Outlook Is Bleak for Vietnam Veterans," *New York Times*, June 5, 1971; John Herbers, "Critics of Veterans Administration Say Ouster of Johnson as Chief Will Not End Public Uproar Over Policies," *New York Times*, April 25, 1974; John Herbers, "Nixon Urges Aid for Vietnam Veterans," March 25, 1973; Mary McGrory, "Amnesty and the Unpopular War," *Washington-Star News*, March 12, 1974; Mary McGrory, "Nixon: Ungiving to Warriors, Unforgiving to Dodgers," *Washington Star-News*, March 29, 1974; Mary McGrory, "Cheers for POW's Then — VA Cuts," *Evening Star and Daily News*, February 13, 1973; William Steif, "GI Bill Failing to Attract Viet Vets," *College & University Business*, September 1969. Many of the important early pieces have been collected in *Source Material on the Vietnam Era Veteran*, Senate Committee Print No. 26, 93rd Congress, 2nd Session, February 12, 1974.

8. From late 1977 through early 1979, *Boston Globe* ran at least nine editorials. See "Making Benefits Beneficial," July 31, 1977; "Evening Up Veterans' Benefits," September 21, 1977; "Memorial Day Reflections," May 29, 1978; "Inaction on Vietnam Vets," September 15, 1978; "A Standard for Vietnam Vets," October 4, 1978; "Rethinking Veterans' Pensions," November 4, 1978; "A Veterans Day for Veterans," November 11, 1978; "GI Bill Needs Review," January 8, 1979; "The Continuing Vietnam Trauma," February 11, 1979.

9. Nina McCain, "Vietnam's Forgotten Casualties," *Boston Globe*, September 10, 1978; Hoag Levins, "Coming Home," *Philadephia*, September 1978; Thomas J. Brazaitis, "Time Deepens Anger, Resentment of Vietnam Veterans," *Plain Dealer*, October 26, 1978; Sam Meddis and Janet Thompson, "The Rifles Are Silent, but the Memories Won't Fade," *Courier-News*, December 6, 1978; Judy Rosenfield, "Victims or Victors?" *Louisville Times*, December 27, 1978; Sandy Rovner, "Since Vietnam: Years of Quiet Desparation," *Washington Post*, May 4, 1979; Bob Dart, "Vietnam Aftermath: The Warrior Victims," *Atlanta Constitution*, December 10, 1979.

10. Tracy Kidder, "Soldiers of Misfortune," *Atlantic Monthly*, Volume 241, No. 3, March 1978, pp. 41-52, 87-90; Marlene Cimons, "Delayed Stress: Vietnam's Deadly Legacy," "Two Stories of War Veterans as Victims," July 29, 1979; "Rap Session as Therapy," "A Mother to the World," July 30, 1979, *Los Angeles Times*; David Friend and John Neary, "Six Who Came Home: The Unforgettable Faces of Vietnam — Then and Now," *Life*, Volume 2, Number 10, October 1979.

11. Bernard Weinraub, "Now, Vietnam Vets Demand Their Rights," *New York Times Magazine*, May 27, 1979.

12. "After Vietnam: Voices of a Wounded Generation," *Washington Post*, May 25, 1980.

13. "The Forgotten Warriors," *Time*, July 13, 1981; "What Vietnam Did to Us," *Newsweek*, December 14, 1981.

14. *Myths and Realities: A Study of Attitudes Toward Vietnam Veterans*, conducted by Louis Harris and Associates, Inc., for the Veterans Administration, July 1980, reprinted by the Veterans Administration, pp. 60 and 87.

15. Ibid., pp. 251 and 37.

16. See Paul Starr, *The Discarded Army: Veterans after Vietnam* (Charterhouse: New York, 1973), p. 234.

17. Ibid., pp. 232-235; Sar A. Levitan and Karen A. Cleary, *Old Wars Remain Unfinished: The Veteran Benefits System* (The Johns Hopkins University Press: Baltimore and London, 1973), pp. 10-12.

18. David S. Broder, "Vietnam Vets: An Unpopular War Rubs Off," *Washington Post*, February 13, 1973.

19. William Raspberry, "Aiding the Vietnam Vets," *Washington Post*, April 3, 1974.

20. Among other articles, see, "A Fair Shake for Vietnam Veterans," *Washington Post*, October 22, 1973; "Fairness to Veterans," *Washington Post*, June 28, 1974; "Fairness for Viet Vets," *New York Times*, June 28, 1974. Several regional papers wrote important editorials during the early 1970s. See, for example, "Nam Benefits," *Houston Post*, February 5, 1974.

21. David S. Broder, "Vietnam Veterans and the GI Bill," *Washington Post*, December 2, 1973.

22. Provisional results from the VA study were secured under the Freedom of Information Act by the Vietnam Veterans of America and released in 1979. See Bernard Weinraub, "Vietnam Veterans Found to Have Major Problems," *New York Times*, September 26, 1979; Ward Sinclair, "Study Says Vietnam Vets Face Difficulties," *Washington Post*, September 26, 1979. The theme was reflected in editorials. See, for example, Colman McCarthy, "Survivor's Syndrome," *Washington Post*, March 14, 1979, or the title given a later piece by McCarthy, "Casualties Still," October 30, 1979. The final VA study was released in 1981. See Robert D. McFadden, "Lingering Difficulties Still Plague Veterans of Combat in Vietnam," *New York Times*, March 23, 1981; Thomas O'Toole, "Vietnam Aftershocks: 8-Year Study Finds Combat Vets Suffer More from Alcohol, Drug Abuse," *Washington Post*, March 24, 1981.

23. See Mike Sager, "Convicted Building-Scaling Office Burglar is Suspected in 725 Cases," *Washington Post*, July 15, 1981. The AP story ran December 3, 1980, in the AM cycle. The UPI story ran on February 12, 1981, in the AM cycle. The *Post* has subsequently been quite sensitive to the use of "Vietnam veterans" as a characterization in news stories. A letter from Congressman David E. Bonior to the *Post*'s ombudsman, Robert J. McCloskey, about a 1982 article, prompted an immediate response from McCloskey and a letter from the story's author, a Vietnam veteran, which carefully justified the use of the label.

24. Tim O'Brien, "The Violent Vet," *Esquire*, Volume 92, Number 6, December 1979, p. 100.

3   Films

> Like the dog that attracted Sherlock Holmes'
> attention by *not* barking, it's perhaps the very
> absence of movies [about the Vietnam War] that
> is most deserving of study.
>
> Gilbert Adair
> *Vietnam on Film*[1]

ABSENCE

The curious nature of a new generation of Americans fighting
in the jungles of distant Southeast Asia would seem certain to
attract attention. Through the Tet Offensive of early 1968, combat
in Vietnam was reported widely in newspapers and covered almost
nightly on the evening news. Yet during the Vietnam War, there
would be only *one* war film.

During World Wars I and II, there were scores of war films. Those
movies played a historic role in shaping public support for the war
effort and encouraging public respect for the soldiers fighting in
battle. As Jack Valenti, president of the Motion Picture Association
of America, recalled:

[World War II] was a popular war. We were defending honor. We had
been bombed at Pearl Harbor. There was a general agreement in the
populace that we must win. And I was a young man in those days, and

49

I, like a lot of my friends, was eager to get in — volunteered — and went off to cheers.

Vietnam was different, as Fay Kanin, an acclaimed screenwriter and president of the Academy of Motion Picture Arts and Sciences, noted:

So you had a whole different feeling about wars [in World War II]. You could be romantic about war, as many films were, and almost escapist about war. War had a sort of glory to it. You sang songs about it. There were some very realistic and very strong films about war, . . . but many were, you know, "service films" and "hero films" and "our boys films." I think a public could accept and enjoy them because the wars seemed remote. . . . It was, I think, the first time, in Vietnam, that we had a different kind of war.

Even the medium of television, which might have been viewed as building a market for war movies, actually discouraged film makers. As Jack Valenti explained:

The reason why you didn't see many Vietnam movies was that nobody liked Vietnam and you already saw the movie. Now, if World War II had been on television every evening in living color, I do not think that would have been such a popular war. War is an inhumane, grisly, and squalid occupation, and people who came back from war usually only remember those fragments of good moments they had and don't want to talk about the misery. Therefore, I think that the movie makers rightly thought why make a movie about Vietnam when everybody says, "Hell, I saw that for the last year."

Films are expensive and must be funded by attracting investors. An industry consensus that the United States was not interested in a Vietnam War film surely would have made financing hard to attract. Fay Kanin said simply, and with an insider's confidence, that money for a Vietnam War film "would have been a tough dollar to raise."

Yet the one film made during the Vietnam War years, *The Green Berets* (1968), was quite successful. Produced by Michael Wayne, the son of John Wayne (who starred in the film), the movie was John Wayne's second largest money-maker. It was a very big hit for one of the industry's biggest stars.

During the war years, a group of talented young filmmakers were emerging, including Francis Ford Coppola, Brian De Palma, George Lucas, John Milius, Steven Spielberg, Martin Scorsese, and Paul Shrader. The talent was there to make films about Vietnam, and these directors did not have great difficulty attracting money. Among them there would be several expensive films that were commercial failures, like *The Conversation* (1974), *New York, New York* (1977), and *1941* (1979).

As Gilbert Adair concluded in his major study of Vietnam War films:

> If they had been so inclined, they could certainly have raised financing for movies about the war. But while it would be self-righteously puritanical to censure them for failing to seize this opportunity of becoming the spokesmen of their contemporaries drafted to (and sometimes killed in) Vietnam, it can't be denied that their record on this matter is disappointing, to say the least.[2]

The consensus against Vietnam War films existed because no one chose to challenge its truth. To better understand the opportunity lost by the failure to seriously address the abundance of Vietnam War themes, a historical review of the industry's previous war efforts is helpful.

HISTORY

As early as 1914, movie attendance had reached 15 million a day, according to a generous estimate. The industry was grossing $1 million a day. There were 100,000 people producing and marketing movies.

By 1926, the still infant film industry had become a giant, ranked variously as the fifth to the eighth largest industry in the country. In their famous 1929 study, *Middletown: A Study in Modern American Culture*, Robert and Helen Lynd suggested that the theaters in Muncie, Indiana took in 30,000 admissions per week out of a population of 38,000.[3]

By the time of World War I, movies were a major force in U.S. society. That force was put to work in support of the war effort.

Although there were early films that supported neutrality, such as *War is Hell* (1914) and *Be Neutral* (1914), they soon gave way to a tide of films devoted to war preparedness.

Leading the charge was J. Stuart Blackton, a major producer of World War I films. An immigrant from England with the reputation of a dandy with hawkish views, Blackton in 1915 began to produce and direct films designed to involve the United States in the new war.

His 1915 epic, *The Battle Cry for Peace*, grossed millions and had a profound impact on the nation. The film begins with a warning about our vulnerability to invasion, and then a Teutonic enemy with spiked helmets invades New York harbor.

Once the output began, the number of films with war themes jumped sharply. In his recent study, *War on Film*, Michael T. Isenberg has catalogued and reviewed the films on World War I. There were over 197 films with major war themes from 1914 through 1918.[4]

The film industry was not a neutral observer. It was a part of the war effort. Popular among the war films were movies that set a negative image of the Germans — often through an unflattering characterization of the kaiser — seeking to build support for the war among the nation.

After the war, disillusionment followed the astronomical loss of life and property caused by the massive war to end all wars. Films such as *All Quiet on the Western Front* (1930), which won the Academy Award for best picture, and *Ace of Aces* (1933) paused to take a reflective look back at the effect of modern war on its soldiers.

In 1941, *Sergeant York* told the story of a Tennessee woodsman who won the Congressional Medal of Honor during World War I. In the film, York's congressman, Cordell Hull, foreseeing another storm on the horizon, says: "Some day, your people may ask you to serve them again. None of us can tell what we may be called on to do in the years to come."

Sergeant York straddled two eras: World War I and the not-too-distant entry of the United States into World War II. It bridged the eras by following the soldier back home as he becomes the veteran and grows old. Ready again to argue for war preparedness, it put the veteran's story to use in the service of a new war effort.

The country was attacked at Pearl Harbor, and the "Day of Infamy" ensured national unity, but the nation was not prepared for battle. As a result, the military and the film industry were remarried, working together to move the nation toward readiness.

Sacrifice became the theme of the moment as Bing Crosby paraded across the country singing "Buy, Buy, Buy a Bond" or "Your Country Needs Taxes to Beat the Axis." Even Donald Duck quacked out the themes of sacrifice and patriotism.

As a recruiting inducement, Bette Davis sang "What's Good Is in the Army, What's Left Won't Have Me." In a series of basic training films, new enlistees like Jimmy Durante, Phil Silvers, Bob Hope, and the team of Abbott and Costello clowned their way in and out of boot camp, always proud to be soldiers, always certain of the war's cause.[5]

The weekly newsreels at the local theaters reported proudly of the courageous Yanks fighting the evil enemy. Just as World War I films set a negative image of the kaiser, no viewer of World War II films would be left long in doubt about the moral character of the Germans and the Japanese.

Once again, however, the end of the war brought a period of reflection, and a series of films focused on the new veteran. In 1945, Delmar Davis's *Pride of the Marines* showed the difficult adjustment of a blinded marine to civilian life. In Fred Zimmermann's *The Men* (1950), Marlon Brando played a paraplegic who struggles to find a new life. In *The Best Years of Our Lives*, William Wyler followed three veterans with mental and physical scars as they return to a small town in the United States.

Hollywood was ready to turn the Korean War into a remake of World War II. As Gilbert Adair uncovered:

In September of the same year [1950], a delegation of Hollywood notables was dispatched to the White House to acquaint the President with the industry's unanimous support. . . . They declared notably that: "We are at your service, at the service of the country and the United Nations."[6]

A remake, however, proved impossible. The weariness of war was fresh on the minds of Americans who had, it seemed, just finished World War II. It was harder to define the nature of the U.S. involvement in Korea. The complexity of the situation caused hesitancy in the nation's filmmakers.

At the same time, the structure of the U.S. film industry was changing. The Justice Department was divesting the industry. As Jack Valenti recalled:

> Before 1948, when the Justice Department broke up the ownership of studios, production, and theaters, there was a monolithic industry. It was controlled by a handful of maybe six or seven men who owned all the studios and owned all the theaters. When the divorcement was forced upon the industry, all of that power collapsed, and from 1950 on, the movie industry was a collection of fragments. It was an assembly of a mutually antagonistic group of people. There was no power center.

Despite the patriotic intent of the Hollywood establishment that walked into President Harry Truman's office, Korea was left in a somewhat foggy limbo. It was more financially rewarding to do films about World War II because the public found them easier to accept. The pattern begun during the Korean War would culminate during the Vietnam War.

There were more films made about World War II during the Vietnam War than were made about Vietnam. Considering only the epics and major money-makers, the lone Vietnam combat movie, *The Green Berets*, was outnumbered by *Von Ryan's Express* (1965), *The Battle of the Bulge* (1966), *The Dirty Dozen* (1967), *Where Eagles Dare* (1969), *Patton* (1970), and *Tora! Tora! Tora!* (1970). The comfort of old settings had triumphed over the immediacy of the nation's disturbing experience in Vietnam.

The unsettling nature of the war years set the background for a counterculture milieu. Rebellion through drugs, sexual liberation, and opposition to the war were colorful themes. The movie industry, facing the same choice as network news executives, joined television in concentrating on the cultural war at home, not on the battle in Vietnam.

In place of the boot camp escapades of Bob Hope, the Vietnam War would see counter-enlistee films focused on those avoiding the draft: *Greetings* (1968); *Alice's Restaurant* (1969); *Hail, Hero* (1969); *The Strawberry Statement* (1970); and *Summer Soldier* (1971). The only parallel to Phil Silvers would be the counterpoint of *M*A*S*H* (1969). Ostensibly set in Korea, but really about Vietnam, the film put humor to the purposes of a decidedly tragic theme.

Even when the Vietnam War and its U.S. soldier, nearly absent from these films, finally entered the plot, the setting remained at home in the United States. The soldier was always a returning veteran who was exploited as a crazed criminal or as a noble outcast.

Vietnam veterans were integral to the new motorcycle movies. In 1966, Peter Fonda and Michael J. Pollard starred in *Wild Angels*, where a Vietnam veteran is involved in a Nazi motorcycle gang. In the films *Angels from Hell* (1966), *Crome and Hot Leather* (1971), and *Welcome Home Soldier Boy* (1971), the veteran is ignoble and avenging, damned by his war experience.

Born Loser (1967), *Billy Jack* (1971), and *Hard Ride* (1971) were more sympathetic. The veteran in these films is a social outcast, struggling to reform a corrupt United States. The war and its impact, however, are not in focus, and the veteran's nobility, consciously made colorful through his social rebellion, is a prop quickly forgotten when the action begins.

Because it was easier to exploit the veteran than grapple with the real issues the war posed, these films predate the first string of films about the war itself. The pattern set in World Wars I and II was reversed. Instead of beginning with the war and following the soldier home, Vietnam films began at the end, with the veteran, and worked backward to the war itself.

The end of the Vietnam War would eventually lead to several films exploring the lives of returning veterans, and a few films were about the war itself, but during the war years, there would be near silence broken only by a few moments of cheap exploitation and *The Green Berets*.

THE EXCEPTION

In *The Green Berets* (1968), John Wayne put his money where his politics were. With his son's help, he made a propaganda film that put the issues in simple terms, black and white, our guys versus the bad guys, and glossed over the complexity of the war.

Given the Waynes' involvement, there was little chance of an anti-U.S. film, but the government was nevertheless hesitant to cooperate in the film's production. That hesitancy was quite a contrast from World War I and II, where, as Jack Valenti noted, "There was lots of cooperation."

Cooperation benefited both parties. The film industry, seeking combat realism and increased ticket sales, gained the use of government facilities, personnel, and equipment. In return, the government won a large audience for a message that almost always supported the war effort.

Another producer had originally acquired the film rights to Robin Moore's novel, but, according to Michael Wayne, the producer was unable — for an unknown reason — to win Pentagon cooperation. Nor did Michael Wayne win support easily. As he remembered:

> It was like they were going to tell us, if you want our cooperation, if you want to use some of our equipment and film on our facilities, then you must do it this way. So, we did. We created a script around that. We didn't tell my father, but we created a script around what they told us was suitable for them, showed it to my father. He didn't like it too well, but then we told him, this is kind of the way we have to do it and everything else, and so he said, "Fine."

Even before its release, the film sparked concern on both sides of the war issue. In Congress, leading liberals were concerned that Pentagon cooperation amounted to taxpayer funding for propaganda. A Congressional investigation was launched.[7]

War planners at the White House feared the film as well. Jack Valenti, who was a close adviser to President Johnson, related the story:

> I told the President that I thought Wayne was not for us. He was not an LBJ man, not a Great Society man, but I said, "If he makes a movie about Vietnam, I have a feeling that it would not be pro Viet Cong."
> . . . At least the American fighting man would be a hero and not some slovenly, sadistic beast, and I think that he did get some cooperation out of the Defense Department. . . . He put his own money on the line.

Controversy followed the film after its release. Antiwar groups protested at some theaters showing the film, and the protests received extensive coverage. The movie did well. It grossed close to $10 million in the United States alone, a large percentage for 1968. It did particularly well in the South and Midwest.[8]

Surveyed in 1979, 38 percent of Americans said they had seen the film. Veterans, in particular, sought it out. Sixty-seven percent of Vietnam-era veterans had seen the movie. Among veterans who had served in Vietnam, the percentage exceeded 70 percent.[9]

Jack Valenti had been right. The Wayne family had been careful to paint a positive picture of the U.S. soldier. As Michael Wayne recalled:

> We really made an effort to show the American fighting man as the best fighting man. We wanted to show him as a solid citizen. We wanted to make a film supporting the soldier, and we didn't give a damn about the war. People were getting killed over there just like in World War I and World War II, and if they were heroes in those wars, they were heroes in Vietnam, and that's what we tried to show.

In the 1979 survey, 70 percent of the general public and 73 percent of the Vietnam-era veterans felt that the movie's image of the Vietnam veteran was positive. The Waynes had succeeded in creating heroes. The only movie about the U.S. soldier in battle made during the war years was positive.[10]

TRUTH DELAYED: FILM DOCUMENTARIES

During World War II, the U.S. government commissioned Frank Capra to produce a series of films documenting the need for America's involvement in the war. Capra's series, *Why We Fight*, was successful in its mission, not because it changed U.S. attitudes toward the war, but because it complemented what Americans already felt.[11]

During the Vietnam War, the U.S. government produced about 100 movies. These films usually ran between seven and thirty minutes and centered on military training, the heroism of our fighting men, the military's positive role in reconstructing South Vietnam, and the military's important civic role back in the United States.[12]

Building a Nation (1968) documented a civic action program run by the Air Force in Vietnam that helped the Vietnamese raise their standard of living. In *The Gentle Hand* (1968), a U.S. navy surgeon gives medical aid and instruction to the South Vietnamese in a small village. *Medal of Honor — One for One* (1968) paid tribute to Major Benard Fisher, the first U.S. soldier in Vietnam to be awarded the Congressional Medal of Honor.

The Pentagon, like the film industry in general, was making films about other wars and other issues. The Vietnam War was only part of the Defense Department's agenda even as the war was being played out. After 1968, *only five films* were made about the Vietnam War.[13]

In 1967, the United States Information Agency enlisted the talents of John Ford to create a propaganda documentary entitled *Vietnam! Vietnam!* The goal was to match Frank Capra's success in *Why We Fight*. Yet after four years of production, the agency's director, Frank Shakespeare, delayed release of the film.[14]

In the years since the film was begun, deepening division within the United States had brought into question the film's potential value. Commissioned before the Tet Offensive and Vietnamization, it hardly made sense to release the film in 1971, when the only question was the date of the eventual U.S. withdrawal.

At the Pentagon, it seemed nearly impossible to make a film that complemented the national mood and that could help shape national attitudes. The Vietnam War simply would not stand still long enough to be captured on film.

Frank Capra's *Why We Fight* was not the only major documentary of the World War II era. In 1945, John Huston made *Let There Be Light*, a documentary about veterans of World War II suffering from shell shock — the war's "casualties of the spirit."

Opening with the day that a new group of World War II soldiers enter a special government-run clinical program, *Let There Be Light* follows the group through the program, day by day, week by week. Slowly the darkness of the war's memories breaks, and the viewer watches as individual soldiers recover their confidence and their humor, are reunited with their families, and then leave the program ready for a new life.

Let There Be Light was a powerful film of spiritual triumph. Yet the film was not released until *after* the Vietnam War. It had been impounded by the Pentagon until Jack Valenti, the president of the Motion Picture Association, secured its release at the request of Ray Stark, a leading producer.

Asked why he thought it was impounded, Jack Valenti said:

Somebody stamps on a file, "Not to Be Released," and nobody asks why. My own judgment is that at that time, in our environment, the

Pentagon didn't want to show the mental anguish the war provisioned you with. We know about getting your leg blown off, or a bullet going in your belly, but people in those days didn't know too much about mental illness. . . . So I would guess — this is only a surmise, a wild surmise — that the Army decided that this was a film better unviewed.

One soldier in *Let There Be Light* covers his Purple Heart and campaign ribbons under the flap of his shirt pocket. The veteran could just have easily been Sergeant Jackson (portrayed in the play *Medal of Honor Rag*), a Detroit Vietnam veteran awarded the Congressional Medal of Honor who was unable to rationalize the medal's value.

The readjustment problems faced by Vietnam veterans were not unique and should have surprised no one. Yet the discovery of combat stress among Vietnam veterans by the nation's media was not made until 1978, and then was understood only as a special problem created by a special war.

Whether it was suppression or not, the failure to release *Let There Be Light* played a role in the perpetuation of a myth — the pleasant fantasy that war's horrors were limited only to the physical. Not surprisingly, the first documentary on the Vietnam War concentrated on bringing home the human side of the war.

Winter Soldier (1972) documented a hearing held in Detroit during January 1971. In the film individual Vietnam veterans testify to their own brutality (described in incidents like dropping live prisoners from helicopters) and to the war's brutality on them.

The Detroit hearing provided a cathartic release for deeply tormented men and women who yearned for an opportunity to express their war experiences and guilt. Above all else, the film was both a demand that the United States listen to its soldiers and a plea for psychological counseling through neighborhood outreach centers.

The counseling program documented in *Let There Be Light* was established *immediately* after World War II. It treated veterans while they were still soldiers, directly on their return from the war. The Vietnam veterans counseling program urged in *Winter Soldier* would not actually be implemented until 1980, more than a half decade after the war had ended and nearly two decades after the war had begun.

The advent of a Vietnam veterans counseling program would have to overcome the attitude of both the nation and the Congress, that good soldiers — meaning the soldiers of World War II — simply did not have mental or readjustment problems. False myths have their price. The problems of Vietnam veterans would be left untreated because the nation could not accept mental pain as anything more than a coward's excuse.

Peter Davis's *Hearts and Minds* (1974) won the Oscar for best documentary. Its focus was the war's impact on the Vietnamese people, but it also addressed the U.S.'s prosecution of the war. *Hearts and Minds* documented the failure of U.S. policy from the commander-in-chief on down.

The film suggested powerfully that America's policy was based on the premise that the Vietnamese, mere "Gooks," were inferior. A former French foreign minister recalled that John Foster Dulles asked in 1954 if the war might be ended "if we were to give you two atomic bombs." The Vietnamese casualties resulting from the use of atomic weapons were implicitly dismissed as irrelevant by Dulles. National Security Adviser Eugene Rostow suggested a position more measured in degree, but still similar, when he recommended that the United States should have used a firmer military policy.

In a classic interview, General George Patton III, the son of the World War II hero, commented that his troops were a "bloody good bunch of killers." General William Westmoreland asserted that the Oriental value of life is inferior to our own. Together, the interviews captured a pervasive leadership attitude that assumed the indifference of Vietnamese life.

This attitude was held despite its moral implications, and interviews throughout *Hearts and Mind* subtly evoke its price. In one, a Vietnamese father returns home to find his family dead, killed in a bombing attack. In the second, an emotionally drained U.S. bomber pilot explains that his job was merely a matter of technical expertise. "I never heard the explosion," he says, "never saw the people."

ARRIVAL

Around 1977, the United States began to take a look at the Vietnam War and its veterans. The longer they looked, the more curious they became. There was an almost simultaneous rush to remember the war and its warriors.

Vietnam veterans began to assume leadership positions in their communities. The Veterans Administration had a decorated triple-amputee Vietnam veteran at its head. A caucus was formed among the Vietnam-era veterans in Congress. A new veterans organization, eventually to be called the Vietnam Veterans of America, was formed.

Veterans began to write about their experiences, culminating in such powerful books as *A Rumor of War* by Philip Caputo and the National-Book-Award-winning classic *Going After Cacciato* by Tim O'Brien. They were joined by other works like *Dispatches*, by Michael Herr.

Prominent national newspapers as well as local papers editorialized about the forgotten warrior of Vietnam. The three major networks each featured stories on the varying readjustment problems facing Vietnam veterans.

The film industry was no exception. It joined in the awakening, as Fay Kanin noted:

> It's funny, we all kind of blossomed at the same time. . . . It was fascinating to me that these [films] all came alive at the same period. It was almost as if creative people felt, and then people who make decisions and can implement felt, at the same time, there was a readiness on the part of the public's part to look at this.

The late 1970s saw six major films about the war and its veterans. Three centered on the war: *The Boys in Company C* (1977), *Go Tell the Spartans* (1978), and *Apocalypse Now* (1979). Two centered on the veteran: *Rolling Thunder* (1977) and *Coming Home* (1978). One, *The Deer Hunter* (1978), followed young men to battle and their return home.

The films were a gamble. Fear that the nation might not yet be ready to face the war or its veterans had delayed release of *Rolling Thunder* and *The Boys in Company C*. After debuts in the early 1970s, they were distributed only in 1977 and 1978, just as the other films were being released.

Despite the industry's fears, 12 years of watching the war on television had not entirely dulled the nation's interest. Though they did not break any records, these six films made at least a respectable showing, according to *Variety*.

Go Tell the Spartans and *Rolling Thunder* (even after its delayed release) did poorly. Badly promoted, the films were neglected among expectations over the release of *The Deer Hunter* and *Apocalypse Now*. Both of these films did well. *The Deer Hunter* grossed $30 million in the United States.

Although two of the films, *Apocalypse Now* and *The Deer Hunter*, came close, there is no definitive Vietnam War film. Pieced together, however, the six films give a composite picture of the war and its impact on Vietnam veterans.

The movies, however, unlike television, would never be put to work for Vietnam veterans. Of the four films that commanded decent audiences, both the general public and Vietnam veterans agreed that the image of the veteran in *Apocalypse Now* was negative, according to the 1979 Louis Harris survey.[15]

In two others, *The Boys in Company C* and *The Deer Hunter*, the public was almost evenly divided, with those who thought the films presented a positive image holding narrow leads. Among Vietnam veterans, a narrow majority either felt uncertain or were convinced that the image was negative.[16]

The pattern of negative portrayals was reinforced by three other films released during the same period: *Taxi Driver* (1976), *Heroes* (1977) and *Who'll Stop the Rain* (1978). In contrast with the motorcycle sagas or the *Billy Jack* films, these three movies were each feature films, with substantial budgets and major stars.

They were widely promoted and two, *Taxi Driver* and *Heroes*, were successful at the box office, according to *Variety*. These three films are not without artistic merit, but each fails, in varying degrees, to reach past exploitation. Asked in the 1979 survey about *Who'll Stop the Rain* and *Taxi Driver*, both the general public and veterans agreed that the portrayal of Vietnam veterans in the films was negative.[17]

In *Taxi Driver*, Travis Bickle, a veteran played by Robert De Niro, is a psychopath bent on violence. *Who'll Stop the Rain*, starring Michael Moriarty and Nick Nolte, portrays the veteran as a drug smuggler. The hero of *Heroes*, played by Henry Winkler, is a mad young Vietnam veteran with "survivor guilt," who escapes a psychiatric ward.

Of all the feature films made about the Vietnam War and its veterans, the general public and veterans found a positive image of the Vietnam veteran in just two: the early film *The Green Berets* and *Coming Home*. Yet neither the public nor Vietnam veterans were looking for films that reduced Vietnam veterans to one-dimensional characters or that hid the questions about the war behind a patriotic veneer.

Indeed, *The Green Berets* and *Coming Home* presented decidedly different images of the Vietnam veteran. *Coming Home* portrays two veterans decidedly unsure of the war's purpose, doubts absent from *The Green Berets*. The attitude toward the war in the films was also diametrically opposite. *Friendly Fire*, the made-for-TV classic about a family that opposed the war, was also perceived as presenting a positive image of the veteran.[18]

By the time of the 1979 Harris survey, the public was clearly prepared to accept diverse roles and diverse views about the war. Having avoided the issue of the war for so long, however, the film industry's late revival would be hesitant and uncertain. The industry, unable to catch up with its audience, would never recover the confidence that pervaded World War I and II films.

Sidney Furie's *The Boys in Company C* chronicled a platoon of young and diverse U.S. "boys" as they move through basic training and into combat in Vietnam. The characters in the film grow, emerging as courageous and rejuvenated, despite the war's failures.

The film, however, dealt almost exclusively in stereotypes — a flower child and a good old boy from the South, to pick just two. The complexities of the issues raised by the war were reduced to a droning pacifism.

In contrast, Ted Post's *Go Tell the Spartans* sought to locate the war historically and attempted to develop individual characters. Eschewing both anti- and pro-war ideology, the audience learns to respect in victory and defeat the courage of U.S. soldiers dying in defense of an obscure village garrison.

On the arch above a French cemetery near the village is written, "Go Tell the Spartans, those who passest by, that here, obedient to their law, we lie." The film's final scene is a long shot of the cemetery. As U.S. soldiers replace the French predecessors, the cemetery scene evokes both the war's futility and the soldiers' quiet heroism.[19]

Rolling Thunder, a movie by John Flynn, tells the story of a U.S. POW, Major Charles Rane, who returns home to find himself a stranger to his son and deceived by his wife. The military tries to force him out of the service. The people in his hometown seek to express their respect, but with an awkward sense of what is proper they succeed only in shaming him with false fame and a tinsel fortune (a red Cadillac convertible).

Through flashbacks of Major Rane's years in the prison camp, including torture scenes, the film reminds us how strong we can be, but in the end, *Rolling Thunder*, like the community it portrays, does not know how to resolve the emotions it evokes. The film settles for reconciliation through violence. Major Rane's wife is killed, and in the film's graphic conclusion, he hunts down the killers.

Coming Home tells the story of two veterans: a paralyzed veteran named Luke (played by Jon Voight) and Bob Hyde, a gung-ho officer (played by Bruce Dern). Luke and Bob Hyde's wife, Sally (played by Jane Fonda), fall in love, establishing a traditional love triangle.

Luke's treatment in the VA hospital is dramatically portrayed, reminding the nation of the deplorable care Vietnam veterans have received. In an opening scene, Luke lies face down on a rolling stretcher with a nearly overflowing urine bag. Later, a friend whom Luke made in the hospital commits suicide.

Coming Home is the only film to address in detail the readjustment problems Vietnam veterans faced. Asked by his wife to explain what the war was like, Bob Hyde can only respond, "I don't know what the war is like. I only know what it is. TV shows what it's like. It sure as hell don't show what it is."

These scenes are extraordinary, but as critic Peter Marin noted in *Harpers*, "What may have begun as a straightforward and somber attempt to deal honestly with the problems of returning veterans is reduced to a ritualized love story and vehicle for Ms. Fonda's perpetual moral posturing."[20]

Yet Sally's attempt to love both her husband and Luke is a quiet invitation for the audience to embrace both, whether hawk or dove, officer or enlisted man, as caring beings and not as political symbols. Like the ambiguity of the war itself, the film ends mysteriously with Bob swimming naked into the ocean, perhaps to his suicide death. There are no storybook endings in any of the major Vietnam War films.[21]

Francis Ford Coppola's *Apocalypse Now* has been described by one critic as a "prolonged hallucination" and by another as a jungle town of scary rides.[22] Structured after Joseph Conrad's *Heart of Darkness*, it tells the story of one U.S. soldier, Willard (played by Martin Sheen), who is sent into the depth of the jungle to kill Colonel Kurtz (played by Marlon Brando), a once brilliant West Point officer, who has gone mad and is holding court in the Cambodian jungle.

Coppola's ability to clash cultures gives the audience a taste of the incredible shock the soldier suffered. Together with the clash of combat, the audience begins to understand something of the extremes men can be driven to.

In the film, a quiet village near the sea is attacked by helicopters — with Wagner's "Ride of the Valkyries" blaring from the lead chopper — all to ensure "good surf" for the unit's beach-bound commander. Playboy bunnies are deposited at a spectacularly lighted supply depot in the jungle to tease sex- and emotionally starved GIs.

More than the film's visual power — which at times is immense — its production and the effect of its long labor were telling. *Apocalypse Now* was Coppola's personal Vietnam. Like the war, the film took years to complete and exceeded budget. Originally projected to cost around $13 million, it actually cost $30 million.[23]

The intensity of the project prompted Martin Sheen to comment that he had become a changed man. And Coppola said that while making the film, he began to identify first with Willard and then with Kurtz. If the mere production of this film could so significantly alter the lives of these artists, it is not difficult to understand how the jungle changed U.S. soldiers in Vietnam.

The Deer Hunter is a film about three young working men from a Pennsylvania steel town, who grow up together and leave together to fight in Vietnam. Their return home is marked by the scars of their experiences in the war.[24]

Despite its artistic acclaim, *The Deer Hunter* has been criticized almost universally for its historical misrepresentation and racist viewpoint. Although it is hard to justify the film's decidedly Western slant, it is nevertheless an extraordinary film about war and its impact.

In a key prison scene, the young men are required by their North Vietnamese captors to play Russian roulette. Surviving the harrowing encounter, one of the three, Nick (played by Christopher Walken) disappears into the Saigon underground, where he plays Russian roulette for money.

It is arguable whether the film's director, Michael Cimino, needed to take such poetic license with the Russian roulette metaphor. But it is also arguable whether, in fact, Russian roulette was not played in Vietnam. What is clear is that the film's battle scenes come across the screen with electrifying intensity.[25]

The film's success, however, lies principally in the first and third parts which are set in a steel town in the United States. No movie of the Vietnam War more successfully developed the character of the soldier who went to fight. The ethnic orthodoxy of a Slovak community is seen through work at the steel mills, through play at a wedding dance, through religion at the wedding ceremony and at a wake, and through life and death in two deer hunts.

As opposed to the other Vietnam films that, with the exception of *Coming Home*, either ignored the problem of reconciliation or reduced it to drugs and violence, *The Deer Hunter* struggled with the role of family, community, and ritual.

Beginning with the celebration of Steven's marriage, the lives of the three young men are torn asunder by Vietnam. Nick is lost to the Saigon underworld. Steven (played by John Savage) is paralyzed from a combat wound. He tries to hide from his wife, family, and community in a VA hospital.

Director Cimino has a decided political slant, but through the character of Michael (played by Robert De Niro), he overcomes his ideology. Michael, as the hero-reconciler, tries valiantly to save Nick. When that fails, he brings Nick's body home for burial. Michael seeks out Steven at the VA hospital and forces him to come home and resume his life.

In the movie's last scene, after Nick's funeral, the characters join together in a private wake at the grill of the local bar. Together, they begin to sing "God Bless America," their voices growing slowly stronger. It then becomes clear that united they will grow past their grief.

The final scene, it has been argued, merely perpetuates the trite cultural symbols, like "God Bless America," which will only lead another generation of soldiers into another Vietnam. Although that may be true, the film suggested that only the simplest rituals, carrying the deepest meanings, can give people the strength necessary to survive a war.

"God Bless America" is part of a rich heritage that ties the film's final survivors together. If the strength of that heritage also helps to create war, then that is a paradox in life and not merely in the film. It is also a paradox that the film carefully notes.

The pathos of the final wake is a contrast to the joy at the dance following Nick's marriage at the beginning of the film. Set at the hall of a major veterans organization, the three young men are urged on to the horror of the Vietnam War in the name of the colorful patriotic symbols that hang from the walls.

CONCLUSION

Tom Bird grew up in Freeport, Long Island, where Dominican nuns taught him to defend both country and church. At home, his father recounted his own service in the medical corps under General George Patton. At 18, Tom volunteered for the draft and ended up in Vietnam, where he served in an aviation outfit and then in an infantry unit.

After returning from Vietnam, Bird began a career in the theater. In the United States, he found members of a theater establishment who were certain of their conclusions about the Vietnam War and its veterans, but who were uncertain how to face a real veteran, one who did not conform to their preconceived ideas.

Tom Bird studied with Lee Strasberg for several years. In an exercise called "emotional memory work," Strasberg encouraged actors to recall, to work through, and to retain the emotions of past events, forming – in Tom Bird's words – "a sort of savings bank" of feelings. When Tom suggested that he might use his Vietnam experiences in the exercise, Strasberg told him that he should see a psychiatrist. The war and its memories were evidently not worth saving.

Bird earned an interview with Francis Ford Coppola to try out for a part in *Apocalypse Now*. An exciting and open discussion came to a quick halt when Coppola learned that Tom was a Vietnam veteran. Surprisingly, although Coppola had interviewed several hundred actors for the film, Tom Bird was the first Vietnam veteran.

Coppola asked Bird if it were not true that all actors were against war. He also asked Bird if he personally was against war. Bird said yes, and Coppola responded that despite Bird's opposition to war, Bird seemed proud of his military service. Bird felt no need to deny his pride, adding only that this was a paradox that all veterans faced. The interview ended with Coppola's statement that he did not want to involve Vietnam veterans in the film because they might know too much about Vietnam and might not respond to his direction.

Only a year or so later, Tom Bird was working with Wynn Handman, artistic director of the American Place Theatre. The play they were doing was set in the 1960s. To help set the tone of the production, Handman emphasized that the 1960s were a complex and difficult time in the United States, the time when the United States had lost its soul in Vietnam. Bird asked if that meant that Vietnam veterans were lost souls. Yes, Handman responded, those poor boys are all lost souls.

Separated by years, these three experiences spurred the development in Tom Bird's mind of a Vietnam veterans theater company. In early 1978, the corporation was formed. Called the Veterans Ensemble Theatre Company, it has continued to grow.

The theater has provided a showcase for moving plays written by Vietnam veterans, like Jonathan Polansky's *In Pursuit of Liberty*, and has developed a continuing company where veterans can bring their war memories to enhance their diverse roles. It has even started an irregular program of poetry readings.

In 1981, the company was strengthened by a growing relationship with Joseph Papp, the New York theater producer. Over time, Papp has provided a challenge grant, free performing space, and a contract to produce two plays by the company at his New York Shakespeare Festival's Public Theater.

Most of all, however, Papp has helped them grow. "Joe Papp," explained Tom Bird, "has led us past didacticism to good theater. More narrative and less preaching. More character development and less relying on powerful images. We needed to resolve our plays, to bring them together in a final emotion that the audience can take home, can use."

Tom Bird's own convictions have been deepened by opposition. He is certain that the theater and films are crucial to the nation's development and are especially crucial to addressing problems, like the Vietnam War, which people are trying to avoid:

> I think the arts probably have the greatest potential for exploring the issues of war and peace, both in Vietnam and in current affairs, of anything in America. I think it has the potential because it is immediate, it is direct, but it is not a straight encounter with a reality that most of us put off, shut out, try to avoid. Things can be structured

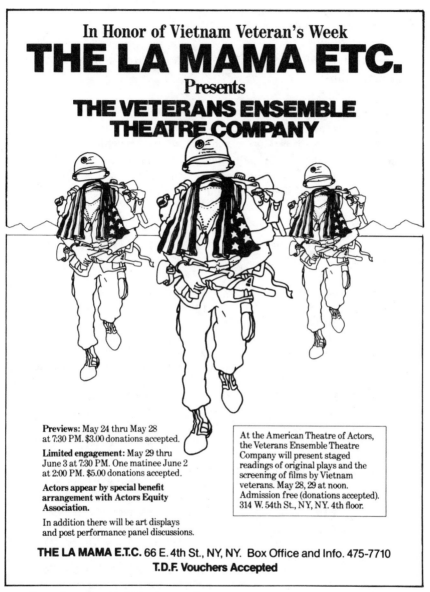

In Honor of Vietnam Veteran's Week

THE LA MAMA ETC.
Presents
THE VETERANS ENSEMBLE THEATRE COMPANY

Previews: May 24 thru May 28 at 7:30 PM. $3.00 donations accepted.

Limited engagement: May 29 thru June 3 at 7:30 PM. One matinee June 2 at 2:00 PM. $5.00 donations accepted.

Actors appear by special benefit arrangement with Actors Equity Association.

In addition there will be art displays and post performance panel discussions.

At the American Theatre of Actors, the Veterans Ensemble Theatre Company will present staged readings of original plays and the screening of films by Vietnam veterans. May 28, 29 at noon. Admission free (donations accepted). 314 W. 54th St., NY, NY. 4th floor.

THE LA MAMA E.T.C. 66 E. 4th St., NY, NY. Box Office and Info. 475-7710
T.D.F. Vouchers Accepted

Typography contributed by **Tri-Arts** Press, Inc. Printing contributed by **City University** Printing Department

This poster, designed by Vietnam veteran James A. Victorine, was the first VETCO billboard.

in the theater in a way that makes them more palatable than reality, and that allows people to learn from them.

Tom Bird is equally certain that the theater can benefit from Vietnam veterans:

If America is going to make something of that war, if we are going to grow from it, then we cannot run from Vietnam and everything about it. We have to face it creatively, and that means through the arts. How can we do that if we exile the bearers of the experiences, the Vietnam veterans themselves, from the screen or stage? If Vietnam is still stuck in our mind, part of the reason is our failure to absorb it through the arts.

NOTES

1. Gilbert Adair, *Vietnam on Film: From the Green Berets to Apocalypse Now* (Proteus: New York, 1981), p. 12.

2. Ibid., p. 64.

3. Michael T. Isenberg, *War on Film: The American Cinema and World War I* (Fairleigh Dickinson University Press: Rutherford, Madison, Teaneck, New Jersey, Associated University Presses: London and Toronto, 1981), p. 16; Robert S. Lynd and Helen Merrell Lynd, *Middletown: A Study in Modern Culture* (New York: Harcourt, Brace and World, Inc., 1929), pp. 358, n. 20; 359, n. 22, cited by Michael T. Isenberg, *War on Film: The American Cinema and World War I*, ibid.

4. Michael T. Isenberg, *War on Film: The American Cinema and World War I*, op. cit., pp. 250-260.

5. See the TV special, *Oscar Presents the Movies*. A copy of the special was provided to us by Charles Champlin and Sheila Benson of the *Los Angeles Times*.

6. Gilbert Adair, *Vietnam on Film: From the Green Berets to Apocalypse Now*, op. cit., pp. 13-14.

7. See the letter from the comptroller general of the United States to the Honorable Benjamin Rosenthal, of June 19, 1969, with attachments; and *Military Assistance to Commercial Film Projects*, House Committee Print, Military Operations Subcommittee Staff Memorandum (with Department of Defense commentary), 91st Congress, 1st Session, December 1969.

8. Gilbert Adair, *Vietnam on Film: From the Green Berets to Apocalypse Now*, op. cit., p. 15.

9. *Myths and Realities*, op. cit., p. 172.

10. Ibid.

11. Michael T. Isenberg, *War on Film: The American Cinema and World War I*, op. cit., pp. 46-47.

12. See *A List of Audiovisual Materials Produced by the United States Government for History*, General Services Administration, National Archives and Records Service, National Audiovisual Center, Washington, D.C.

13. Ibid.

14. Peter McInerney, "Apocalypse Then: Hollywood Looks Back at Vietnam," *Film Quarterly*, Volume 33, Number 2, 1980, pp. 21-32, p. 23.

15. *Myths and Realities*, op. cit., p. 172.

16. Ibid.

17. Ibid.

18. Ibid., pp. 171-72.

19. Peter McInerney, "Apocalypse Then: Hollywood Looks Back at Vietnam," op. cit., p. 29.

20. Peter Marin, "Coming to Terms with Vietnam," *Harper's*, December 1980, Volume 261, Number 1567, pp. 41-56, at p. 46.

21. Peter McInerney, "Apocalypse Then: Hollywood Looks Back at Vietnam," op. cit., p. 26.

22. Ibid., p. 31; Gilbert Adair, *Vietnam on Film: From the Green Berets to Apocalypse Now*, op. cit., p. 150.

23. Gilbert Adair, *Vietnam on Film: From the Green Berets to Apocalypse Now*, op. cit., p. 145.

24. The opportunity to enlist and to serve together, pictured in *The Deer Hunter*, was actually rare during the Vietnam War. Although there were "buddy" plans of one sort or another, soldiers in almost all cases went to war and returned home alone. Most veterans were robbed of their friends and lacked the sense of community that stays with the three men in *The Deer Hunter*. The other Vietnam War films, like *Go Tell the Spartans* and *The Boys in Company C*, are tragically more accurate.

25. Whether or not the Russian roulette scenes are historically accurate may not relate directly to the question of their actual artistic use or to the question of the writer's and director's actual intentions. The fact that something is historically accurate does not mean that the director knew that it was historically accurate or cared that it was historically accurate. Nevertheless, because the scenes were dismissed as fiction, it is interesting to note that accounts of Russian roulette have emerged. See "The High Cost of Survival," a review of *Conversations with the Enemy: The Story of PFC Robert Garwood*, by Winston Groom and Duncan Spencer, Putnam, in the *Washington Post*, "Book World," September 25, 1983.

II Failed Leadership

4   The White House

IN YOUR END IS YOUR BEGINNING

On August 18, 1980, candidate Ronald Reagan, fresh from his victory at the Republican National Convention, delivered a major address before the Veterans of Foreign Wars (VFW). He had come to receive their endorsement for the presidency. It was a night of triumph.

He began his speech with the ritual promise of increased funding for the programs of concern to the VFW and then turned to his major theme, peace through strength, and the Vietnam War:

> For too long, we have lived with the "Vietnam syndrome." . . . It is time that we recognized that ours was, in truth, a noble cause. A small country, newly free from colonial rule, sought our help in establishing self-rule and the means of self-defense against a totalitarian neighbor bent on conquest.[1]

Recognizing the value of the Vietnam War will help the nation recognize the courage and service of its Vietnam veterans:

> We dishonor the memory of 50,000 young Americans who died in that cause when we give way to feelings of guilt as if we were doing something shameful, and we have been shabby in our treatment of those who returned. They fought as well and as bravely as any Americans have ever fought in any war. They deserve our gratitude, our respect, and our continuing concern.[2]

The year 1980 seemed a turning point. The media had rediscovered Vietnam veterans. National polls showed overwhelming support for new benefits. Just since 1978, three organizations had appeared almost simultaneously to advance the cause of Vietnam veterans.

Vietnam veteran advocates were badly outnumbered in Congress. In 1978, those Vietnam veterans in Congress united together in an informal caucus, called the Vietnam Veterans in Congress, to provide leadership on Vietnam veterans issues.

The nation lacked a forceful national advocacy organization dedicated to the special contribution of Vietnam veterans. In 1978, the Vietnam Veterans of America was founded. The nation had yet to build a national memorial to Vietnam veterans, but in 1979 the Vietnam Veterans Memorial Fund was founded.

The awakening was surely late. The Vietnam War had officially begun in 1965, a decade and a half earlier. The last U.S. combat soldier had been withdrawn in 1973, nearly a decade before. The war era had been officially ended two presidents earlier, by Gerald Ford in 1975.

However late, the new attention was sincere. In 1979, Congress enacted legislation to establish Readjustment Counseling Centers across the country. A special outreach program had been established to help disabled Vietnam veterans find jobs. In 1980, Congress set aside a beautiful piece of land, between the Lincoln and Washington Monuments, for a Vietnam veterans memorial.

With his inaugural in 1981, President Reagan had the opportunity to seize the nation's growing support for Vietnam veterans. Committed publicly in his speech to the VFW, President Reagan's first act in office was to impose a hiring freeze on the new Readjustment Counseling Program.

President Reagan's first budget message went one step further and proposed the total elimination of the program. With a thoroughness that almost defied belief, the Reagan White House then went after every single special outreach program for Vietnam veterans, including the special employment program for disabled veterans.[3]

The personnel freeze in the Readjustment Counseling Program was illegal. Congress had specifically prohibited such reductions in the lifesaving VA medical system in 1979. The independent General Accounting Office (GAO), the agency that had the specific task of interpreting the 1979 act, formally ruled against the freeze.[4]

Litigation was filed by 11 members of Congress and the Vietnam Veterans of America, seeking to overturn the freeze. The White House remained firm as the courts worked slowly toward a decision. In the end, it took another act of Congress to bring compliance.[5]

The issue was not partisan. The Republican-controlled Senate joined the House in enacting the final legislation that overturned the freeze and independently passed a separate resolution, by a unanimous vote, that specifically made reference to the legality of the administration's action.[6]

The freeze overturned, Congress rejected the administration's request to end the program. The Disabled Veterans Outreach Program was saved as well. In the end, the administration succeeded in killing only one Vietnam veteran program.

David Stockman, the new director of the Office of Management and Budget, managed the president's budget proposals. Stockman's background made the Reagan cuts in Vietnam veterans programs particularly unacceptable to some.

Active in the antiwar movement at Michigan State University, Stockman had attended divinity school during the course of the Vietnam War. A reporter on the prestigious *Meet the Press* wondered if the administration's proposed cuts for Vietnam veterans would not have a "particularly divisive effect coming from someone who was in divinity school when they were in Vietnam."[7]

Vietnam veterans were less polite. Rick Heilman, legislative director for the Disabled American Veterans, said: "I deeply resented someone of Stockman's background, who was waving antiwar placards while I was over there being shot and seeing some of my friends die, making major decisions about our benefits programs."[8]

In 1981, Congress created a small-business loan program for Vietnam veterans. The initiative merely copied similar efforts for both World War II and Korean veterans. It was long overdue, yet the Reagan administration opposed the bill, only grudgingly signed it into law, and then blocked its implementation. Today, it is a dead letter law, engraved on the statute books, accomplishing nothing.[9]

To help Vietnam veterans without a high school diploma, the Congress in 1981 gave them an additional two years to use their GI Bill benefits for secondary education. At the same time, veterans with continuing employment problems were given more time to use the job training provisions of the GI Bill.

The Reagan administration opposed the measure. Once enacted, the program was implemented through regulations that made almost all Vietnam veterans ineligible. Projected to help 20,000 veterans, only 169 were awarded benefits in the program's first quarter.

Members of Congress wrote the president, seeking a change in the regulations, but that effort proved fruitless. Finally, in 1982, another law was passed mandating new eligibility standards.[10]

In 1983, a series of bipartisan initiatives were passed to address the impact of the deepest recession since the Great Depression. A special Vietnam veterans employment program was designed to augment the 1981 measure. The administration opposed the bill.[11]

In 1981, the Congress took a major step forward in addressing the Agent Orange issue. It passed legislation mandating VA health care for veterans with Agent Orange-related medical problems. The administration opposed the bill. The president carefully noted his dissent when he reluctantly signed the measure into law.[12]

In 1982, the first phase of the Vietnam Veterans Memorial was completed. A national dedication ceremony was scheduled for the week of Veterans Day. Hundreds of thousands of individuals participated, yet the president declined to join the formal ceremonies and did not speak during the memorial's dedication.[13]

*   *   *

The Congress has never declared war except on the petition or concurrence of the president of the United States. As the primary formulator and executor of foreign policy, and as commander-in-chief of the Armed Forces, the president is a highly visible and identifiable embodiment of the U.S. government for those serving in the military.

In fact, in "police actions," such as those in Lebanon, the Dominican Republic, Korea, and Vietnam, the president has unilaterally committed U.S. troops without a Congressional declaration of war. Granted, the Congress had to provide appropriations for such actions, but the president initiated the actions and left Congress to debate funding after the fact when U.S. soldiers were already involved in life-and-death battles.

Vietnam veterans could reasonably expect the president to be a forceful advocate for recognition and benefits. Under any circumstances, the president and the men who formulated the policies for the war would be expected to be grateful to those who attempted to carry out those policies.

From a purely pragmatic point of view, it would be important to be appreciative of veterans simply because they become the fathers of those who may be called on to serve in the future. A generation hewn from the bitterness of their fathers' experience may not be willing to volunteer in the next foreign policy crisis.

Since the beginning of the Vietnam War, no president has been as determinately hostile to Vietnam veterans programs as President Reagan, yet each previous administration would do by inaction part of what the Reagan White House did as a matter of clear policy. For many Vietnam veterans, the long passage of time, culminating in the Reagan administration, had only made explicit the attitudes that had been implicit in previous administrations.

Administrations that spent billions of dollars per week prosecuting the war each vetoed or threatened to veto proposals for the benefit of the war's veterans on the basis of expense. Each administration in its own way had recognized Vietnam veterans, but each, on balance, had committed little to lead the temperament of the country with regard to their return and readjustment.

FALSE START: THE JOHNSON AND NIXON YEARS

In 1966, during the beginning of the Vietnam War, 116 members of the House of Representatives (one out of every four) had studied under the World War II GI Bill, as had 12 of the nation's governors (again, one in four), and five of President Johnson's senior White House advisers.[14]

The World War II GI Bill opened the doors of colleges and universities to a generation of young Americans. It was a revolutionary effort, the *first* major government program to provide direct aid to the students themselves, not merely grants to colleges.[15]

The program was generous. Up to $500 a year was available to cover the costs of tuition for veterans. In addition, a veteran received an additional $75 a month for living expenses, more if he were married, and even more if he had children.

Compared to today's multithousand-dollar tuitions, $500 seems a small amount, but in 1946 it covered the full tuition at nearly every college and university in the United States, public or private. Benefits were available for 48 months, more than five academic years. Those few veterans who could not meet the full cost of their tuition were allowed to accelerate their benefits, receiving a higher payment for fewer months.

As President Johnson signed the Vietnam GI Bill into law in 1966, he confidently asserted that the World War II GI Bill and its successor, the Korean GI Bill, had been a success:

> The first two GI Bills cost $21 billion. Our economists now estimate that they resulted in a return of some $60 billion in federal taxes for that $21 billion invested.
>
> The education level of World War II and Korean war veterans averages about 2 years above the level of nonveterans. The difference exists primarily because of what the GI Bills were able to do.
>
> We made the most promising investment that a nation can make, an investment in the talent and ambition of our citizens. The return on that investment has doubled and has redoubled ever since.[16]

The Vietnam GI Bill that President Johnson signed into law provided $100 a month to cover both tuition and living expenses. The payment worked out to almost exactly the amount that World War II veterans had received: $75 a month for tuition plus the earlier $500 a year for tuition.

The benefit levels had been frozen. Unfortunately, inflation had not stood still. The general inflation rate, as reflected in the Consumer Price Index, had jumped more than 50 percent. The cost of higher education rose even faster. The cost of attending a public four-year college had doubled. The cost of attending a private four-year college had increased four times.[17]

The inadequate benefit levels affected Vietnam veterans' ability to use the GI Bill. Despite the general increase in the percentage of people attending college, the percentage of Vietnam veterans using the GI Bill was lower than that for both the World War II and Korean programs.[18]

Although the public image still exists that Vietnam veterans are uneducated draftees, 79 percent had a high school diploma at the time of their discharge, compared to only 45 percent of those who had served during World War II. The problem was not the soldier. It was the benefits.[19]

In time, there were increases in the benefit levels, but the increases would never match the gap in benefits that already existed in 1966. Indeed, by the early 1970s, inflation would be boiling. The benefit increases would barely match the yearly increase in the cost of education.

Even in 1977, the VA found that 42 percent of those Vietnam veterans using their benefits to go to college had to work part time in order to make ends meet. Over half of these part-time students were not able to complete their degrees. The principal problem, the VA discovered, was financial.[20]

Unfortunately, there was an additional catch-22. Ten years after a veteran was discharged, he automatically lost his right to benefits. In the technical language of veterans benefits, he was "delimited." Veterans who went back to school to try again discovered that they had few years of eligibility left.

One study after another concluded that those who needed the GI Bill the most were able to use it the least. The World War II bill had opened new opportunities for working families across the country. Those Vietnam veterans encouraged by their fathers' experiences after World War II were disappointed.

For veterans from families with enough income to help pay the cost of tuition, the Vietnam GI Bill provided a payment that rounded out the cost of tuition and expenses. It eased the way. For those families who could not afford to help their sons, the Vietnam GI Bill was a paltry sum, good only as a symbol of neglect.

Although 20 percent of the soldiers who served in Vietnam did not have a high school diploma, they made up only 8 percent of those who had actually used the GI Bill, the VA discovered in 1972. Although 35 percent of the eligible white veterans discharged from July 1, 1968, through the end of 1970 had used the GI Bill by 1973, only 26 percent of black veterans were able to use their benefits.[21]

As early as 1969, a Committee on the Vietnam Veteran, established by President Nixon, concluded:

Available data show that participation in G.I. Bill training is inverse to need. Nearly 50% of the veterans who already have college training at the time of discharge and therefore have the best prospects for immediate employment seek to upgrade their education under the G.I. Bill. On the other hand, those who have serious education deficiencies show participation rates as low as 10%.[22]

In 1978, as the long saga of the Vietnam GI Bill neared its final stage, the VA found that World War II veterans were 46 percent more likely to have a college diploma than were their nonveteran peers. Vietnam veterans were 45 percent less likely. There had been a total reversal. Military service, once a step up, had become a handicap.[23]

The World War II GI Bill had set the measure of leadership in veterans affairs. A revolution in its time, its accomplishment should have made replication easy, an almost obvious course of action. Somehow, the obvious had proved impossible.

Abraham Lincoln, President Johnson once noted, had given his country the grand promise of emancipation, "but it was a proclamation, and not a fact." Lincoln's promise became real only when it was backed by the federal government and the Civil Rights Act. As President Johnson said, "Today, where once some people were afraid to vote, they now proudly walk into the polling place with their chin up and their chest out."[24]

The Great Society program took the basic American values of justice, liberty, and union and backed those values with the support of an aggressive government. The result was an activist decade that would change U.S. society.

Central to the Great Society was the effort to expand education. In a special message to Congress, President Johnson proposed that we "declare a national goal of Full Educational Opportunity." The nation must recognize, in Johnson's words, that "higher education is no longer a luxury, but a necessity."[25]

The nation's greatest educational program, President Johnson often noted, was the World War II GI Bill, yet creating a new GI Bill involved more than mere benefits. A Vietnam GI Bill would be a clear declaration that the skirmish in Vietnam was not likely to end soon. It would move the government one step closer to stating publicly that Vietnam had been a real war, even if it had lacked the trappings of a formal declaration.

Throughout most of 1965, the Johnson administration opposed any GI Bill. By 1966, the need could no longer be avoided, but the administration was still hesitant. Although the World War II GI Bill had helped all veterans, President Johnson proposed that traditional benefits now be limited to only those veterans who had served in a combat zone. Other veterans would receive a flat grant that would defray just some of the cost of tuition.[26]

Congress rejected the administration's proposal almost immediately. The Senate, under the leadership of Senator Ralph W. Yarborough (D-Texas), was independently advancing a stronger measure.

The president's view, however, could not be dismissed. Veto threats were reported, and a replication of the World War II GI Bill was precluded. The administration insisted that costs had to be controlled.[27]

The final compromise was developed in large part by the chairman of the House Committee on Veterans' Affairs, Congressman Olin E. (Tiger) Teague (D-Texas). Its limited benefits held the first-year cost to $325 million, but even that seemed high to President Johnson, whose proposal would have run just $150 million.

Asked in a press conference to list his budget disputes with Congress, President Johnson noted the high cost of the finally enacted Vietnam GI Bill. When he signed the bill, over half of his statement was devoted to its budget implications.[28]

As early as 1966, the cost of the Great Society and the Vietnam War were beginning to collide. In the next few years, the conflict increased. The Johnson White House placed increasing pressure on domestic programs. To enact a full GI Bill would not only add to the immediate cost of the war but would also build in an obligation that would continue long after the fighting had stopped.

Yet President Johnson was prepared to change his mind. Although his signing statement emphasized the bill's budget impact, he finished with candor:

> I am going to sign this measure this morning notwithstanding the fact that it goes further than I was willing to ask for this year, because, paraphrasing what Secretary Rusk said the other day in response to a question from Congress, he said, "Well, Senator, could it be that they could perhaps be wrong?" And it just could be that the president was wrong when he made his original request.[29]

President Johnson backed his candor with action. Within a year, he submitted a special message to Congress calling for a 30 percent increase in GI Bill benefits. When action was delayed, he reiterated his request in another special message. The increase was enacted into law.[30]

It would be a long time before a president would once again take the lead on the Vietnam GI Bill. In 1969, the Senate sought a 46 percent increase in benefits. The new Nixon administration opposed the measure and threatened to veto the bill. In the final law, the increase was cut back nearly 25 percent.[31]

In 1972, the Senate sought a 43 percent increase. The Nixon administration wanted to hold the line at 8.6 percent. The final law cut the Senate increase nearly in half. The Vietnam GI Bill had been behind from the beginning. Now the White House was cutting down long overdue increases.[32]

President Nixon was a Republican, but to the anger of the more conservative wing of his party, during his administration the Johnson vision of a Great Society continued to drive government programs. Government expansion in the service of human needs would continue, but Vietnam veterans would somehow be forgotten.

In its May 22, 1970 issue, *Life* documented the squalid conditions at a Veterans Administration hospital in the Bronx. Paralyzed veterans were left unattended while meals grew cold. Rats crawled along the walls. Filthy linen sat in piles. Veterans unable to control body functions were forced to lie in their own waste for hours.

"It's like you've been put in jail or been punished for something," one veteran commented. The problem was money. "We're just not being funded in a way that we can adequately give and fulfill our services," the hospital director complained, but over $100 million in increased funding was on the way.[33]

The *Life* article struck the nation's conscience, yet less than three months later, on August 11, 1970, President Nixon vetoed an appropriation bill because, among other complaints, he said that it contained $105 million more than he had requested for the VA medical system.[34]

No citizens have a greater claim on their government than the soldiers who protect the nation in battle. Vietnam veterans legitimately expected that their needs would receive priority attention during a new era of government activism. It was a fundamental paradox of the Great Society that it would do so much for so many and then be struck by sudden caution in helping those to whom it owed the most.

PARTIAL RECONCILIATION: PRESIDENTS FORD AND CARTER

Gerald Ford's first major act as president of the United States was to announce a conditional pardon for draft resisters and military deserters. His last act in office, signed on January 19, 1976, the day before the inauguration of Jimmy Carter, was to extend the pardon for deserters.

Jimmy Carter's administration shared this symmetry. As he noted in his autobiographical account of his term in office, President Carter's first and last meetings in the Oval Office were with Max Cleland, the triple amputee Vietnam veteran who had run the Veterans Administration for him.[35]

It was a "time of healing," as Gerald Ford termed it, from Vietnam and Watergate, from costly failure abroad and corruption at home. In their different ways, both Presidents Ford and Carter tried to be reconciling forces. For both, it proved to be a difficult job. The strength of their personal commitment would be felt to the nation's lasting benefit, but both would meet with only partial success.

The very problems that divided the country made reconciliation difficult. The credibility of the national government itself had fallen because of the dual crises of Vietnam and Watergate. Official government actions would not evoke the spontaneous trust required for truly bold initiatives.

The turbulence of the times was reflected in Gerald Ford's strange road to the White House. He is the only person in U.S. history to become president without winning a national election. He had been appointed vice president on the resignation of Spiro Agnew, who was facing corruption charges. Ford rose to the presidency on the resignation of Richard Nixon, the first president ever to resign from office.

The tenor of the time itself urged caution. Gerald Ford's status as an appointed president with no electoral coalition reinforced the suggestion. A pardon for draft resisters would be a risky initiative. Yet President Ford chose to proceed carefully, keeping his intentions secret from all but a select group of senior counselors.[36]

President Ford was aware of the rifts that remained in U.S. society. Those rifts had reached into his own home:

> My two oldest sons who were in college were sympathetic to those who raised questions about the Vietnam War. We at the dinner table as a family would often discuss the pros and cons. Fortunately, we were able to have a rational discussion. They challenged some of my views, which were hawkish, and I tried to understand their views.

President Ford's pardon program was carefully drawn. Its theme was "earned reentry." Draft resisters and deserters would be pardoned, but only if they made individual applications, cleared a special process, and did alternative service. The deserters were made ineligible for veteran benefits.

To those supporting a pardon, the Ford program was too limited. Its caution, however, won no friends from those opposed in principle to letting the resisters come home, a group already concerned that President Ford might be too moderate. Congressman Robert Bauman (R-Maryland), a leading Congressional conservative, noted that he was particularly "concerned with [Ford's] amnesty stand."[37]

Republican Party chairmen from the South were so concerned that they called an emergency meeting in Washington. California governor Ronald Reagan, in town to speak at a fund raiser for Congressman Bauman, had begun to talk "privately of becoming a national spokesman for conservative alternatives," according to the *Washington Post*.[38]

Governor Reagan, no doubt, would have found a reason to run against President Ford for the Republican nomination in 1976. The Ford pardon program, however, made finding a reason easy.

At the end of President Ford's term, Jane Hart, the widow of the recently deceased senator Philip Hart (D-Michigan), urged him to broaden his pardon program. Jane Hart was a personal friend. Senator Hart had represented President Ford's home state of Michigan.

The White House staff counseled no action, but President Ford insisted that options be developed. Among the deserters were veterans who had been wounded in combat and some who had been decorated for valor. President Ford made them eligible for veteran benefits.[39]

President Carter completed the task. While he was still a candidate, Carter announced that he would grant a pardon to all draft resisters. The day after his inauguration, the pardon was issued. It was nearly total and unconditional. The draft resisters could finally come home.[40]

Given the response to the more limited initiative by President Ford, the resulting reaction could be expected. But President Carter benefited from the earlier Ford action. President Ford had survived his critics, beating Ronald Reagan for the Republican nomination, and had come back to extend the program. He had demonstrated that it could be done.

Gerald Ford, Jimmy Carter, and Ronald Reagan are our nation's three post-Vietnam presidents. Each had chosen the national convention of a major veterans organization to deliver a significant address. President Ford announced his decision to grant a pardon before the Veterans of Foreign Wars (VFW). Candidate Carter announced his intention to grant a total pardon before the American Legion. Candidate Reagan took his revisionist history of Vietnam to the VFW.

Reagan received standing ovations, as he almost certainly expected. President Ford was careful to keep any mention of the pardon initiative out of the prepared text made available before the address. The surprised VFW was struck dumb, but no more. An organized group within the American Legion was ready for Carter. He was booed.[41]

For both Presidents Ford and Carter, the choice of audience had its price, but it also reflected their message. If there was to be true reconciliation, then organizations like the VFW had to forget the war's hatred, just as draft resisters had to understand that a pardon would never mean total acceptance.

As they prepared a pardon initiative for President Ford, the White House staff secured research on earlier amnesties. There were no exact parallels. The Civil War had divided the nation, but the issue after the war was clemency for Southern leaders, not draft resistance. World War II had brought the modern draft, but the war did not divide the nation.

Reconciliation after Vietnam presented unique problems. Acting almost as a relay team, with one runner from each of our nation's political parties, Presidents Ford and Carter were prepared to break new ground. Reconciliation was won for at least one group — those whose opposition to the war forced violation of their nation's laws.

However united or divided on the war itself, the nation faced the entirely separate problem of its still unmet debt to Vietnam veterans. The country needed to reconcile itself with its veterans as well as with its war resisters.

Amnesty seems the more controversial of the two tasks, yet reconciliation with Vietnam veterans would actually prove the hardest. It would require billions of dollars. Amnesty was nearly free. The onus was different in each case. In letting resisters come home, the nation was the judge offering forgiveness. In facing its Vietnam veterans, the nation was the guilty party.

Pardon for draft resisters, couched in terms of the need to put the war behind us, also was consistent with the nation's rush to forget Vietnam. At the price of momentary controversy, it completed a task that otherwise would have hovered over the United States, requiring further action. For veterans, however, the war was still present. Facing its veterans would require the nation to help those veterans shoulder the war's memories.

As it returned for business in 1973, the Congress was prepared to try again to increase benefits under the Vietnam GI Bill. In 1974, it cleared a 23 percent increase and sent it to the nation's new president, Gerald Ford, for signature. Bent on winning the fight against inflation, President Ford vetoed the bill.

The 23 percent increase, the first in two years, would barely match the spiraling cost of higher education, then jumping 14 percent a year. Naturally, it would not move to close the gap that had existed in 1966, but it would slightly exceed the jump in the general inflation rate over the previous two years.[42]

The Office of Management and Budget, the president's cost control managers, urged a veto, as did the Treasury Department. The only arguments for the bill came from the Veterans Administration and a few key White House advisers. Their counsel, however, was almost purely political.

Even for those supporting the bill, the needs of Vietnam veterans were not the principal issue. The entire argument over the inadequacy of the Vietnam GI Bill was dismissed in a two-page memo by a junior staffer. The advisers wondered instead whether the president could sustain his veto in Congress. The President did lose, and the increase became law.[43]

President Carter had a personal sense of the problems faced by Vietnam veterans:

> My oldest son, Jack, voluntarily left college and enlisted in the Navy as an enlisted man, electronics specialist, went to Vietnam and spent a long time there. . . . However, when Jack came home, in spite of my pride, he was pretty well condemned and ridiculed by his peers — the other college students and his former friends in high school, and so forth, because he had gone. Instead of it being a source of pride for him and admiration when he went to public events in his uniform, as it had been for me before, he soon found that he was better off to take his uniform and replace it with civilian clothes.

From his son's experiences, and the experiences of other Vietnam veterans, President Carter drew a firm conclusion:

> Even before I began my campaign for president, I was concerned, I don't want to say obsessed, but I was at least concerned with the stigma that had been attached to Vietnam veterans and with the realization that even greater than those who served with me during the time of the preceding war, they had to be especially courageous and their sacrifice was even greater because they were not heroes and also because they were not appreciated.

President Carter understood the need to join reconciliation with those who had fought the war with reconciliation with those who had opposed it. He carefully joined the appointment of antiwar activist Sam Brown as head of Action — the nation's volunteer service program — with the appointment of Max Cleland as the first Vietnam veteran to run the Veterans Administration.[44]

The Carter administration sought to balance the pardon initiative for draft resisters with an employment initiative for Vietnam veterans. The president then commissioned a comprehensive review of all Vietnam veterans programs within the federal government.

Termed a PRM, for Presidential Review Memorandum, the review brought the GI Bill debate into the Carter White House. The newly formed Vietnam Veterans in Congress, as well as the Vietnam Veterans of America, both argued for comprehensive GI Bill reform. The proposal was rejected.

In the end, the PRM's GI Bill initiative was reduced to a measure that helped Vietnam veterans without a high school diploma and veterans with serious employment problems. Those veterans surely needed help, but equally sure, there was considerably more to be done.[45]

The PRM was a paradox. Self-consciously labeled a presidential initiative, the high level of the effort was incongruous with its results. It seems almost bizarre that a president would begin an effort so large and so public while intending in the end to do nothing.

The explanation seems, simply, to be that the president had no intentions beyond the concern that the problems facing Vietnam veterans be thoroughly explored. The effort was begun with an implicit understanding that *any* conclusion was acceptable as long as it was carefully justified. Lacking was a presidential commitment that the final action must seem bold and be publicly recognized as significant.

Explaining his decision-making process, President Carter stated: "My general procedure for handling these kinds of things was to defer to recommendations of my most trusted advisers unless I had an overwhelming reason for not accepting them."

Clearly, if the president was willing, the staff was not. Yet, the Carter years saw progress on Vietnam veterans issues. To help reach more veterans, and to provide important psychological help, the Readjustment Counseling Program was enacted. The Labor Department developed a successful special outreach program to help disabled Vietnam veterans find jobs.

Like the PRM's GI Bill proposal, these changes were important, but they were carefully limited. They expanded outreach but left the basic benefits untouched. More Vietnam veterans were found, but once found, the tools to help them were essentially the same.

The Carter White House was seeking small changes that they hoped might combine to make a real difference. Vietnam veterans were hoping for more. Reaching 30 years old, they had a growing sense that time was running out. Vietnam veterans were seeking major reforms that would suggest a dramatic new beginning.

President Carter began reconciliation between the nation and its Vietnam veterans, but he would take only the first step, comparable to President Ford's first step on the pardon issue. President Carter's successor, however, would not be prepared to complete the job with Vietnam veterans as President Carter had completed the job with draft resisters.

The dramatic new beginning never came.

PUBLIC AND PRIVATE ACCOUNTABILITY

In 1979, Louis Harris asked Americans what they thought were the principal "effects of the war in Vietnam on the United States and American society?" Thirty-four percent of the replies emphasized a common theme: "the deterioration of the nation's confidence in its institutions, especially the government."[46]

The response was surprising because the question was open-ended. The answer was not suggested, yet a third of the nation came back with the same response. Vietnam had rocked our nation's faith in its government.

Based on the response, the Harris organization asked Americans whether they believed the war added to "young people's hostility toward the government." Fifty-seven percent said, "Yes." Fifty percent felt that the war increased "people's lack of trust in government to do what's right."[47]

The nation was clear that the war's failure lay at the feet of government leaders, not of Vietnam veterans. An overwhelming 73 percent felt that the "trouble in Vietnam was that our troops were asked to fight in a war which our political leaders in Washington would not let them win."[48]

It was the nation's sense of betrayal by its leaders that helped produce the growing cynicism about government. The American people were clear where accountability lay, but their sense of accountability was not reflected in the actual distribution of public blame.

No public distinctions would be drawn between those who had taken risks to focus their leaders' attention on the war's problems (such as, most publicly, George Ball) and those who had simply pursued the war despite its costs. Those who had led the nation would not be left untouched by the war, but they would also be almost equally honored.

When the Falkland Islands were taken by Argentina in a surprise attack in 1982, Britain's Lord Carrington resigned his post. This act is common in most countries where a government is embarrassed by poor foresight or poor execution.

Yet throughout the Vietnam War, only one figure would interrupt his ambitions to acknowledge the war's controversy or its failure — President Johnson. Although Vietnam would be the military's most controversial modern war, no general or admiral resigned in protest over war strategy.[49]

In contrast, the consequences for veterans would be severe, although private. Vietnam veterans would be held accountable for the nation's rejection of the war through an inadequate GI Bill, unemployment and underemployment, divorce and suicide.

Not surprisingly, the disillusionment that swept the United States after Vietnam would be especially severe among Vietnam veterans. They felt betrayed. For many, the pride they felt in their own medals hardly matched the anger they felt over the Presidential Medals of Freedom that hung from the chests of so many leaders who had made the war. (See Table 1.)

Table 1
Postwar Honors for War Policymakers

Officer	Position	Postwar Career
McGeorge Bundy	National Security Adviser, 1961-66	President, Ford Foundation 1966-1979; Professor of History, New York University
Walt Rostow	National Security Adviser, 1966-68	Professor of Economics and History, University of Texas; Recipient of Presidential Medal of Freedom
Henry Kissinger	National Security Adviser, 1969-72 Secretary of State, 1972-74	Faculty of Georgetown University; Consultant to NBC, Goldman Sachs and Co., Chase Bank; Senior Fellow, Aspen Institute, 1973-76; Trustee, Metropolitan Museum of Art, New York City; Recipient of Presidential Medal of Freedom
Robert McNamara	Secretary of Defense, 1961-68	President, World Bank; Director, Royal Dutch Petroleum, the *Washington Post*, TWA, Corning Glass, Ford Foundation, Brookings Institute, California Institute of Technology; Recipient of Presidential Medal of Freedom
Clark Clifford	Secretary of Defense, 1968	Senior Partner, Clifford and Warnke; Recipient of Presidential Medal of Freedom; Director, Financial General Bankshares, Knight-Ridder Newspapers
Melvin Laird	Secretary of Defense, 1969-73	Senior Counselor of National and International Affairs, *Readers Digest*; Director, Northwest Airlines, Phillips Petroleum, Metropolitan Life Insurance, Communications Satellite Corporation; Board of Directors, Thomas Jefferson Foundation, University of Virginia, George Washington University; Trustee, Kennedy Center; Recipient of Presidential Medal of Freedom

Table 1, continued

Officer	Position	Postwar Career
Dean Rusk	Secretary of State, 1961-68	Professor of Law, University of Georgia
William Rodgers	Secretary of State, 1969-72	Senior Partner, Rogers and Wells

Veterans benefits do more than provide help. They are the principal way our nation tries, perhaps desperately, to humanize war by limiting its costs in the lives of those who fight. Benefits are the way the nation steps forward to share some of the private cost of war by pledging its tax dollars to extend help.

Nations, like individuals, can get lucky. They can be saved from their leaders' failures by their people's ability to endure. But the people's ability to rebound from war is conditioned on generous benefits that help soldiers find new lives.

The United States was not lucky after Vietnam. The war changed everything. That consequence, however, was not made necessary by the war alone. More was required. In part, it was made for us by Watergate. In part, we made that consequence for ourselves because as a nation we chose to limit our ability to adjust and grow past the war's horrors.

NOTES

1. Address by the Honorable Ronald Reagan, Veterans of Foreign Wars, Chicago, Illinois, August 18, 1980, pp. 6-7.

2. Ibid., p. 7.

3. See *Additional Details on Budget Savings*, April 1981, Executive Office of the President, Office of Management and Budget, pp. 319-320; Statement of the Honorable David E. Bonior, March 10, 1981, *Congressional Record – House*, H. 845-846; and Philip Geyelin, "A 'Noble Cause' Lost?" *Washington Post*, March 23, 1981.

4. General Accounting Office, letter of February 19, 1981, to the Honorable G. V. Montgomery, chairman, Committee on Veterans' Affairs, B-198103;

General Accounting Office, *Impoundment Report Responding to the President's Sixth Special Message, of March 10, 1981*, April 13, 1981, B-200685.

5. *Congressman David E. Bonior, et al., v. David A. Stockman*, Civil Action No. 81-0979, District Court, District of Columbia. The suit was brought, *pro bono publico*, by Joseph Zengerle. A partner in the firm of Bingham, Dana and Gould, Zengerle is a Vietnam veteran and was assistant secretary of the Air Force under President Carter.

6. *Congressional Record – Senate*, June 2, 1981, S. 5657-5658, for passage of S. Res. 120. The House, in an action accepted by the Senate in conference, acted earlier in the Supplemental Appropriation Bill, P.L. 97-12. The House also specifically addressed the legality of the impoundment. See *Supplemental Appropriations and Rescission Bill, 1981* – Committed to the Committee on the Whole House on the State of the Union and ordered to be printed, 97th Congress, 1st Session, Report No. 97-29, pp. 172-173. *Congressman David E. Bonior, et al., v. David A. Stockman* was ruled moot by Judge Charles R. Richey on February 9, 1982, following the administration's decision to obligate the funds.

7. Jack W. Germond and Jules Witcover, "Tempers Flare on Plan to Cut Veterans' Help," *Washington Star*, May 6, 1981.

8. Ibid.

9. See *Veterans' Health Care, Training, and Small Business Loan Act of 1981*, Statement on Signing H.R. 3499 into Law, November 3, 1981, Weekly Compilation of Presidential Documents, Monday, November 9, 1981, Volume 17, Number 45, p. 1217; and statement of the Honorable David E. Bonior, "Abandoned Again," and "Veterans' Administration Fails to Properly Implement Vietnam Veteran Legislation," the Honorable Bob Edgar, "Vietnam Veterans," the Honorable Thomas A. Daschle, "Veterans Business and Employment," May 20, 1982, *Congressional Record – House*.

10. See statements of the Honorable David E. Bonior, Bob Edgar, and Thomas A. Daschle, May 20, 1982, op. cit.; statement of the Honorable David E. Bonior, "Extended Eligibility for Vietnam Era Veterans: H.R. 6915," *Congressional Record – Extension of Remarks*, August 5, 1982, E. 3706-3709; statement of the Honorable David E. Bonior, *Congressional Record – House*, September 28, 1982, H. 7798-7799. The effort to mandate changes in the eligibility standard through new legislation was led by Senator Alan Cranston. It was enacted as Section 206 of P.L. 97-72.

11. See letter of the Honorable Harry N. Walters, administrator of Veterans' Affairs, to the Honorable G. V. (Sonny) Montgomery, chairman, Committee on Veterans' Affairs, May 11, 1983, *Emergency Vietnam Veterans' Job Training Act of 1983*, May 13, 1983 – Committed to the Committee of the Whole House and ordered to be printed, 98th Congress, 1st Session, Report No. 98-116.

12. See "Statement on Signing H.R. 3499 into Law," op. cit., p. 1217; and *Veterans' Health Care Act of 1981*, May 19, 1981 – Committed to the Committee of the Whole House and ordered printed, 97th Congress, 1st Session, Report No. 97-79, pp. 31-32.

13. Lou Cannon, "White House Team No Longer Pulling Together in the Traces," *Washington Post*, November 15, 1982.

14. "Remarks Upon Signing the 'Cold War GI Bill' (Veterans' Readjustment Benefits Act of 1966)," March 3, 1966, *Public Papers of the Presidents of the United States, Lyndon B. Johnson, 1966* (in two books), Number 100, pp. 263-265, at p. 264.

15. Paul Starr, *The Discarded Army: Veterans after Vietnam* (Charterhouse: New York, 1973), p. 232.

16. "Remarks upon Signing the 'Cold War GI Bill' (Veterans' Readjustment Benefits Act of 1966)," March 3, 1966, op. cit., p. 264.

17. *Final Report on Educational Assistance to Veterans: A Comparative Study of Three G.I. Bills* (conducted by the Educational Testing Service, Princeton, New Jersey, pursuant to Section 413 of Public Law 92-540), Submitted to the Committee on Veterans' Affairs, United States Senate, September 20, 1973, 93rd Congress, 1st Session, Senate Committee Print No. 18, pp. 27-29.

18. Paul Starr, *The Discarded Army: Veterans after Vietnam*, op. cit., p. 228. Mr. Starr found rates lagging as late as 72 months (six years) after the Vietnam GI Bill had begun.

19. Ibid., p. 240.

20. See *Veterans Benefits Under Current Educational Programs*, April 1977, Veterans Administration; and *Completion Rates For Education and Training Under the Vietnam-era GI Bill*, June 1976, Veterans Administration.

21. Sar A. Levitan and Karen A. Cleary, *Old Wars Remain Unfinished: The Veteran Benefits System* (Johns Hopkins University Press: Baltimore and London, 1973), pp. 141-144.

22. *Report of the President's Committee on the Vietnam Veterans*, processed, pp. 8-9.

23. *Education and Income Characteristics of Veterans*, March 1978, Reports and Statistics Service, Office of Controller, Veterans Administration; see especially, pp. 16-17.

24. "Remarks at the Post Office in Jeffersonville, Indiana," July 23, 1966, *Public Papers of the Presidents of the United States, Lyndon B. Johnson, 1966* (in two books), Number 353, pp. 778-784, at p. 781.

25. "Special Message to the Congress: 'Toward Full Educational Opportunity,'" January 12, 1965, *Public Papers of the Presidents of the United States, Lyndon B. Johnson, 1965* (in two books), Number 9, pp. 25-33, at pp. 25-26, 30.

26. See "Cold War Veterans' Bill Passed by Senate," *1965 CQ Almanac*, pp. 401-404, and "Congress Approves 'Cold War GI' Benefits," *1966 CQ Almanac*, pp. 313-316.

27. Ibid.

28. "Remarks Upon Signing the 'Cold War GI Bill' (Veterans' Readjustment Benefits Act of 1966)," March 3, 1966, op. cit., pp. 264-265. See also, *Education and Other Benefits for Veterans of Service after January 31, 1955*, February 3, 1966 — Committed to the Committee of the Whole House on the State of the Union and ordered to be printed, 89th Congress, 2nd Session, Report No. 1258.

29. "Remarks upon Signing the 'Cold War GI Bill' (Veterans' Readjustment Benefits Act of 1966)," March 3, 1966, op. cit., 265.

30. "Special Message to the Congress: America's Servicemen and Veterans," January 31, 1967, *Public Papers of the Presidents of the United States, Lyndon B. Johnson, 1967* (in two books), Number 25, pp. 108-113; and "Special Message to the Congress — Our Pride and Our Strength: America's Servicemen and Veterans," January 30, 1968, *Public Papers of the Presidents of the United States, Lyndon B. Johnson, 1968-1969* (in two books), Number 40, pp. 112-118.

31. See *Veterans Education and Training Assistance Amendments Act of 1969*, October 21, 1969, — Ordered to be printed, 91st Congress, 1st Session, Senate, Report No. 91-487, pp. 70-73; "Veterans Benefits," *1969 CQ Almanac*, pp. 555-558; and, "Veterans Education Assistance," *1970 CQ Almanac*, p. 271.

32. See *Vietnam Era Veterans' Readjustment Assistance Act of 1972*, July 26, 1972. — Ordered to be printed, 92nd Congress, 2nd Session, Senate, Report No. 92-988. The administration was prepared to oppose even a 14.1 percent increase as provided in the House Bill, H.R. 12828. See pp. 95-98. See also "Veterans' Education Benefits," *1972 CQ Almanac*, pp. 856-857.

33. "Assignment to Neglect," by Charles Child, photographed by Co Rentmeester, *Life*, May 22, 1970.

34. *Message from the President of the United States Returning Without Approval, An Act (H.R. 17548) Making Appropriations for Sundry Independent Executive Bureaus, Boards, Commissions, Corporations, Agencies, Offices, and the Department of Housing and Urban Development for the Fiscal Year Ending June 30, 1971, and for Other Purposes, Together With a Statement Thereon*, August 11, 1970. — Message, together with accompanying bill, ordered to be printed as a House document, 91st Congress, 2nd Session, Document No. 91-377.

35. Jimmy Carter, *Keeping Faith: Memoirs of a President* (Bantam Books: Toronto, New York, London, Sydney, 1983), pp. 24 and 596.

36. Robert T. Hartmann, *Palace Politics: An Inside Account of the Ford Years* (McGraw-Hill Book Company: New York, St. Louis, San Francisco, Dusseldorf, Mexico, Toronto, 1980), pp. 209-215; Gerald R. Ford, *A Time to Heal: The Autobiography of Gerald R. Ford* (Harper & Row and The Reader's Digest Association, Inc.: 1979), pp. 141-142.

37. Lou Cannon, "Amnesty and Health Plan Stir Disenchantment," *Washington Post*, August 25, 1974.

38. Ibid.

39. The original staff letter provided for no further action. A January 8, 1977 memo from Jim Cavanaugh to Ed Schmults noted, "The President reviewed the letter and feels that it needs to be modified slightly so that the average reader will not get the impression that he has closed off doing anything later about the other two options you are working on." January 1977 Folder, Amnesty, Staff Files, Schmults, Ford Library. A return memo from Schmults to Dick Cheney provided a new draft letter, which suggested, "I thus have decided to maintain my position on earned clemency and hope you will understand. However, this does not preclude my taking further action to address any area of concern within the clemency program before completion of my term as President." January 1977 Folder, Amnesty, Staff Files, Schmults, Ford Library.

On January 14, a new draft letter went into the Oval Office with a briefing package on the two options to expand the program. The package contained a cover memo from Schmults to Jim Cavanaugh. "Please convey to the President my recommendation that he do nothing at this date." The new draft letter provided that veterans who were wounded in battle receive veteran benefits. January 1977 Folder, Amnesty, Staff Files, Schmults, Ford Library. The package was returned with a new memo dated January 18, 1977. "Mr. Marsh advises that the President wants to include those decorated for valor." Only after this third modification was the final letter signed and the paperwork done to implement the president's requests.

40. "Presidential Proclamation of Pardon," Proclamation 4483, January 21, 1977, *Public Papers of the Presidents of the United States, Jimmy Carter, 1977*, (in two books), p. 5. The accompanying Executive Order is printed at p. 6.

41. President Carter noted in an interview, "I was booed by an organized claque there, but I went ahead." On President Ford's strategy, see Robert T. Hartmann, *Palace Politics: An Inside Account of the Ford Years*, op. cit., p. 211; Gerald R. Ford, *A Time to Heal: The Autobiography of Gerald R. Ford*, op. cit., pp. 141-142.

42. See *Vietnam Era Veterans' Readjustment Assistance Act of 1974*, June 4, 1974. – Ordered to be printed, 93rd Congress, 2nd Session, Senate, Report No. 93-907, "Need for Increases in Educational Assistance Benefits."

43. Letter, the Honorable Richard L. Roudebush, administrator of Veterans Affairs to the Honorable Roy L. Ash, director, Office of Management and Budget, H.R. 12628 Folder, White House Records File, Ford Library. "I am convinced that, despite the large increase in cost engendered by the enrolled enactment, it represents the best compromise that can be reached and, on balance, is realistic." Memorandum, William E. Timmons to Warren Hendriks, November 23, 1974, H.R. 12628 Folder, White House Records File, Ford Library. "The question for the President is whether he gains from making the issue and can blame Congress for inflation – or if by losing another veto he further weakens his position on other issues before Congress and embarrasses his natural Hill supporters." Memorandum, Ken Cole to the President, November 27, 1974, "Comparison of GI Bill Educational Benefits," VA 3, Education Programs Folder, 10/23-12/31/74, White House Central File, Ford Library.

44. "Swearing-In Ceremony: Remarks at the Swearing In of the Administrator of Veterans' Affairs, the Director of Action, and the Chief of Protocol," March 2, 1977, *Public Papers of the Presidents of the United States, Jimmy Carter, 1977* (in two books), pp. 272-273.

45. "Vietnam Era Veterans: Message to the Congress," October 10, 1978, *Public Papers of the Presidents of the United States, Jimmy Carter, 1978* (in two books), pp. 1737-1742, at p. 1740.

46. *Myths and Realities: A Study of Attitudes Toward Vietnam Era Veterans*, printed by the Veterans Administration, July 1980, pp. 63-65.

47. Ibid., p. 69.

48. Ibid., p. 61.

49. Richard A. Gabriel and Paul L. Savage, *Crisis in Command: Mismanagement in the Army* (Hill and Wang: New York, 1978), pp. 97-116.

Veterans Organizations

NUMBERS THAT SCARE

The president of the United States wields great power, but even the president faces limits, sometimes from surprising sources. So President Carter learned when he opposed the largest of the nation's veterans organizations, the American Legion.

In an effort to hold down the rising federal budget, President Carter vetoed a Veterans Administration (VA) health care bill. Bob Spanogle, the Legion's national adjutant, its highest staff position, told the story of the veto aftermath:

> Carter appeared at our convention on Thursday and went home that evening, and actually on Friday, about 3:30, vetoed that piece of legislation. Now we were prepared for that veto. . . . We were in convention. We had our Legislative Council members ready and primed. When they went home, they could make private phone calls to their Congressmen. . . . I think that was the second time that a Democratic president had been overridden by a Democratic Congress in almost thirty years.

The story is impressive. A Congress manipulated. A president defeated. Yet it is only one story that Robert Spanogle and the small group that led the nation's major veterans organizations told. Cooper T. Holt, the executive director of the nation's second largest veterans organization, the Veterans of Foreign Wars (VFW), proclaimed with droll understatement, "I do feel we have a wonderful relationship with members of the House Veterans' Affairs Committee and their

'What do you guys want?! You've got your own week
and now they're coming out with your own postage stamp!'

Reprinted with permission from the *Minneapolis Star and Tribune*.

staff. I do believe we are effective." Asked if he could remember
ever losing a legislative battle, Holt quickly replied, "I can't think
of one that's major."

Any Washington-based interest group has some power. The busy
schedules of congressmen, with varying interests constantly com-
manding their attention, leave little time for actions that are not
responsive to at least one of those interests. Congress seldom origi-
nates. It reacts to outside suggestions, and the interest groups are
the chief source of both ideas and demands.

Yet the major veterans organizations have more power than do
most other interest groups. The source of that special power lies,
in part, in the patriotic aura that surrounds the needs of veterans,
an aura that shines on the veterans groups as well as on the needs
they represent. As Max Cleland, the administrator of the Veterans
Administration under President Carter, often put it: "I think veterans groups start out in a special category. I think the average member
of Congress puts the veteran on a pedestal."[1]

The aura is only part of the equation, however, for it shines on several of the largest membership organizations in the United States. The VFW has 2.0 *million* members, with an auxiliary of 700,000 more. The American Legion has 2.5 million members and a 930,000 member auxiliary. Membership in the Disabled American Veterans (DAV), the third and last of the major organizations, is limited to veterans with service-connected disabilities. Even with that restriction, it claims 880,000 members.

In comparison, many of the groups that have become household names in the United States have relatively small memberships. Common Cause reports a membership of 255,000, the National Organization of Women (NOW), a membership of 250,000.

The massive membership of the major veterans organizations translates into an equally massive impact on members of Congress who, with one eye toward reelection, must often defer to constituency pressure. In 1977, for example, the three major organizations generated a mail and phone-in campaign that literally jammed the huge Capitol Hill switchboard.[2]

The impact of the massive membership of the veterans organizations is further magnified by the fact that their voice is almost unopposed. The AFL-CIO must often face off against the Business Roundtable, and vice versa. The National Rifle Association must respond to a welter of smaller but persistent organizations seeking handgun control. In contrast, the veterans organizations share a common agenda, and nonveterans organizations seldom even address veterans legislation.

Blessed with the special deference that flows from their patriotic appeal — without opposition and carrying the weight of millions of members — the major veterans organizations do, indeed, have substantial power, as President Carter learned. When that power is focused specifically on veterans issues, it is almost unassailable.

The very clarity of their power, however, gives rise to increased accountability. Able to win so often, the veterans organizations can seldom appeal to impotence as an excuse for inaction or for action wrongly taken. The very clarity of their power, accordingly, gives rise to the question of their purposes. What do the major organizations want? Where do they throw their weight?

A HISTORY OF NEGLECT

"To honor the dead by helping the living," runs the motto of the Veterans of Foreign Wars, but the real question is whether Vietnam veterans were counted among the living. Cooper T. Holt, the organization's executive director, insisted that they were and that the VFW has been an advocate for Vietnam veterans.

In a revealing moment, however, he listed the "major problems we look at in this office." These major problems constituted the VFW's agenda and the interests it served. Three programs were mentioned: the pension program, the VA health care system, and the compensation system.

Conspicuous by its absence was any mention of any readjustment program for Vietnam veterans. There was no mention of the GI Bill. And, of course, there was no mention of readjustment counseling. If Vietnam veterans were counted among the living, they had only a toehold on life at the VFW.

Of those programs that were mentioned, two — the pension program and the hospital system — benefit principally (but not exclusively) older veterans. Only the compensation system, which provides income to veterans disabled during their service, equally helps veterans of all eras.

Eligibility for the pension program is triggered in large part by age and principally serves older veterans. Among the more than one million veterans receiving pensions, only 12,000 (around 1 percent) are Vietnam veterans. All veterans are eligible for VA health care if they cannot afford care elsewhere. This general health care, however, primarily benefits older veterans, who because of their age, have greater health needs. For younger veterans, seeking to find their way in society, health care was not the priority problem.

Each of the three programs mentioned by Holt are huge. Together, they made up nearly 80 percent of the VA's total budget, and their cost pushed that budget up to a staggering $24 billion in 1982.

The massive VA budget, as well as the three programs that generate most of it, have placed pressure on the federal budget and set the agenda for the major veterans organizations. The organizations have to ensure that the country continues, year in and year out, to spend scores of billions of dollars. "I think you've got a lot of members of the Congress who feel that when you talk about $24 billion, that's an awful lot of money," Cooper T. Holt explained.

In the competitive environment of Washington, just maintaining government spending is difficult for most interest groups. The power of the veterans organizations makes that task relatively easy, but even the veterans organizations cannot win budget increase after increase. If they can maintain present programs, they still have to set priorities in the formation of new programs.

From the perspective of the VFW, Vietnam veterans create a budgetary problem. Vietnam veterans need new programs, over and above the principal existing programs that serve older veterans — new programs that will cost billions of dollars in additional money. Yet, at the same time, older veterans are also seeking to expand their programs also at the cost of additional billions. Combined, their cost is prohibitive. Even the veterans organizations cannot push the government's budget up that high. That leaves a stark choice: hold back the growth of programs for older veterans, or block the development of Vietnam veterans programs.

The years 1977-78 demonstrated this choice at work. Two important proposals were being considered by the Congress. One proposal would have expanded the pension program that provided income support for older veterans. The other would have finally achieved equity for Vietnam veterans by reforming the Vietnam GI Bill and making it comparable to the World War II GI Bill. Both proposals were expensive. The pension increases would have cost $9.7 billion over five years, according to the VA's budget estimate. The GI Bill reform would have cost $7.5 billion.

For the VFW, the GI Bill reform was simply too expensive. "The anticipated cost thereof," the VFW asserted, "alone would be sufficient cause in the existing fiscal climate to oppose passage."[3] In contrast, no cost was too great for the pension program. The VFW could "not in good conscience support" a cheaper, $5.8 billion pension increase. It simply did not go far enough.[4] Even the full $9.7 billion package needed further expansion. The VFW proposed a list of improvements that would have cost hundreds of millions of dollars more, according to the VA's budget estimates.[5]

The pension program was important and was responsive to compelling needs. It demanded substantial national support, but clearly its funding should not have been won at the expense of Vietnam

"YOU AIN'T GONNA CLOSE YOUR POCKETBOOKS TO US VETERANS, ARE YOU?"

"You ain't gonna close your pocketbooks to us veterans, are you?" — from *Herblock • On All Fronts* (New American Library, 1980).

veterans. The error implicit in the VFW's choice was accentuated by the nature of the two programs at stake.

The pension program was specifically designed to serve veterans who had *no* service-connected problems, and it reflected the nation's generous commitment to help veterans whenever possible. The GI Bill, on the other hand, responded to the immediate and service-connected need of veterans seeking to return to civilian society. It reflected the nation's deep obligation to those whose lives and careers had been disrupted by wartime service.

The VA budget pitted the generations against each other. Faced with the conflict, the VFW chose to favor older veterans over younger veterans. That choice condemned Vietnam veterans to a history of neglect.

In 1977, with pressure mounting to meet the needs of Vietnam veterans, the VFW took extraordinary action to make sure that Congress understood where the VFW wanted the VA budget spent. Referring to a group of pending proposals to create new veterans programs, the VFW passed an unprecedented resolution announcing active opposition to funding *any* new programs out of the existing, by then nearly $20 billion, VA budget.

In case there was any ambiguity as to which were the threatening proposals, the VFW listed them in a "Whereas Clause," which created the impression of the VFW facing a swarm of vexing demands. If Vietnam veterans were not so lucky as to be listed in Holt's group of major problems, they were surely listed here. With just one exception, the "Whereas Clause" listed *only* Vietnam veterans initiatives – GI Bill reform, readjustment counseling and additional employment assistance.[6]

The VFW was not unique. The American Legion has supported GI Bill reform proposals, providing important leadership, but it was cautious leadership at best. The Legion joined the clamor for pension increases but chose to sit out the House hearings on the GI Bill reform, seemingly unwilling to join in the heat of the battle.

Asked to list his principal concerns, Legion leader Robert Spanogle stated: "Our primary belief is full funding for veterans' programs. . . . Full funding means those programs that are in place, that have proven accountability. We like to see full funding for those programs, plus cost-of-living." At the Legion, too, the problem was to maintain the existing program base and to ensure full funding for the programs created decades ago, whose vast cost benefited principally older veterans.

That the government failed the Vietnam veterans is significant and, given the importance attached to veterans programs, even remarkable. In the end, however, the real check on government is not government. It is those outside of government, like the major veterans organizations, who are responsible for the interests of special groups, for spotting their needs, for focusing attention on failure, and for arguing for reform.

The Marine Corps motto "Semper Fidelis" (Always Faithful) has special meaning for many Vietnam veterans. It captures their firece loyalty to each other. Asked for an example of "semper fi," Marines often mention their traditions of never leaving their dead and of visiting the wounded in the hospitals.

It is not unusual for a government to fail to meet real human needs. It is even less unusual for a government to be cautious, unwilling to venture new money on new problems. For Vietnam veterans, the difficulty was not only that the government had failed them, but that other veterans, forgetting bonds of fidelity, had chosen to abandon them as well.

DRUG ADDICTS AND DESERTERS

Among the very few members of the U.S. Congress in 1977 who had served in Vietnam, one, Congressman John Murtha (D-Pennsylvania), rose on the House floor to tell his colleagues the story of one hero from the Vietnam War:

> I had a young fellow in my district. That fellow was in combat over thirteen months. He came back home. His father was dying of cancer. The young man had a very serious wound in Vietnam. He deserted, in [the] technical sense of the military. . . . He had been decorated, wounded, and [when he returned to the military] was kept in the brig and given an Undesirable Discharge.[7]

Most veterans, notably decorated and wounded ones, have not received an Undesirable Discharge, and fortunately so. Among the five types of discharges (Honorable, General, Undesirable, Bad Conduct, and Dishonorable), surveys have demonstrated that employers discriminate against veterans with less than an Honorable Discharge.[8] Veterans with less than a General Discharge are effectively barred from the GI Bill. Called "bad paper," a less than Honorable Discharge guarantees a rough return home.

Although Bad Conduct and Dishonorable Discharges require formal court-martials, Undesirable and General Discharges are awarded administratively with few procedural safeguards, sometimes even without a hearing. Among legal authorities, there is almost universal agreement that the discharge system was abused during the Vietnam War. Even the Department of Defense concurred, recognizing, among other problems, the system's racial bias.[9] Over one-half million veterans received General or Undesirable Discharges during the Vietnam era.

The pressures of war have always strained the fabric of military justice. Command requires discretion, and that discretion is inevitably abused by some. The nation has responded to abuses that emerged in earlier wars. World War II was followed by the landmark Uniform Code of Military Justice (UCMJ), which established courts independent of command influence. The basic procedures for reviewing discharges were also established.

After the Korean War, discharge procedures were tightened, prodded along by proposals from Senator Sam Ervin (D-North Carolina), who subsequently gained national recognition as chairman of the Senate Watergate investigation, and Congressman Charles Bennett (D-Florida). In the late 1960s legislation passed that continued the reforms begun by the UCMJ increasing procedural protections for soldiers being court-martialed.

Both the post-World War II and the post-Korean War reforms had carried extensive national support, including the support of the major veterans organizations, whose members, after all, had seen the abuses first hand. Indeed, veterans organizations like the American Legion courageously insisted through the early 1960s that General and Undesirable Discharges be carefully investigated or eliminated entirely.

After the Vietnam War, presidents of both parties recognized the problems that had emerged in the discharge system. In 1974, shortly after taking office, President Ford created a very limited program of amnesty for some veterans with bad discharges. As one of the last acts of his presidency, on the day before the inaugural of Jimmy Carter, President Ford responded to a last-minute special request by the widow of Senator Philip Hart, a Democrat from Ford's home state of Michigan, and expanded the program slightly.

It fell to President Carter to implement a more comprehensive approach. In 1977, he created the Special Discharge Review Program (SDRP) to seek out and upgrade discharges that had been inequitably given during the Vietnam War. The reform program, it was hoped, would gather the same nationwide support that had met the UCMJ and earlier military justice reforms. It did not.

Almost on the day of the president's announcement, the opposition began. Congressman Robin Beard (R-Tennessee) successfully offered an amendment in the House to the VA appropriation. Called the "Beard Amendment" after its author, the provision, if adopted by the Senate, would have created a one-year ban against paying veterans benefits to anyone whose discharge was upgraded under President Carter's program. Legislation was introduced to make the one-year ban permanent, and hearings were quickly scheduled.

The source of the opposition to the president's program was familiar to Vietnam veterans. Once again, it was the major veterans organizations. This time, however, their concern was not money. Although the VFW made a faint-hearted effort to argue against the program because of its cost, it quickly abandoned that effort. The American Legion, to avoid even the appearance of pursing financial self-interest, explicitly noted that its opposition was not based on the cost of the program at all.[10]

The problem for the major organizations ran deeper than money. It had emotional roots. The president's program had captured all of their ambivalence about these strange, new, sometimes long-haired veterans, some of whom had thrown their medals away and seemed to hold nothing sacred. Vietnam veterans with less than Honorable Discharges were the loser veterans who had lost the "little" war in distant Vietnam. Somehow, their attitude toward Vietnam veterans led to a change in their long history of concern over the discharge system.

The American Legion called the program "inherently unjust, inequitable and dangerous . . . an insult to all those who served in combat," a theme picked up by its allies in Congress.[11] Congressman Beard asserted that the president's program would "blanket in and include thousands" who had received bad discharges for "willful misconduct or desertion."[12] During the hearings, Congressman Chalmers Wylie (R-Ohio), a ranking Republican member of the

House Committee on Veterans' Affairs, summed up the opposition by asking point-blank, "Isn't the president's program, in effect, a blanket pardon for those who deserted during the Vietnam War?"[13]

In the rhetoric was forgotten that a veteran who deserted in a combat zone faced a nearly absolute bar to upgrading under the president's program. In the rhetoric was forgotten that a veteran who displayed cowardice faced similar bars, as did a veteran who committed an act of violence. On the House floor, Congressman Beard conceded the facts, but the rhetoric was repeated nevertheless. Emotions prevailed.[14]

In the rhetoric was also forgotten the heroism of Vietnam veterans. The combat desertion rate among Vietnam veterans had been *lower* than that of any earlier war. About 80 percent of Vietnam veterans had been volunteers. World War II had been fought principally by draftees.[15]

It fell to a small organization, the National Association of Concerned Veterans (NACV), to champion the president's program, to remind Congress and the Committee on Veterans' Affairs of the rights and dignity of the veterans who were involved. In testimony before the House Committee it stated: "Vietnam era veterans with less-than-fully-honorable discharges have suffered enough. They have, in many cases, suffered inequitably. It is time to address those cases of inequitable punishment. The president has begun that process, and we urge the Congress to assist him."[16]

The NACV did not have the resources of a paid staff or a vast Washington office to bring to bear against the VFW's marble palace a block from the Capitol, nor the American Legion's claim to 2.9 million members. It did have one crucial characteristic. Its board was made up almost exclusively of Vietnam veterans. Against the arsenals of the major organizations, the NACV raised only the claim of legitimacy – of being Vietnam veterans speaking for Vietnam veterans.

The claim was a mighty one. The major organizations scrambled to respond, yet only the DAV could actually produce a Vietnam veteran to testify before Congress. The VFW, for example, had to settle for the conjured ghost of an absent junior staffer during testimony before the House Committee:

Mr. Hammerschmidt: Fine. Well, I assume for the record, you are speaking for that portion of your membership as well. I am speaking of the Vietnam veterans — you are speaking for him as one of his representatives here?

Mr. Schwab: Yes, sir. My special assistant, Mr. Poteet, is a Vietnam veteran who was a helicopter pilot, and he subscribes to our position wholeheartedly.[17]

As a substitute for the presence of an active, independent Vietnam veteran as spokesman, each of the major organizations emphasized the size of its Vietnam veterans membership. What was carefully left unsaid, and emerged only in private interviews in 1981, was the fact that in 1977, not one of the organizations had ever elected a Vietnam veteran to its major leadership positions, nor did many Vietnam veterans hold senior staff positions.[18]

The Vietnam War did not create the generation gap. There had always been a difference between younger and older veterans. The older veterans had always controlled the major veterans organizations and had been hesitant to grant power to the young.

Returning from World War II, the famous war cartoonist Bill Maulden discovered a generation gap in the American Legion. As he recalled in his autobiographical account, *Back Home*:

> Since practically all the top Legion brass that boast World War II service can also boast World War I duty, the original criticism should be reworded: *youth* has no voice in the Legion. . . .
>
> One of the Legion's high dignitaries was pretty frank about this at the 1946 San Francisco Convention. "This is a billion dollar corporation," said he. "You don't turn something like that over to a bunch of inexperienced kids."[19]

Yet the World War I veterans, who had received no GI Bill themselves, fought for the landmark World War II GI Bill. Although young veterans like Bill Maulden might have chafed at the condescension of their older World War I brothers, there is a clear distinction between paternalism and neglect.

Beyond the competition for control of the veterans organizations, beyond the competition for scarce federal dollars, there was a deeper generational conflict during the Vietnam era. There was a fundamental division in the attitudes of younger and older veterans. The Vietnam War had produced a difference in its veterans.

That difference was reflected in the fundamental shift in attitudes toward authority and especially toward government. Vietnam veterans, often uncertain of the war's meaning, shared in the national attitude of suspicion that was deepened by Watergate. The leadership of the older veterans organizations seemed untouched by the war and by the doubt it engendered.

That difference found expression in the dispute over discharge upgrading. Older veterans, having forgotten their own problems with the military justice system, instinctively assumed that commanders had been right and discharges had been deserved. Vietnam veterans, fresh from a war whose conduct was deeply questioned, were prepared to side with almost any private against almost any general.

The result was a crisis of leadership within the major organizations. Although the fiscal competition could have been ultimately overcome by the gradual realization that older veterans had an obligation to younger veterans, the generation gap was not so easily closed. In fact, the generation gap meant that older veterans might be incapable of liking and respecting Vietnam veterans, and so were unable to speak out for them.

That difference could have been bridged by bringing Vietnam veterans into leadership positions, but, as the major organizations' inablity to produce Vietnam veterans spokesmen during the hearing had demonstrated, in the major organizations, Vietnam veterans were still invisible. Where present, they were not able to change the organization's policies, but were used to give credibility by creating the facade of Vietnam veteran support. For Vietnam veterans, there was a leadership vacuum that meant that their views and their emotions went unspoken.

As the debate over President Carter's Discharge Review Program ground to its first discouraging conclusion, Congressman Murtha rose to the House floor again, to speak in frustration:

> I remember a young fellow, who was from Texas. This fellow extended by one month his tour of duty in Vietnam. He said he wanted to be with the troops on this one last operation. . . . I happened to be in the Command Point when this young man stepped on a mine. We heard a loud explosion, and he said over the radio, "Skipper, I am going to have to give up my command because I just lost both my legs." . . .
> I will tell the Members the difference between [the Vietnam War and] what went on in World War II and Korea. . . . It is a terrible feeling for

a man who served his country to come back here and receive criticism for fighting. There was a tremendous difference.[20]

The debate over this program proved to be decidedly one-sided. Carter was unable or unwilling to commit the vast political resources of the presidency to the defense of the program. In the end, the White House's role was that of a leader who had proposed the idea, had initiated the long overdue action, but who had required that the program sustain itself on its own political capital.

That capital was scarce. Congressman Murtha did not speak alone. In the House, he was joined by Congressmen Don Edwards (D-California), Bob Edgar (D-Pennsylvania), and Thomas J. Downey (D-New York); in the Senate by Gaylord Nelson (D-Wisconsin), Edward Brooke (R-Massachusetts) and James Abourezk (D-South Dakota). If not alone, however, Murtha represented a minority faction that was limited to obstructionist strategies.

Together they won important concessions; but, in the end, the major veterans organizations prevailed. All veterans who became eligible for benefits under the president's program had to have their cases reviewed again under tighter standards. They would not be able to appear in their own defense unless the Department of Defense first ruled against them.

The final bill was so onerous that the Department of Justice considered recommending a veto on the grounds that the bill violated the U.S. Constitution. The Department of Defense, however, recommended a veto. Another bill, with fewer concessions, however, was waiting in the wings. A veto could only be effective if it signaled a willingness to fight the entire battle over, with a new level of presidential commitment. The president signed the bill.[21]

THE LAST HOLDOUT

The first business of those seeking to help Vietnam veterans was to understand the need. That was certainly one of the first tasks faced by the Senate Committee on Veterans' Affairs. Yet the committee could find little help in so basic an effort, even as late as 1977, four years after the last American combat soldier was withdrawn from Vietnam.

Asked as simple a question as whether he felt there was a serious readjustment problem among Vietnam veterans, then-VA administrator Max Cleland could only respond with bureaucratic double-talk and a half-decade-old assumption:

> Yes, sir, Mr. Chairman, you might recall that back in the early 1970s the Veterans Administration did reveal that one out of five veterans that came back from service during the Vietnam era had readjustment problems severe enough to be of concern.
>
> I have *seen no real data* to *either reinforce* that or *to challenge* that assumption. And that is the basic assumption under which the Veterans Administration is proceeding. [Emphasis added] [22]

In 1977, the VA had yet to do a serious, empirical study of the actual readjustment needs of Vietnam veterans. The Senate committee could not turn to the VA in its search to better define and address the needs of Vietnam veterans. The VA simply did not know.

Nor, with one exception, could the committee turn to the veterans organizations. The one exception was a study funded by the Disabled American Veterans (DAV) and conducted by Dr. John Wilson of Cleveland State University. A quarter-million-dollar effort called *The Forgotten Warrior Project*, the DAV study was the first major empirical mental health study of Vietnam veterans.

Its results were overwhelming and discouraging. Forty-nine percent of the black veterans surveyed reported a serious alcohol or drug problem. All veterans displayed deep alienation. As Dr. Wilson explained in his testimony: "And interestingly enough, we asked the men the question, if there was another Vietnam tomorrow, would you go? And across the board . . . over 95 percent of the men answered absolutely not."[23]

Responding to the study results, the DAV began a nationwide effort to create a special Vietnam veterans outreach effort. It established store-front centers outside of VA facilities. It made persistent efforts to hire Vietnam veterans as service officers, the front-line workers who handle the needs of individual veterans. Three Vietnam veterans were given visibility in the organization — Ronald W. Drach, the employment director; Robert H. Lenham, special projects director; and John (Rick) Heilman, legislative director.

The source of the DAV's concern for Vietnam veterans was simple enough. To the obvious needs of Vietnam veterans, documented in their own study, was added the element of self-interest. "You have to consider your future," explained Norman B. Hartnett. With few World War I veterans left, and World War II veterans reaching age 65, Vietnam veterans were clearly the organization's future membership base.

To an outsider, the DAV's decision seems the obvious and only choice. Yet despite its obviousness, the DAV was the first to implement it. The DAV was followed by the American Legion. In 1981, Robert Spanogle, a Vietnam veteran, was appointed national adjutant, the American Legion's highest staff position. Two years earlier, in 1979, he had been appointed the executive director of the Legion's Washington office.

The actions of the two organizations demonstrated a recognition that there was a leadership vacuum and that problems of political habit and of a generation gap separated older and younger veterans. The gap could be closed only by a conscious effort to reach out and involve Vietnam veterans. Both organizations were prepared to make the effort.

Precisely the degree of their earlier indifference defined the measure of the DAV's and Legion's accomplishment in finally addressing the needs of Vietnam veterans. Entrenched attitudes had to be abandoned. The attitudes of two major organizations were being shifted, a testament to their underlying creativity and adaptability. Not every organization was prepared to make such changes.

In 1978, when the DAV was responding to the results of *The Forgotten Warrior Project*, the new priority for the VFW was the formation of a national Political Action Committee (PAC). The VFW was the first veterans organization to form a PAC. The landmark event was watched with care and then with some surprise.

Although the PAC might have been expected to support candidates who fought for veterans issues, it *opposed* the ranking Democratic member of the House Committee on Veterans' Affairs, Don Edwards (D-California), despite his 100 percent voting record on veterans issues.

When Cooper Holt was asked if he had found anything incongruous in a veterans organization opposing the strongest Congressional leaders on veterans affairs, he responded, "No, not really." Asked a follow-up question, he explained that the VFW ratings really had very little to do with votes on veterans legislation. The PAC of the VFW, the nation's second largest veterans organization, was simply not about veterans issues. It was about foreign policy and defense spending.

The other major veterans organizations were among the first to diagnose the problem and criticize its impact. Asked if it was the wave of the future, Norman Hartnett quickly said, "Not for the DAV." John Heilman elaborated on their concerns:

> First of all, their criteria, in terms of choosing their PAC candidates, was totally wrong. They did it on their conservative bent. It was national defense oriented, generally conservative. That is whom they supported. They really didn't look at, really look at veteran legislation.

However belated the change, the DAV and the American Legion had remained focused enough on specific veterans issues to perceive and address the role of Vietnam veterans in their own organizations. The VFW, in contrast, was preoccupied with power politics and foreign policy. Its attention diverted, the VFW remained the last holdout, playing a game of politics as usual, which failed to reflect the changes under way in veterans affairs.

The difference in results was significant. While the DAV was seeking to serve Vietnam veterans, the VFW was worrying about troop strengths in Korea. While the DAV and the American Legion were grappling with the vital veteran-related need to bring Vietnam veterans into their organizations, the VFW was worrying about the mechanics of power politics. As Rick Heilman of the DAV put it, "We could care less whatever happened to that Panama Canal. We never involved ourselves in that, and the VFW went to the wall."

As late as 1981, the VFW did not have a *single* Vietnam veteran in a single senior staff position. Nor had a single Vietnam veteran been elected to one of the major representative positions that rotate each year. Holt noted with pride that a Vietnam veteran might be elected to the third-ranking position in late 1982 or 1983, some 20 years after the war had begun. In fact, he was elected in 1982, but that lone Vietnam veteran will reach the VFW's highest position only after 1985. The DAV had elected a Vietnam veteran to its highest position in 1980.

Like all political dinosaurs, the VFW risks the extinction that follows steadily declining respect. Speaking of his ten-point rating,

Congressman Thomas A. Daschle (D-South Dakota) called it "probably [the one I am] the most proud, of all my ratings," and quickly added that he had the overwhelming support of the VFW in his district. Looking at the results of recent polling, he noted, "We broke it down into 'favor' and 'unfavor' and 90 some percent favor. . . . So you know, they can rate me any way they want to out here [in Washington]. Cooper Holt's credibility against mine is fine with me."

Asked about their past record on behalf of Vietnam veterans, both the DAV and the Legion pointed to change and accomplishment. As Robert Spanogle put it for the Legion, when asked about its opposition to the Readjustment Counseling Program, "We were opposed to the initial concept of the psychological outreach centers, but I don't think, you know, I think that if you look back in the testimony during the last year and a half, you will find that we have championed that cause."

Able to point to change, Legion spokesmen need not lie. The VFW seemed to have fewer options. Asked if the VFW had ever opposed readjustment counseling, Cooper T. Holt stated: "Oh no, Lord no. We fought for it tooth and toenail. As a matter of fact, I don't think you can name anything the Congress had over there relative to the Vietnam veterans that the VFW opposed."

Yet perhaps even a dinosaur can evolve. In 1982, under the prodding of its new commander-in-chief, James R. Currieo, the VFW became the first traditional veterans organization to endorse Agent Orange compensation. In 1983, the American Legion followed Commander Currieo's leadership.

In 1983, the bill (H.R. 1961) began to advance, but the opposition remained strong. Weaker compromise legislation was advanced. After a heated subcommittee debate, the sponsor of the original bill accepted the weaker measure, which was supported by the committee's respected chairman.

Defeated in subcommittee, the advocates regrouped for another try in the full committee. A new amendment was drafted and carefully shared with the VFW and the American Legion. National commanders at the VFW, however, are elected for only one year, and in the interim Commander Currieo had retired.

Currieo's personal commitment proved to be the missing ingredient. Without him, the organization moved quickly to retrench and refused to endorse the amendment. The American Legion was left alone, the only major organization prepared to stand fast with Vietnam veterans.

At the VFW, old habits die hard.

NOTES

1. Bill Keller, "Chinks in the 'Iron Triangle'? How a Unique Lobby Force Protects over $21 Billion in Vast Veterans' Programs," *Congressional Quarterly*, June 14, 1980, pp. 1627-1634, at p. 1627.

2. Ibid., p. 1628.

3. *H.R. 2231 Proposing Accelerated Entitlement and Other Changes in Veterans Education and Training Programs; H.R. 8419 Proposing Tuition Assistance; and Related Measures*, hearings before the Subcommittee on Education and Training of the Committee on Veterans' Affairs, House of Representatives, 95th Congress, 1st Session, September 15-16, 1977, p. 261.

4. *Veterans' and Survivors' Pension Improvement Act of 1978*, hearings before the Subcommittee on Veterans' Affairs, United States Senate, 95th Congress, 2nd Session on S. 2384, February 3, 1978, pp. 120-127, especially p. 120.

5. *Review of the Non-Service Connected Pension Program*, hearings before the Subcommittee on Compensation, Pension and Insurance of the Committee on Veterans' Affairs, House of Representatives, 95th Congress, 2nd Session, February 7-9, 1978, pp. 249-255, p. 250.

6. *H.R. 2231 Proposing Accelerated Entitlement and Other Changes in Veterans Education and Training Programs; H.R. 8419 Proposing Tuition Assistance; and Related Measures*, op. cit., pp. 263-264.

7. *Congressional Record – House*, June 15, 1977, H. 19079.

8. Congressman Sieberling (D-Ohio) surveyed employers and found, for example, that 61 percent would have discriminated against veterans with an undesirable discharge. See also Major Bradley K. Jones, "Gravity of Administrative Discharges: A Legal and Empirical Evaluation," *59 Military L.Rev.* 1 (Winter 1973), pp. 1-25; and Peter Slaven, "The Cruelest Discrimination," Summer 1975, Number 14, *Business and Society Review*, pp. 25-33.

9. See Andrew S. Effron, "Punishment of Enlisted Personnel Outside the UCMJ: A Statutory and Equal Protection Analysis of Military Discharge Certificates," *9 Harvard Civil Rights-Civil Liberties Law Review* 227 (1974) pp. 237-324; *People Get Different Discharges in Apparently Similar Circumstances*, report of the comptroller general of the ULSL, April 1, 1976, B-184890. *Report of the DOD Task Force on the Administration of Military Justice in the Armed Forces*, 1972.

10. *Upgrading of Discharges under Special Programs Implemented by Former President Gerald Ford and President Jimmy Carter*, hearings before a

Select Committee on Veterans' Affairs, House of Representatives, 95th Congress, 1st Session, June 20, 21, 27 and 28, 1977, p. 274 for the statement of the VFW, and pp. 131-132 for the statement of the American Legion.

11. Ibid., p. 125.

12. *Congressional Record — House*, June 15, 1977, p. H-19078.

13. *Upgrading of Discharges under Special Programs Implemented by Former President Gerald Ford and President Jimmy Carter*, op. cit., p. 81.

14. The regulations and other material implementing the program are printed in *Upgrading of Discharges under Special Programs Implemented by Former President Gerald Ford and President Jimmy Carter*, op. cit., pp. 2-40. In response to questions from Congressman Edgar (D-Pennsylvania), Congressman Beard conceded that veterans who had been separated from the military for reason of acts of violence and desertion were barred from upgrading. *Congressional Record — House*, June 15, 1977, H-19078. However, the charge that deserters were receiving upgrades was raised again on the very next page in a speech by Congressman Hillis (R-Indiana).

15. On the combat desertion rate, see Lawrence M. Baskir and William A. Strauss, *Chance and Circumstance: The Draft, the War and the Vietnam Generation* (Alfred A. Knopf: New York, 1978), p. 112. On numbers drafted during World War II and the Vietnam War, see ibid., p. 5; and *Statistical Abstract of the United States*, 103rd Edition, U.S. Department of Commerce, Bureau of the Census, p. 361.

16. *Upgrading of Discharges Under Special Programs Implemented by Former President Gerald Ford and President Jimmy Carter*, op. cit., p. 240. Coauthor Steven M. Champlin appeared on behalf of NACV.

17. Ibid., p. 125.

18. For the claims of the American Legion, see ibid., p. 128. The Disabled American Veterans, ibid., pp. 232-233; the Veterans of Foreign Wars, ibid., p. 269.

19. Bill Maulden, *Back Home* (William Sloane Associates: New York, 1947), pp. 89 and 90-91.

20. Statement of the Honorable John P. Murtha, *Congressional Record — House*, June 15, 1977, H-19085.

21. See statement of the Honorable Edward P. Boland, *Congressional Record — House*, September 28, 1977, H-31329; and Barry W. Lynn, "Carter and the Veterans," *The Nation*, December 24, 1977, pp. 678-682.

22. *Veterans Health Care Amendments Act of 1977*, hearings before the Subcommittee on Health and Readjustment of the Committee on Veterans' Affairs, United States Senate, 95th Congress, 1st Session on S. 1693 and H.R. 6502, June 22, 1977, p. 39.

23. Ibid., p. 266.

III Coconspirators

6   Congress

CLOSED PROCEDURES: THE TEAGUE ERA

In the early 1970s, as the chairman of the House Judiciary Committee, Congressman Peter Rodino (D-New Jersey) led the House Watergate hearings on the possible impeachment of President Richard M. Nixon. In 1949, however, more than 20 years earlier, he was just one more new member of Congress seeking his first committee assignment.

As a World War II veteran, Rodino won a seat on the House Committee on Veterans' Affairs. It was a choice·assignment. Congressman Melvin Price (D-Illinois), who also served on the committee, recalled that the "assignment was so good politically that membership was open but allocated by state."

When Peter Rodino came to Congress, the World War II GI Bill was already a half-decade old. The Korean War was years away. During this interlude of peace, the principal issue before the Congress was not readjustment, but the veterans pension program.

The pension program is not related to any service-connected need. As its name implies, it is principally a program to supplement the income of older veterans in need. The program derives from the nation's generous commitment to those who have defended their country during time of war.

Because all veterans and their dependents are eligible, the program also poses a potential budget problem. A delicate balance has to be maintained between meeting the needs of older veterans and controlling costs.

The chairman of the House Committee on Veterans' Affairs, Congressman John Rankin (D-Mississippi), however, was not interested in balance. With the support of the major veterans organizations, he was readying in 1949 a massive increase in the pension program.

The Rankin Bill, H.R. 2681, would have given *every* veteran a pension at age 65. There would have been *no means tests*. Whatever his income, any veteran was eligible, providing that he had served only 90 days in the military during World Wars I or II.[1]

New members of Congress are called freshman as though they were youngsters just entering college. Like all freshmen, the 39-year-old Rodino had been told to "go along to get along for the first term. Why, just be quiet, listen, learn."

Rodino wanted to abide by the informal etiquette of the House, but it was hard to be quiet when he "heard the astronomical figures being projected" for the pension bill. Costs might reach $6 billion per year, and opponents ultimately argued that the bill's total cost could run to $110 billion, in 1949 dollars.[2]

As Rodino recalled: "We [veterans] didn't come back to be looking for a handout or to be rewarded materially, and that was my pitch when I came to [the] Committee. . . . I thought that I would speak out and wanted to offer a reasonable kind of amendment during the course of discussion."

He never had a chance. Chairman Rankin did not allow committee members to see the proposed bill until the day the committee met to adopt the legislation. The entire bill was then pushed through in less than 15 minutes.[3]

When Rodino tried to speak during the committee deliberation, he was gaveled down by Rankin. Rodino recalled, "I took exception and said I was going to take an appeal from the ruling of the chair. Imagine me, fresh upstart, you know. He gaveled me down again. . . . And I said to myself, 'My God, this isn't representative government. This is a tyrant.'"

With no opportunity to participate in the committee debate, Rodino took an extraordinary step. He walked out of the committee. Six other members of the committee joined him, a total of one-quarter of the committee's 27 members.

The controversy swept onto the House floor, with charge and countercharge being made regarding Rankin's handling of committee procedures, as well as on the bill itself. The *Washington Post* entered the fray with a scathing editorial cartoon of Rankin.

A strong supporter of the then dominant House Committee on Un-American Activities, Rankin was prepared with a reply:

> Mr. Speaker, I see a hideous cartoon of myself in this morning's Washington *Post* − the uptown edition of the Communist *Daily Worker*.
>
> You will remember that we chased some of the Communists off the editorial staff of that publication; but they still have a Communist cartoonist.
>
> This publication is doing more to stir race trouble here in Washington than all other forces combined, by its communistic propaganda for wiping out all race segregation and forcing Negroes into the white hotels and white schools of the District of Columbia.[4]

Opposing Rankin was clearly a high-risk game. He was prepared not only to debate facts but also to attack reputations. Those seven members who left the committee, the chairman claimed, had "walked out on the veterans."[5] Rodino disagreed: "I did not walk out on the veteran. I shall never walk out on the veteran. I shall always fight for the welfare of the veteran. But I shall also continue to fight for the things the veteran fought for − the preservation of our democratic principles."[6]

The seven members who walked out of the committee were not alone in their opposition to the Rankin Bill. They were joined by President Truman and the speaker of the House. A full campaign was waged to defeat the Rankin Bill.

When Rodino left the committee debate, among the six who joined him was Congressman Olin E. Teague (D-Texas). Nicknamed "Tiger," Teague also was a World War II veteran. First elected in 1946, two years before Rodino, Teague helped lead the opposition to Rankin.

In contrast to Rankin's attempt to inflate veterans pensions exclusively, Teague reminded his House colleagues of the needs of all older Americans:

> Mr. Chairman, sooner or later this Congress must decide between our old system of direct pensions to veterans and some kind of a system

"We'll All Get A Big Bang Out Of This, Boy"

Copyright © 1949 by Herblock in the *Washington Post*.

for all our old people, veterans and nonveterans. Certainly in a country such as these United States, our old people and our crippled people, whether or not they are veterans and who cannot care for themselves, must be cared for in some way. . . . If there is a group in America today who should have the public interest at heart, it is the veteran group.[7]

Veterans bills are rarely defeated. In a dramatic effort, after several days of debate, the Rankin Bill was beaten. The final vote came on a dramatic motion offered by Teague. After a recount, the Teague motion carried by one vote, 208-207.[8]

Although Rodino left the Committee on Veterans' Affairs to begin his distinguished career on the Judiciary Committee, Teague remained. In 1955, Teague became chairman of the committee, a position he held for nearly two decades.

When Teague left the chairmanship of the full Veterans' Committee in 1973 to take control of another House committee, he retained control of the key Veterans Subcommittee on Education and Training. Although no longer chairman of the full committee in title, he still controlled GI Bill legislation and had an effective veto on nearly all other veterans bills.

Through a long era that began with the successful defeat of the Rankin Bill and that stretched through the entire Vietnam War, Tiger Teague effectively ran Veterans' Affairs in the House. He shaped not just a few bills but the entire structure of our nation's veterans programs.

*　　　*　　　*

When Silvio Conte left the military in 1944, after World War II, his home town turned out in welcome. He used the generous World War II GI Bill to earn a college and law degree, which helped him win election to the Massachusetts State Senate in 1950. Eight years later, he was elected to the United States Congress as a Republican.

As Conte noted, without the World War II GI Bill, "I certainly would not be in Congress today." In 1973, he headed a special group studying the Vietnam GI Bill to determine whether Vietnam veterans were receiving the same chance.[9]

Conducted for the National League of Cities and for the United States Conference of Mayors, this study was based on public hearings in several cities across the country. Not only had the general benefit levels been low, the Conte committee discovered, but the benefit structure under the Vietnam GI Bill compounded the problems created by the low benefits.

The World War II GI Bill had provided a fixed payment to veterans to meet their living expenses and also provided a separate payment to the schools to meet the cost of tuition. The Vietnam GI Bill, in contrast, provided a fixed payment to each veteran to cover the cost of both tuition and living expenses.

The change in benefit structure created serious inequities. Under the World War II Bill, the payment to the schools could *vary* according to tuition levels, while leaving the payment to each veteran the same. Under the Vietnam GI Bill, veterans facing higher-than-average tuition payments were abandoned.

Without a separate payment to meet tuition, many Vietnam veterans simply could not afford private colleges. Although World War II veterans had made up 59 percent of Harvard's enrollment in 1947-48, Vietnam veterans were only 1.5 percent of Harvard's enrollment in 1971-72.[10]

Some states provided college education to their residents at little or no cost through their state universities. Others required students to help finance the public universities through higher tuition payments. In Arizona, where tuition was low, 54 percent of eligible veterans attended college. In Vermont, where tuition was higher, the rate was only 17 percent – one in six.[11]

While the president and Congress fought over general funding levels for the Vietnam GI Bill, a second battle was developing in Congress. The question was not the amount of money paid, but whether all the money should be paid in equal lump sums or whether some should be set aside to meet the needs of veterans facing higher tuition payments.

In 1951, before he became chairman of the House Veterans' Committee, Teague had run a special investigation of abuses under the World War II GI Bill. The World War II Bill included a broad range of programs. In addition to the college program, veterans could also use their benefits for on-the-job training, vocational education, and farm training.

The Teague report found that both guaranteed payments for the cost of tuition at profit-making business training schools and guaranteed payments under the on-the-job training program had encouraged abuse. The Veterans Administration, in turn, had difficulty administering the new programs that sprang up in a few short years, involving millions of veterans and billions of dollars.[12]

Yet the Teague report also specifically concluded that the college program, in contrast to some of the others, "had been successful." "Participating colleges and universities," the report concluded, "have rendered outstanding service in training veterans under many adverse conditions."[13]

Despite the contributions of the colleges, the Teague report recommended that separate payments be stopped to *all* schools, not only to the profit-making business training programs. The report's recommendations were adopted in the Korean War GI Bill. When it came time for the Vietnam GI Bill in 1966, Teague stuck with his new formula.

Joined by Congressman Albert H. Quie (R-Minnesota) and others, Conte argued that the time had come to reassess the Teague committee recommendations. Conte's recommendation was far less generous than the World War II GI Bill had been. It would not meet all the cost of tuition. Yet it was still costly enough to win the opposition of Teague.

Reform proponents hoped to offer their legislation as an amendment when the 1972 GI Bill amendments came to the floor. They never had a chance. Using his power as the committee chairman, Teague barred any amendments at all.[14]

The bill was brought to the floor under a procedure called the suspension of the rules. Designed to whisk noncontroversial measures into law, suspension procedures do not allow amendments. Debate is limited to a total of only 40 minutes, giving each side 20 minutes. In return for the streamlined procedure, two-thirds of the House is required to pass a bill under suspension, instead of a simple majority. Yet the two-thirds can be easily won if a chairman makes clear that the House has but one choice: accept his bill without amendment or get no bill at all. Not surprisingly, Teague's bill passed.

In 1974, the reform advocates regrouped, but Teague resorted to the suspension procedure again. Blocked from offering any amendment at all, Quie noted:

Mr. Speaker, I am very disappointed that the House of Representatives is today considering H.R. 12628 under suspension of the rules procedures, which does not allow the House to work its will. This is the second time the committee has brought out a veterans education assistance bill under this procedure, and I certainly hope it is the last.[15]

It was not. In 1975, despite strong objections from other members of the House, Teague resorted to the suspension procedure again to ram GI Bill amendments through the House without the opportunity for any amendments or extensive debate.[16]

In 1977, reform proponents tried again. Without even allowing hearings on alternative proposals, Teague forced his bill through committee and again resorted to the suspension procedure. Conte rose in protest:

> Mr. Speaker, I rise to express my vigorous objections to the way that this GI Bill legislation, which will control the expenditure of some $10 billion over the next five years, is being handled. It was scheduled without warning. . . . No amendments are being allowed on an expenditure that involves billions of dollars.[17]

In the Senate, members of the Committee on Veterans' Affairs backed reform proposals. In 1974, and then again in 1977, the Senate adopted reform legislation, opening the possibility of a compromise with Teague.

Differences between the House and the Senate are normally resolved through a conference committee. Usually including several members of each party from both the House and the Senate, conference committees meet in the open, subject to the scrutiny of the press.

Those seeking some sort of separate tuition payment were almost guaranteed representation on a conference committee over the GI Bill amendments, yet no conference was held on the 1977 bill. The differences between the House and Senate bills were resolved in private through direct negotiations between Teague and his staff, and the Senate leadership and its staff.

Outraged at the failure to proceed through an open conference, 13 members of the House committee, nearly a majority, wrote Teague requesting a full conference. Editorial pages usually reserve their space for the discussion of policy, but the abuse was so significant that the *Washington Post* wrote an editorial supporting the call for a conference committee.[18]

Teague was not deterred. He not only refused to confer with the Senate but also forced crippling concessions in the Senate bill. The provision addressing the cost of tuition in the final measure was so complex that literally no Vietnam veteran has ever been able to use it. It is a program in name only.[19]

In a column for the *Washington Post*, Colman McCarthy captured the attitude implicit in the chairman's strategy:

Asked a few days ago by the Dallas *Morning News* how compromises were reached on a major and current piece of legislation that affects almost three million Vietnam veterans, Teague said it was done "around a breakfast table." . . . For those who believe that Senate and House versions of a bill should be worked out in an open-to-the-public conference committee by senators and representatives who are accountable, Teague said, "It's just quicker and easier" to do the compromising "without a whole lot of people."[20]

His victory at hand, Teague rushed the final bill to the floor. He sought to increase his power by forcing consideration of the bill in the waning days of the 1977 session when any debate could only have been won late at night while Congress struggled to adjourn.

Margaret Heckler became secretary of Health and Human Services in the Reagan administration in 1983. In 1977, however, she was a Republican congresswoman from Massachusetts and a ranking member of the House Veterans' Committee. When the final bill was brought up for a vote she noted:

For the second consecutive year, members of this distinguished body have been presented veterans educational and employment assistance legislation during the closing moments of the Congress. . . . No formal conference has been held on the bill which is before us. The large majority of the members of this Committee on Veterans' Affairs have not been consulted on how best to resolve critical differences between the two bodies regarding veterans programs of education and employment assistance.[21]

As Heckler noted, this was not the first time Teague forced a bill through at the last minute. Like his use of the suspension procedure, there was a pattern of abuse. When Conte objected to the consideration of the 1977 bill under suspension, he was careful to note the long history: "I might point out that this argument about the suspension situation preventing amendments raises the same point that Congressman Albert Quie and Neal Smith raised in the GI Bill debate of February 1974."[22]

Tiger Teague, once the young champion struggling against abusive committee leaders, had become the abusive chairman himself. On four different occasions, over eight long years, culminating in the 1977 bill, Teague won by simply precluding debate.

In 1978, Public Affairs Analysts, Inc., the respected consulting firm of Joe Napolitan, polled the members of the House on Vietnam veterans issues. It found that a clear majority would have supported a tuition provision if they were given the opportunity. They never were. During the entire Vietnam era, the House was never able to vote on GI Bill policy.[23]

A ONE-HOUSE CONGRESS: THE ROBERTS YEARS

Charles Kurchek could not sleep at night. He could not eat meat. He constantly felt anxious. He was plagued by constant repetitions of the same nightmare. In that nightmare, he was being held by Vietnamese soldiers who were slowly flaying him alive, beginning with his stomach.

The nightmare arose out of real events. In Vietnam, Kurchek was with South Vietnamese troops when they took an area containing the mutilated bodies of tortured Americans. Prompted by rage and revenge, the South Vietnamese interrogated a captured North Vietnamese soldier by slowly peeling his skin off, starting with his stomach area. Kurchek was watching.

Throughout 1970-71, he took his problem to the VA. He was relentless in his insistence that something be done, that his nightmares be ended. The VA did offer help of a sort. It sent him to a psychiatrist, who placed him on medication.

For Kurchek, that began a traditional program of psychotherapy. Incredibly, the dream was assumed by the VA psychiatrist to reflect domestic problems in his family or in his childhood. The war was conveniently overlooked, and, not surprisingly, Charles Kurchek's problem was not resolved.

Unfortunately, by the early 1970s, the Vietnam War, then over six years old, had yet to reach the VA. The VA still did not understand and, apparently, did not want to understand what had happened to many Vietnam veterans. Its therapy reflected this failure of understanding.

In 1971, several U.S. senators, led by Senator Alan Cranston (D-California), tried to bring the war to the VA. They introduced legislation seeking to create a new health care program providing readjustment counseling specifically focused on Vietnam veterans, and a new program for alcoholism and drug abuse treatment.

The bill was the product of disturbing hearings. "Significant numbers of Vietnam veterans . . . have . . . suffered severe psychiatric problems," the committee concluded in its 1972 report. Charles Kurchek was not alone.[24]

The major veterans organizations disagreed. They opposed the legislation. The program could only be created if it were separately funded and, in the words of the Veterans of Foreign Wars, "shall not be taken from existing funds," or, in the words of the American Legion, "should not be allowed to have any impact on other health services."[25]

Propelled by the overwhelming need, the Senate committee, chaired by Senator Vance Hartke (D-Indiana), overlooked the dissent of the veterans organizations. The bill was brought to the Senate floor, passed, and referred to the House.

In the House, however, the veterans organizations were able to find champions for their point of view. The House Committee on Veterans' Affairs refused to accept the Senate-passed measure, killing the program.

The concerns over funding of the veterans organizations and of their House allies are hard to understand. No VA health care programs are separately funded, except for the special Nobel Prize-winning research programs.

In an agency with a $12.7-billion budget in 1973, proposed as the first year of the program, the *total five-year cost of the program* would have been $550 million, or less than one percent (0.66 percent) of the VA's projected budget during those five years. The House committee was either exceedingly stingy, or their opposition to the program ran deep.

*   *   *

Peter Long is a Vietnam veteran. He can remember the day when he knew that he could no longer push the war's memories away:

It was the day President Ford announced we were pulling out of Vietnam, and you saw the guy come out of the embassy and fly away, and he was the last American. There was something inside me that tore me to pieces. That's when I wanted to see the brass bands. . . . I knew that wasn't going to happen. So I thought, well, what I'll do is go to church tomorrow. And the priest will say something. He says prayers for every SOB in Washington, you know; he'll say one for the people who've come back from Vietnam, or who died at least.

He never mentioned it. Never, never mentioned it. I remember as I was walking out the door, I turned to him, and I said, "You're a heck of a lousy priest." . . . I didn't wait for an answer, and I knew at that moment I had a lot of anger in me that I had not looked into.[26]

When Peter Long took that anger to the VA, it told him that there was nothing to worry about — to forget it. In the VA's opinion, Peter Long, an Air Force officer who had held a position at the White House before he was discharged, simply could not have a problem. If he would just wait a bit, everything would be all right.

Despite the VA's confidence, Peter Long's rage remained. In part, he was angry at himself, an anger born of guilt. Although he had seen his share of combat, he was a rear-echelon Air Force officer who had made important decisions yet had only visited the front. He felt that he had failed to serve those who did the fighting. He had let himself take the easy way out. As he turned to the VA seeking help, however, he found a new source of anger — rage at the VA and at the nation that were abandoning him and other Vietnam veterans.

In 1975, there still was no place for Peter Long to go, as there had been no place for Charles Kurchek to go in 1970. When a new Congress convened in 1973, the Readjustment Counseling Program passed the Senate again, only to die again in the House. The year 1975 brought another Congress. The Senate passed the bill again. It died again at the hands of the House committee.[27]

In 1975, Congressman Ray Roberts (D-Texas) became chairman of the House Veterans' Committee. He held that position for the next five years. Roberts was strongly opposed to the Readjustment Counseling Program. Congressman David Satterfield (D-Virginia), who chaired the subcommittee with jurisdiction specifically over health care, shared Roberts's attitudes.

From 1971 through 1976, the House committee was reinforced in its opposition not only by the major veterans organizations but also by the Nixon and Ford administrations. In 1977, when Jimmy

Carter became president, that changed. For the first time, the country had a president who supported the program.

Accepting the arguments of the major veterans organizations, the leadership of the House committee was not swayed by the new president. Unmoved on the merits, they were nevertheless prepared to strike a deal. They would accept the counseling program if the price were right.

The VA runs the largest medical system in the United States. With more than 170 hospitals, the VA has control over the location of individual facilities, a control that carries political power. Congressmen seeking hospitals for veterans in their areas have to defer to those chairmen who control the hospital system.

Despite its general jurisdiction over veterans benefits, the Committee on Veterans' Affairs did not have control over the location of VA hospitals. Both Roberts and Satterfield wanted a piece of that action.

In 1977, Senator Cranston, author of the readjustment counseling legislation, became chairman of the Senate Veterans' Committee. He was prepared to deal. In exchange for House support for readjustment counseling, he offered his support for House legislation that would give the veterans committees a voice in the location of VA hospitals.

In 1978, the deal was included in comprehensive VA health care legislation, but the House committee proved unable to win the necessary support within the House for the new legislation giving them control over the location of VA hospitals. In the closing days of the 1978 session, the deal began to unravel.

Rather than move the rest of the comprehensive package, leaving the hospital provision for another year, Roberts and Satterfield dropped the entire package. If they could not have control over the location of VA hospitals, then Vietnam veterans could not have readjustment counseling.

Congressman John Paul Hammerschmidt (R-Arkansas), the ranking Republican member of the committee, explained what had been lost:

> At the same time, however, I would like to register my disappointment in this amendment in its present form. Mr. Speaker, this amendment contains only the most absolutely essential portion of a very comprehensive bill. . . . The version originally intended for this body's vote

included a provision that would have given mental and psychological readjustment counseling to Vietnam veterans.[28]

In 1979, the Senate tried again, for the fifth time. The major veterans organizations remained opposed to the program. The Veterans of Foreign Wars, the Disabled American Veterans, and the American Legion repeated the same budgetary complaints expressed in the first round of hearings nearly a decade earlier.[29]

Yet in the few months that had passed since the last days of the 1978 session, the leaders of the House committee had managed to clear the legislative path for the hospital control legislation. The deal was secured, and the objections of the major organizations were suddenly insignificant. In 1979, the measure was enacted into law.

The legislation's final enactment occurred as the nation paused to honor Vietnam veterans during a week of special celebrations. David Broder, a columnist for the *Washington Post*, noted the politics at work in the readjustment counseling victory and its ironic implications:

> What has happened is this: As their price for approving the special treatment for the psychologically damaged Vietnam vets, members of the House Veterans' Affairs Committee have demanded from the president and the Veterans Administration veto power over all significant future VA hospital and medical facility construction. . . .
>
> Next to tipping over a wheelchair, it is hard to imagine a shabbier way for Congress to mark Vietnam Veterans Week.[30]

In 1979 and 1980, while the finally enacted Readjustment Counseling Program was working its way through the always slow process of implementation, Charles Kurchek and Peter Long joined a privately run counseling program called "Back in the World," founded by Jeffrey Jay, Ph.D. and Ken Harbert, PA-C.

At Back in the World, they each found a group of Vietnam veterans and counselors who were prepared to listen, prepared to understand that their problems were real and were related to Vietnam. Over 12 difficult weeks, each began to make his private peace with the war.

Vietnam veteran Ken Harbert said, after describing Peter Long's and Charles Kurchek's struggles:

What happened in our groups did require some sensitivity, some trial and error, some training, but there was nothing magical about it. All we did was provide a place to talk. The VA could have done the same, and years ago.

It's a tragedy, it makes me very mad, when Vietnam veterans come to our groups after so many years, so many problems. How many years did Peter or Charles lose to the Vietnam War? One year, for the year they spent in Vietnam? Several years, for the years they served? Or nearly a decade, for all the time they waited because no one was there to listen.

Nearly a decade. That's my answer. Nearly a decade. Why did it take so long?

*   *   *

During the bulk of the Teague era, there was no Senate Committee on Veterans' Affairs at all. Instead, jurisdiction over veterans issues was divided among several committees, most notably the powerful Senate Finance Committee, which was preoccupied with its control over the nation's entire tax system.

Since no Senate chairman had an exclusive interest in veterans issues, the Senate tended to defer to the House committee leadership for guidance. Gilbert Steiner, a Brookings scholar who has studied the politics of veteran legislation, observed:

Arrangements between House Veterans' Affairs and Senate Finance soon settled into an agreed pattern. All consequential veterans' benefits legislation would first be acted on in the House. Then the Finance Committee would move bills that Teague endorsed and drop the bills he opposed.[31]

Effectively, there was only one Committee on Veterans' Affairs, one which had control over both the Senate and the House. When a separate Senate committee was created in 1970, the habits of power among the House leaders were hard to change.

Asked in 1977 to justify his determined opposition to the Senate-backed Readjustment Counseling Program, Roberts simply dismissed the importance of his colleagues on the Senate committee:

Now, the Veterans' Committee over in the Senate is a new committee, and they almost lost it. As a matter of fact, if it hadn't been for support from [the House], they would have done away with the Committee.

Uh, it is uh, a minor committee over there, compared to the function we perform over here.[32]

In fact, the functions performed by the Senate committee match nearly exactly the House committee's, but the chairman's point has a truth behind its confused facts. As he knew, by tradition the leaders of the House committee are the barons of veterans politics.

Over a long decade, first Senator Hartke and then Senator Cranston slowly built the power of the Senate committee. For Vietnam veterans, however, the power came too late, as was reflected in the Senate's repeated defeats on the Readjustment Counseling Program.

Vietnam veterans had many friends in Congress. They had friends on the Senate committee. They had friends in the House. They even had friends who served on the House committee. But in veterans politics, the only friends who counted were the leaders of the House committee.

The opposition of the House committee leadership to the Readjustment Counseling Program was not an isolated event. Like the story of the Rankin pension bill more than two decades earlier, it was part of a pattern — the close working relationship between the major veterans groups and their friends among the House Committee on Veterans' Affairs.

As Rodino recalled, the battle over the Rankin pension bill pitted the generations against each other. Younger veterans had been prepared to question the pension increase. Older veterans, with important exceptions, had not.

Despite the generation gap, World War II veterans were well positioned in Congress to protect their interests following their war. A mere two years after the end of World War II, there were 92 World War II veterans in Congress, nearly 20 percent of the combined House and Senate.

The make up of Congress following the Vietnam War was decidedly different. In 1980, there were 103 members of Congress who had been eligible for service during the Vietnam War, but just 21 had served on active duty. Only four had served in Vietnam.

The soldiers who fought the Vietnam War were young. The poor, minorities, and middle-class working families contributed disproportionately to combat units. There were few Kennedys or Rockefellers who marched off proudly to battle and returned triumphant to serve in the U.S. Congress.

Essentially, the only personal knowledge Congress would have of the war came from the sons who fought. While the children of congressmen served in the same proportion as the population as a whole, congressmen are older and few had sons eligible for the draft. A 1970 survey by the *Congressional Quarterly* found that just 5 percent of the Congress had sons who served in Vietnam.[33]

The older veterans, however, were united by age with the older members of the House. The older veterans also managed the machinery of the major veterans organizations. On both counts, they carried the allegiance of the senior members who ran the House Committee on Veterans' Affairs.

Tiger Teague was the great exception. Nearly alone among the senior members of the committee, he was prepared to fight against the major organizations, as he had demonstrated in the debate over the Rankin Bill. Teague set his own priorities.

Winning fame through his study of abuses under the World War II GI Bill, schooled in the debate over the pension bill, Teague inherited a world of veterans politics where the roles were fixed and easy to understand.

The veterans organizations constantly sought more. Members of Congress advanced their proposals, earning the organizations' praise and support. Some members of Congress always did just as the veteran groups asked. The role of responsible leadership was to sort out the legitimate requests from the budget boondoggles.

Under these conditions, the chairman's job was to learn to say "No," and then to have the courage to take the heat when he did. The veterans organizations, it was assumed, would not fail to advance needed programs. No chairman would need to argue for programs against hesitant veterans groups.

Abandoned by the major veterans organizations, Vietnam veterans needed an ally among the barons, one who would stand with them against the major veterans groups. The role was almost unintelligible to Chairman Teague. Without his support, Vietnam veterans were left without any friends who counted on the House committee.

Nor did the House ever vote to overrule its veterans committee chairmen and mandate increased attention to the needs of Vietnam veterans. Congress reflected the attitudes of the nation, including the nation's desire to forget the war and its turmoil.

For the Congress, as for the nation, the Vietnam War had been controversial, rancorous, and seemingly endless. The members of

Congress, no less than their constituents, were glad to set the burden down. Ready to be diverted, there were a host of new problems that grabbed their attention.

Hardly were U.S. soldiers withdrawn from Vietnam than Congress was immersed in the constitutional crisis of Watergate. The Vietnam War helped create inflationary pressures in the economy that demanded attention. The Arab oil embargo accentuated the United States's vulnerability to unstable energy sources.

Congress took its cue from the nation, leaving the war and its veteran behind. The Vietnam veteran advocates in the House, like Conte, remained a minority voice. The veterans committee was left alone and the priorities of the veterans organizations became, nearly automatically, the priorities of Congress.

THE MONTGOMERY ERA

In 1978, a group of Vietnam-era veterans serving in Congress formed a new caucus, the Vietnam Veterans in Congress. In the beginning, the caucus had just 11 members. Most were young, first elected to the Congress in 1974 or later. Most were Democrats, progressive and aggressive.

Chaired by Congressman David E. Bonior (D-Michigan), the other founding members of the caucus were Congressmen John P. Murtha (D-Pennsylvania), Les Aspin (D-Wisconsin), John Cavanaugh (D-Nebraska), David Cornwell (D-Indiana), Albert Gore, Jr. (D-Tennessee), Thomas Harkin (D-Iowa), James R. Jones (D-Oklahoma), John LaFalce (D-New York), Leon Panetta (D-California), and Senator John Heinz (R-Pennsylvania).

From the start, the Vietnam Veterans in Congress was a threat to the veterans establishment in the House. The very idea of creating a new caucus was a clear, if nevertheless implicit, declaration that the House Committee on Veterans' Affairs was not doing its job.

As the *Washington Post* noted in an editorial heralding the formation of the caucus:

> Along with the other burdens they bear, many Vietnam-era veterans must confront the reality that few in Congress have any special understanding of the problems they face. ... No organized bloc of Vietnam-veteran advocates was on hand to influence policy until a few weeks

ago, when 11 members of Congress who served during the Vietnam era joined together to work collectively on behalf of the large national constituency composed of their fellow veterans.[34]

Chairman Roberts sensed the message. When the *Post* editorial was submitted into the *Congressional Record*, he responded:

Those of us who deal directly with veteran affairs have given up trying to enlighten the Washington *Post*. Its editorial writers prefer fancy to fact and, I suppose, the prose that drifts up from their pipedreams is more entertaining to their readers than cold, hard facts.[35]

Near the end of his statement, Roberts was careful to announce that the hearings of his committee were open and to urge all members of Congress who were Vietnam-era veterans "to share with this committee any and all views they may have on veterans legislation."

It was a bold promise. Yet Roberts refused repeated requests to meet with the leadership of the new caucus, including a formal request in writing. From the day the caucus was formed until the day Roberts retired, more than two years later, his committee would never hold a single day of hearings on legislation introduced by the Vietnam Veterans in Congress.

Asked about the Vietnam veteran by a network correspondent in 1977, Roberts shot back: "Well, he's a minority — period. In five million veterans that were called during Vietnam, a million of them went over there and saw some — maybe in a combat zone — as against seventeen million in World War II. So, he is a minority."[36]

In fact, there are nine million Vietnam-era veterans, not just five million. In fact, nearly three million served in Vietnam, not just one million. In fact, there were 12.5 million World War II veterans, not 17, and during World War II, as in every war including Vietnam, only a small percentage served in the combat zone, and even fewer faced the horrors of battle.

It is telling enough that the chairman of the House Committee on Veterans' Affairs did not even know how many Vietnam veterans there were. More telling is the tone and occasion of the comment. The chairman had launched into his statement prompted only by the correspondent's remark that, "Of course, the Vietnam veteran is really a minority with veterans organizations."[37]

Without even being asked, Roberts had stopped to explain, in hard, bottom line language, the back-room world of veterans politics. His message was simple. Vietnam veterans had no clout. They just did not count. End of discussion.

In 1978, the Vietnam Veterans in Congress introduced comprehensive legislation entitled the Vietnam Veterans Act. Reintroduced in 1979, the ambitious proposal was not designed to be passed at once, or even to be considered as one bill, but to set out in one place a systematic program.[38]

To those who asked, "What should be done?" the Vietnam Veterans Act proposed an answer. It extended the delimitation date that barred Vietnam veterans from using their GI Bill benefits more than ten years after their date of discharge. It contained legislation to help meet the cost of tuition.

The unemployment rate among Vietnam veterans remained unstable, rising with each economic downturn. The Vietnam Veterans Act proposed stronger employment programs. It included the Senate-passed Readjustment Counseling Program and a companion measure advanced by Senator Cranston to expand alcohol and drug treatment.

The 1979 act contained the first Agent Orange compensation legislation. To help promote national recognition of the needs and accomplishments of Vietnam veterans, the caucus also proposed a Vietnam Veterans Week.

In May 1978, when the Vietnam Veterans in Congress was formed, the House Committee on Veterans' Affairs had yet to hold a single day of hearings on the problem of Agent Orange. As public pressure mounted, the committee held one day of hearings in October 1978.

No representative of the Vietnam veterans groups concerned about Agent Orange appeared. Air Force and Veterans Administration witnesses appeared to defend the status quo, as did the Veterans of Foreign Wars. The hearings lasted just over two hours.[39]

With the doors closed at the House Committee on Veterans' Affairs, Congressman Albert Gore (D-Tennessee), a member of the Vietnam Veterans in Congress, secured hearings before the House Committee on Interstate and Foreign Commerce, with the help of Congressman Robert Eckhardt (D-Texas). The first round of hearings was held in June 1979. A second set was held in September 1980.[40]

The Commerce committee hearings attracted substantial media attention and generated editorials across the country. As public concern increased, Senator John Heinz (R-Pennsylvania), also a member of the Vietnam Veterans in Congress, won Senate passage in 1980 of legislation based on the caucus's Agent Orange proposal. The leadership of the House Committee on Veterans' Affairs, however, refused to accept the Senate-passed measure.[41]

The Veterans' Affairs Committee rejected the caucus proposal for stronger employment programs. Caucus member James R. Jones (D-Oklahoma), however, served on the House Ways and Means Committee. Working with Congressman Charles Rangel (D-New York), he used the tax code to create new incentives for employers to hire disadvantaged Vietnam veterans.[42]

The caucus proposal to create a Vietnam Veterans Week did not require the approval of the House Committee on Veterans' Affairs. All legislation to create commemorative celebrations is handled by the Committee on Post Office and Civil Service. In 1978, Vietnam Veterans Week was passed.[43]

Among the new members of Congress who arrived in 1979 were several Vietnam-era veterans. By the end of 1980, membership in the Vietnam Veterans in Congress had nearly doubled. With members on nearly every important House committee, one committee after another was adopting Vietnam veterans legislation, except for the Committee on Veterans' Affairs.

By the end of 1980, change even reached the Committee on Veterans' Affairs. Roberts, who had chaired the committee since 1975, announced that he would retire. Also retiring was Congressman David Satterfield, the powerful chairman of the subcommittee with jurisdiction over medical care.

Congressman G. V. (Sonny) Montgomery (D-Mississippi) became the new chairman of the full Committee on Veterans' Affairs. In contrast to Roberts, Montgomery was prepared to act on Vietnam veterans issues.

Montgomery was reinforced by new committee leadership. Don Edwards (D-California), long an advocate for Vietnam veterans, became the committee's ranking Democratic member. He was now in a position to quietly ensure that the needs of Vietnam veterans were being addressed.

At the same time, younger members of the committee gained new prominence. Robert Edgar (D-Pennsylvania), first elected in

1974 and a consistent advocate for Vietnam veterans, became chairman of the subcommittee with jurisdiction over the GI Bill.

Thomas Daschle (D-South Dakota), a Vietnam-era veteran who was first elected in 1978, joined the Committee on Veterans' Affairs. In 1980, he became the second chairman of the Vietnam Veterans in Congress. By 1981, he was an active and respected advocate on the Veterans' Committee.

The tight budget climate set by the new Reagan administration precluded expansive proposals. Montgomery, a senior statesman of the so-called "Boll Weevil" caucus of Southern conservatives within the Democratic party, was not inclined to either attack President Reagan or support expensive programs.

Nevertheless, in one short year, the logjam on Vietnam veterans legislation broke. The Veterans' Committee adopted legislation advanced by Congressman Daschle to mandate health care for Agent Orange problems. Although a full extension of the delimitation date was precluded, Montgomery supported another Daschle proposal to provide a limited extension focused on Vietnam veterans with continuing employment problems.[44]

As the recession deepened in 1982 and 1983, the House committee took another look at the employment programs within the GI Bill. Under the leadership of Marvin Leath (D-Texas), the committee in 1983 adopted the proposal in the earlier Vietnam veterans acts to strengthen the GI Bill employment programs.[45]

Having won health care in 1981, the Vietnam Veterans in Congress renewed the push for Agent Orange compensation in 1983. Opposing the provision at first, Montgomery ultimately supported legislation to compensate Vietnam veterans with three specific disabilities related to Agent Orange exposure.

The bill, H.R. 1961, pushed in the Veterans' Committee by Daschle, was reported by the committee on a unanimous vote in 1983. When the Congress returned for the new session in 1984, H.R. 1961 was taken to the floor, where it was adopted by the full House, again on a unanimous vote.[46]

During the long years of defeat, when Vietnam veterans proposals were summarily dismissed by the House Veterans' Committee leadership — indeed were not even granted floor debate nor votes — it was easy for Vietnam veterans to wonder whether their claims had not been wrong all along.

The Montgomery years put the issue back in perspective. The problem was not with Vietnam veterans but with the nation's political leaders. From 1981-84, the new leaders of the House Veterans' Committee revamped the committee's priorities. For the first time, Vietnam veterans had a few friends among the barons. That friendship created a new era in veterans legislation.

NOTES

1. See *Providing Pensions for Veterans of World War I and World War II Based on Non-Service-Connected Disability and Attained Age*, 81st Congress, 1st Session, Report No. 132, p. 2. The issue of a "needs clause" was central to the bill debate. See, for example, the early exchange between Chairman Rankin and Congressman Kearney, *Congressional Record – House*, March 22, 1949, p. 2944.

2. See, for example, statement of the Honorable Walter B. Huber, ibid., p. 2944.

3. Even by the rough and tumble standards of the time, the abuse seemed extraordinary. See statement of the Honorable Walter B. Huber, "Committee on Veterans' Affairs," *Congressional Record – House*, February 15, 1949, p. 1212; statement of the Honorable Olin F. Teague, *Congressional Record – House*, March 22, 1949, p. 2939; and statement of the Honorable James E. Noland, ibid., p. 2951.

4. Statement of the Honorable John Rankin, "The Veterans Pension Bill," *Congressional Record – House*, February 17, 1949, p. 1366.

5. Statement of the Honorable John Rankin, *Congressional Record – House*, February 15, 1949, p. 1212.

6. Statement of the Honorable Peter W. Rodino, Jr., "Committee on Veterans' Affairs," *Congressional Record – House*, ibid., p. 1213.

7. Statement of the Honorable Olin E. Teague, *Congressional Record – House*, March 22, 1949, p. 2960.

8. See ibid., pp. 3110-3115.

9. Congressman Conte's statement is from his personal introduction to the *Final Report: Findings and Recommendations, Special Veterans Opportunity Committee*, National League of Cities/United States Conference of Mayors, September 13, 1973, p. 1.

10. Stuart F. Feldman, *Sunbelt States Reap GI Bill Bonanza: Eastern and Midwestern Vietnam Veterans Lose Scholarship Opportunities*, National League of Cities/Conference of Mayors, December 8, 1976, p. 12.

11. Ibid., p. 5.

12. *House Select Committee to Investigate Educational, Training, and Loan Guarantee Programs under the GI Bill*, February 14, 1952 – Committed to the Committee of the Whole House on the State of the Union and ordered to be printed, with illustrations, 82nd Congress, 2nd Session, House Report No. 1375.

13. Ibid., p. 9 and p. 4. There were problems with the college program surrounding the formulas for calculating tuition payments and payments for books, tools, and supplies. The report specifically concluded, however, "There are probably no cases where the tuition received by the colleges was sufficient to cover the total cost of the veterans' education." Ibid., p. 66.

14. See statement of the Honorable Albert H. Quie during debate on H.R. 12828, *Congressional Record — House*, March 6, 1972, p. 6957.

15. Statement of the Honorable Albert H. Quie during debate on H.R. 12628, *Congressional Record — House*, February 19, 1974, p. 3247.

16. See statement of the Honorable Bob Edgar during debate on H.R. 9576, *Congressional Record — House*, October 6, 1975, p. 31837. In 1975, an effort was made to defeat the bill under suspension, but it failed by less than 35 votes. See ibid., p. 31869.

17. Statement of the Honorable Silvio O. Conte during debate on H.R. 8701, *Congressional Record — House*, September 12, 1977, p. 28229.

18. "A Full Debate for the GI Bill," *Washington Post*, November 2, 1977.

19. The Senate-passed provision allowed Vietnam veterans to use any benefits remaining after completion of their training to pay for student loans secured from the Veterans Administration. The House made payment contingent upon states providing a matching payment. (P.L. 95-202.)

20. Colman McCarthy, " 'Tiger' Teague and the Veterans Compromise," *Washington Post*, November 21, 1977.

21. Statement of the Honorable Margaret Heckler during debate on H.R. 8701, *Congressional Record — House*, November 3, 1977, pp. 36948 and 36949.

22. Statement of the Honorable Silvio O. Conte during debate on H.R. 8701, *Congressional Record — House*, September 12, 1977, p. 28831.

23. The poll, commissioned by the Vietnam Veterans of America, found that 64 percent of the entire Congress (67 percent of the House) favored tuition legislation. See *Survey of Congressional Attitudes on Problems of Concern to Vietnam Veterans*, May 10, 1978, p. 14.

24. *Veterans' Drug and Alcohol Treatment and Rehabilitation Act of 1972*, 92nd Congress, 2nd Session, Senate Report No. 1084 to accompany S. 2108, September 1, 1972, p. 36.

25. *Drug Addiction and Abuse among Military Veterans, 1971*, joint hearings before the Subcommittee on Health and Hospitals of the Committee on Veterans' Affairs, and Subcommittee on Alcoholism and Narcotics of the Committee on Labor and Public Welfare, United States Senate, 92nd Congress, 1st Session, June 15 and 23, 1971, Part I, p. 93 for the statement of the Veterans of Foreign Wars, and pp. 247-248 for the statement of the American Legion. The Disabled American Veterans expressed the same reservations on pp. 84-85.

26. From an interview in Sandy Rovner, "Since Vietnam: Years of Quiet Desperation," *Washington Post*, May 4, 1979. The article profiled "Back in the World," the program described below at pp. 21-22. In the interest of privacy, actual names have not been used in either of the two cases discussed.

27. S. 284, 93rd Congress, 1973-74. See *Veterans' Drug and Alcohol Treatment Rehabilitation Act of 1973*, 93rd Congress, 1st Session, Senate Report

No. 93-56 to accompany S. 284, March 2, 1973. S. 2908, 94th Congress, 1975-76. The report and hearings are published in *Veterans Omnibus Health Care Act of 1976*, hearings before the Subcommittee on Health and Hospitals of the Committee on Veterans' Affairs, United States Senate, 94th Congress, 2nd Session on S. 2908 and related bills, February 18-19, 1976.

28. Statement of the Honorable John Paul Hammerschmidt during debate on H.R. 5029, *Congressional Record — House*, October 13, 1978, p. 37029.

29. *Veterans' Health Care Amendments of 1979*, hearing before the Committee on Veterans' Affairs, United States Senate, 96th Congress, 1st Session, on S. 7, January 25, 1979. See, in particular, p. 313 for the statement of the Veterans of Foreign Wars, p. 379 for the statement of the Disabled American Veterans, and p. 394 for the statement of the American Legion.

30. David S. Broder, "The Pork Barrel Price for Helping Vets," *Washington Post*, June 3, 1979.

31. Gilbert Y. Steiner, *The State of Welfare* (The Brookings Institution: Washington, 1971), p. 254.

32. TV network's unused film, 1977.

33. "Vietnam War Affects Families of Members of Congress," *Congressional Quarterly*, February 13, 1970, pp. 405-13; Don Winter, "A Generation of Leaders Sat Out Vietnam," *Washington Post*, April 6, 1980, p. E1.

34. "Vietnam Veterans in Congress," *Washington Post*, May 8, 1978.

35. Statement of Congressman Roberts, "A Veteran Is a Veteran," *Congressional Record — House*, May 25, 1978, p. 15355.

36. TV network's unused film, op. cit.

37. Ibid.

38. The 1978 Vietnam Veterans Act was H.R. 14164. The 1979 Act was H.R. 3102. Companion legislation was introduced in the Senate by Senator John Heinz (R-Pennsylvania), a member of the caucus.

39. *Herbicide "Agent Orange,"* hearings before the Subcommittee on Medical Facilities and Benefits of the Committee on Veterans' Affairs, House of Representatives, 95th Congress, 2nd Session, October 11, 1978.

40. *Involuntary Exposure to Agent Orange and Other Toxic Spraying*, hearings before the Subcommittee on Oversight and Investigation of the Committee on Interstate and Foreign Commerce, House of Representatives, 96th Congress, 1st Session, June 25-27, 1979, Serial No. 96-139. *Agent Orange: Exposure of Vietnam Veterans*, hearings before the Subcommittee on Oversight and Investigation of the Committee on Interstate and Foreign Commerce, House of Representatives, 96th Congress, 2nd Session, September 25, 1980.

41. See statements of the Honorable David E. Bonior, Thomas Daschle, Robert Eckhardt, and Leon Panetta during debate on H.R. 5288, *Congressional Record — House*, September 25, 1980, pp. 27375-27377, 27391-27392.

42. Based on language in the Vietnam Veterans Act, the provision provided employers with a tax credit if they hired a qualifying Vietnam veteran. It was included in the Targeted Jobs Tax Credit provisions of P.L. 95-600.

43. House Joint Resolution 1147, creating Vietnam Veterans Week, was enacted as P.L. 95-513.

44. Both provisions were enacted as part of P.L. 97-72, *Veterans Health Care, Training, and Small Business Loan Act of 1981.*

45. H.R. 2355, "Emergency Vietnam Veterans' Jobs Training Act of 1983," was enacted as P.L. 98-77.

46. H.R. 1961, "Agent Orange and Atomic Veteran Relief Act," was adopted by the House on January 30, 1984, *Congressional Record — House,* H-218-H-227.

7   The Veterans Administration

CAUGHT IN THE MAZE, STUDIED TO DEATH

John Woods had done more than mark time in the military. He had served for five years and had sought out the distinction of becoming a green beret. He had become a medic and had volunteered for Vietnam in 1966.

While in Vietnam, Woods began to lose weight. He broke out in a severe skin rash and suffered migraine headaches. His problems became worse after his discharge from the Army. He experienced forced heart attacks, went temporarily blind, and permanently lost his ability to distinguish some colors.

Woods' own health problems were not his principal concern. Before he had volunteered to serve in Vietnam, John and his wife Mildred had two children. Both children were normal and healthy. After John's return from Vietnam, the couple had two more children. One suffered from muscle spasms. The other was born with an enlarged right hand and a tumor on the face, and was hypertensive.

John Woods suspected that his children's health problems, as well as his own, might have been the result of his exposure to a herbicide used in Vietnam. Called "Agent Orange," after the orange bands that circled the drums used to store the herbicide, it was formed from equal parts of two chemicals: 2,4-D and 2,4,5-T. It was used from 1961 to 1970 to kill jungle growth, making it more difficult for the enemy to hide. An estimated 12 million gallons were sprayed over three- to four-million acres.

Woods clearly remembered when he was exposed:

> Between the base and us there was a mortar field, but on the other side of us, which we called the suicide zone, that was constantly sprayed with a chemical, and within two to three days the leaves would fall off and we could see maybe 1,000 meters. The chemical would come into our compound, or our area, and whatever trees we had did not grow. The leaves would fall off.[1]

On June 26, 1979, John and his wife Mildred took their fears to Congress. They appeared as the leadoff witnesses in the first major Congressional hearings on Agent Orange and its effects on Vietnam veterans. Joining John and Mildred Woods at the witness table was another Vietnam veteran, Mike Ryan, his wife Maureen, and their daughter Kerrie. Ryan had also served in Vietnam. He, too, felt that he had been exposed to Agent Orange. He remembered the consequences: "I was 178 pounds. Within five weeks I was in the hospital at 128 pounds, fully clothed and fully dressed. I developed a severe skin rash in both eyes and in my groin area. I also had migraine headaches."[2]

Four years after he had returned from Vietnam, Ryan and his wife had their first child, a daughter named Kerrie. She was born with 18 major birth defects, including double reproductive organs, a hole in her heart, a perforated anus, a missing thumb on her right hand, and a left hand attached to her elbow.

Neither John Woods nor Mike Ryan were deadbeats. Both men had been decorated for distinguished service in their civilian careers. Nor were they seeking a handout. They were asking for no more or no less than our nation had historically promised its veterans injured in war: compensation for their service-related disabilities.

Veterans had gone to the VA with Agent Orange claims as early as 1977. By the time of the 1979 Congressional hearings, the VA had its answers confidently in place. When asked to respond to John Woods' concern, a VA spokesman explained, "I would say he's been exposed to things that are more dangerous than that during your [sic] life." When asked about the birth defects, the VA asserted that "birth defects can only be caused by exposure of the pregnant female. We had few pregnant females serving in Vietnam."[3]

Albert Gore (D-Tennessee) captured the committee's reaction to the VA statements: "Years ago, people did not realize that the male had anything to do with procreation. It is just as simplistic to believe that genetic damage can be caused only if the mother is the one exposed."[4]

More than just technically inaccurate, the VA's statement avoided the nation's (and therefore its own) fundamental responsibility to seek out and care for all those caught by war, whether they were fathers injured on the battlefield or children injured because their fathers were on the battlefield. As John Woods put it: "We are not the only veterans. Our children have become veterans. When we hit the battlefield, Mr. Ryan's daughter was with him and my two sons with me. We have to bring them back. They are veterans."[5]

Agent Orange was not the private concern of the VA. The 2,4,5-T contained in Agent Orange was being widely used in the United States throughout the Vietnam era. Regulation of this domestic use fell to the Environmental Protection Agency (EPA). The true measure of the VA's indifference to the needs of Vietnam veterans is found in the EPA's ability to respond effectively to the use of 2,4,5-T at home.

On April 21, 1978, a half year before the first Congressional hearings on Agent Orange, the EPA issued an order announcing its intention to ban the use of 2,4,5-T unless further evidence were presented to the agency demonstrating that the herbicide was safe.[6] In the process of producing 2,4,5-T, a contaminant was created, a particular dioxin referred to as TCDD. All domestic 2,4,5-T, as well as Agent Orange, was contaminated by trace amounts of this dioxin. The EPA had concluded that 2,4,5-T, and, in particular, its dioxin contaminant, posed serious health risks.

The EPA order began a process of public comment, allowing all interested individuals to present new material. Some 3,000 letters were received. One letter was from eight women who lived near the town of Alsea, Oregon, in an area surrounded by forests that had been sprayed with 2,4,5-T each spring:

> The eight of us have suffered a total of ten miscarriages in the spring months, starting in 1973. Of course, a certain rate of miscarriages would be normal, but for a population our size (under 1,000), it seems more than coincidental that so many of us have miscarried in the months of March through June.[7]

The EPA agreed. It responded to the letter by ordering a rapid epidemiological study designed to deny or confirm the women's suspicions. The study, completed in 1979, found that there was a statistically significant increase in miscarriages correlated with the yearly spring cycle of 2,4,5-T spraying.[8]

The EPA's response was dramatic. The agency exercised its ultimate power and issued an emergency suspension order against 2,4,5-T. This order allowed the EPA to ban immediately, without prior hearings, the use of pesticides found to pose an imminent health hazard. In 1979, as a result of the EPA action, almost all domestic use of 2,4,5-T was discontinued.[9]

A scant nine days after the EPA's emergency suspension order, the VA's high-level Steering Committee on Health Related Effects of Herbicides met and concluded that "the studies on which the EPA ban was based do not offer definitive evidence." The EPA's position was characterized as "premature."[10]

It is difficult to understand the VA's justification for this characterization. The 1979 EPA action followed the earlier 1978 order announcing the agency's intention to ban 2,4,5-T, and that, in turn, was not the federal government's first action. As early as 1970, before EPA was created, the Department of Agriculture blocked the use of 2,4,5-T for individual household purposes and in other areas where direct human contact was likely.

Controversy had even specifically followed the military's use of 2,4,5-T in Agent Orange. In October 1969, the Department of Defense itself had restricted the use of Agent Orange, and, in April 1970, had banned its use altogether. No surprise to the women of Alsea, the ban was based on studies demonstrating an increase in miscarriages among laboratory animals exposed to 2,4,5-T.

The dispute between the VA and the EPA, however, was over deeper issues than the quality of the Alsea study alone. The EPA could act decisively on the health risks posed by 2,4,5-T because it was prepared to assess those risks based on laboratory studies of animals as well as on studies of humans. The VA was not. From the beginning, it insisted on exclusively human studies.[11]

When asked to comment on the VA's policy, Eula Bingham, assistant secretary of labor for Occupational Safety and Health, noted, "The entire concept of modern experimental medicine is based primarily upon testing in subhuman species." The use of animal studies to measure the human risk of cancer, she concluded, was "overwhelmingly supported."[12]

In dismissing the research done on animals, the VA cast aside a substantial set of studies. In 1978, the EPA outlined several laboratory studies that related exposure to the dioxin in Agent Orange to cancer, and the evidence continued to mount. In 1980, the government's own National Cancer Institute completed two additional studies finding that dioxin caused cancer in laboratory animals.[13]

In deciding to rely on only human evidence, the VA was subtly, but significantly, raising the burden of proof for Vietnam veterans. Human study is rare because it can only be made when an accident leads to exposure. The Alsea study was exceptional, yet the VA was asking that benefits wait for more exceptions.

Even so, the Alsea study was not unique. As the EPA case evolved, the agency outlined extensive human evidence that related exposure to 2,4,5-T and its dioxin contaminant to a series of health risks. A key component was three Swedish studies that found a marked increase in two specific types of cancers.[14]

The Swedish studies were widely known in the scientific community and had been accepted for publication in professional journals. They had even been discussed in the international press. Yet the VA had, apparently, not even heard of the studies. Its ignorance was hardly accidental. As late as 1980, the VA — in its own words — had "not engaged in any formal correspondence with the EPA regarding its conclusions on the possible effects on human health of 2,4,5-T."[15] The Swedish studies were unknown because the VA had never bothered to review EPA's scientific record on Agent Orange.

When the Swedish studies were brought to the VA's attention in the spring of 1980, the VA administrator immediately dismissed them. Less than two weeks after receiving the studies, the VA administrator concluded that "following preliminary analysis, my scientific advisers have informed me that they do not think the papers make a major contribution." The studies' findings were called the result of mere "random distribution," or, in layman's terms, just plain bad luck.[16]

The Congressional Office of Technology Assessment (OTA) disagreed. It submitted the studies to outside review by Richard Remington, Ph.D., dean of the School of Public Health at the University of Michigan. Remington concluded that the "investigations are among the most carefully conducted investigations of their type that I have ever seen. In toto, the Swedish work is credible if not fully conclusive."[17]

Forced to amend its position, the VA merely regrouped and threw up new barriers. The original assessment of the Swedish studies was recast in more obfuscating language, and new criteria were subtly introduced into VA compensation policy. Benefits would be granted only on the basis of studies specifically focused not just on humans but solely on Vietnam veterans. The Swedish studies and the Alsea study, as well as the entire body of existing research, were summarily rejected by the VA.[18]

Following the VA's earlier decision to disregard studies done on animals, the VA's decision to rest compensation decisions exclusively on studies done on Vietnam veterans raised the burden of proof still higher and further slowed any action. The VA would delay benefits until the veterans themselves became disabled and died, becoming their own evidence of their own needs. Vietnam veterans were to be literally studied to death.

Yet there was still a last chance. If the VA was serious about studies done specifically on Vietnam veterans, there was no agency better equipped to authorize the appropriate research. The EPA, after all, had initiated the Alsea study, but, in the end, it would take an act of Congress, P.L. 96-151, to force the VA to begin a serious study. As late as 1982, the General Accounting Office found that the VA had allocated only $516,000 for Agent Orange research, out of a total research budget of $140 million, a mere one-third of one percent.[19]

The barriers to action were insurmountable. When cornered by congressmen angry at the VA's failure, the agency justified inaction on the grounds that the congressmen themselves had failed to specifically mandate help. If the Congress really wanted benefits, the VA maintained, it could enact a law. Repeated in hearing after hearing, deference to Congress became the VA's ultimate defense.[20]

The VA is a creation of Congress, and so its excuse had some credibility, but Vietnam veterans were seeking more than good excuses. In the face of a nation trying to forget, a Congress in hiding, and a president who seemingly could not be bothered, Vietnam veterans were looking for an advocate.

Surely, the Veterans Administration would be that advocate. Its imposing buildings across the country seemed to proclaim its willingness to serve. Its record of accomplishment following World

War II suggested that the VA was prepared to take the risks necessary to aid and comfort the nation's veterans.

There is no denying the difficulties advocacy would bring. To respond honestly to Vietnam veterans, the VA would have had to abandon a careful role and become the messenger of a truth nobody wanted to hear. In the end, the VA's real choice was between complementing the complacency of the nation or serving the needs of Vietnam veterans. The VA chose complacency.

To the excuses of a Congress that could not be blamed for failing to enact programs that, after all, "the nation did not want," the VA added the excuse that it was, after all, "merely the instrument of Congress." In so doing, it framed a new excuse, for Congress could not be blamed for opposing programs that, after all, "the VA opposed."

And oppose it did. Whatever its claimed deference to Congress, when Congress moved legislation to mandate health care for Vietnam veterans, the VA opposed the proposal. The agency similarly opposed legislation providing disability compensation even though it was a modest bill costing only $5 million a year.[21]

Incapable of exercising the leadership necessary to take independent action, the VA was left with only one option: create a rationale for delay while waiting for someone else to act. The VA sought safety, but there was no way to be safe and still act honestly.

At each turn of the Agent Orange question, the VA faced the choice of accepting the new evidence and becoming an advocate for Vietnam veterans, or building new barriers by dismissing the research. In choosing delay, the VA became not a neutral bureaucracy but part of the problem. Instead of offering help, it built a maze of denials in the path of Vietnam veterans trying to find a way home.

In almost any other federal agency, a policy as important as Agent Orange compensation would be justified on the record and open to public comment. The VA's Agent Orange policy never was, despite a suit filed by the National Veterans Law Center, the group that leads public interest litigation for Vietnam veterans. The VA is *exempt* from the basic laws that dictate administrative due process.[22]

Under normal circumstances, in almost any other federal agency, Vietnam veterans would be able to appeal the VA compensation policy in federal court. Vietnam veterans could not, however, because federal law *exempts* the VA's benefit decisions from judicial review.[23]

Under normal circumstances, in almost any other federal agency, Vietnam veterans would be able to retain counsel to advance their vital interest within the agency. Vietnam veterans could not, however, because federal law *prohibits* a veteran from paying counsel more than $10 for assistance on a benefit claim.[24]

The Bill of Rights states our basic freedoms. Those freedoms, in turn, are protected through our system of courts and the right to due process. It is the courts that turn our laws and our Constitution into working rights instead of eloquent phrases. Vietnam veterans, however, had no protection for their benefit rights.

In 1976, Senator Gary Hart (D-Colorado) introduced legislation to extend to Vietnam veterans the right to judicial review, to administrative fairness, and to representation by counsel. Over the next seven years, Senator Hart's landmark legislation suffered the same fate as the Vietnam veterans Readjustment Counseling Program.

Hart was persistent. In 1978, Senator Cranston joined Senator Hart in developing a new and more detailed proposal. In 1979 and 1981, it passed the Senate. Each time it died in the House. In 1983, it passed the Senate again. Today, in 1984, it is still pending, without action, in the House.[25]

The absence of full legal protection for veterans is a denial of basic rights. It not only violates the cherished symbols of our Constitution, but it also has a specific impact on every single area of Vietnam veterans policy.

For Vietnam veterans, locked in a dispute with the Veterans Administration, the absence of basic legal rights means that there is no exit from the maze, no help in pleading their case, no certainty that the agency will ever disclose the basis for the policy at all. Despite these frustrations, for Vietnam veterans there was no alternative but to return to the VA — almost on their knees — and hope against hope that progress could be made.

WHAT PRICE PROGRESS?

In August 1945, just months after the triumph of the Allied forces in Europe, Five Star General Omar N. Bradley was appointed administrator of Veterans' Affairs by President Truman. Two years later, he retired, only to be called back to veterans affairs in early

1955 by President Eisenhower to head a special Commission on Veterans Benefits.

The "Bradley Commission," as it came to be called, filed its report on April 23, 1956. It was a massive document. The basic report itself ran over 400 pages. Because the data necessary for a comprehensive review of veterans benefits were unavailable, the commission undertook a broad range of special studies.

The existing system of veterans benefits, the commission found, was hardly coherent. It was rather "an accretion of laws based largely on precedents built up over 150 years of piecemeal development." In a candid conclusion, the commission noted: "The public at large has taken little interest and the laws have been enacted in response to minority pressures."[26]

The commission proposed a clear set of national priorities for veterans affairs. The founding principle was a simple belief: "Military service in time of war or peace is an obligation of citizenship and should not be considered inherently a basis for future Government benefits."[27]

Veterans benefits, in the view of the Bradley Commission, did not derive from a national obligation owed to every soldier to meet every need. Their roots were deeper and more permanent. They lay instead in the nation's special obligation to those disabled as a result of service and to those seeking immediate readjustment to civilian life.

To the Bradley Commission, the priority programs in veterans affairs were clear. The first program was compensation and health care for the disabled. Their benefits "should be liberal, even generous." The second program was the readjustment assistance provided by the GI Bill.

The proposal implied a major reform of the VA benefit system. In fact, the GI Bill and the compensation program were only a portion of VA programs. The rest were made up of nonservice-connected programs, including pensions for older veterans and general health care.

Reform was required, the Bradley Commission suggested, because "veterans and their families will soon be a majority" of the nation. Given the expanding demand, the nonservice-connected pension program for older veterans threatened to engulf the VA, channeling resources away from those who had "sacrificed the most or whose needs are greatest."[28]

Nevertheless, the Bradley Commission did *not* recommend ending the pension program. Rather, it proposed that veterans whose needs were unrelated to service should be helped first through the nation's social programs for the general population. Where those programs were inadequate, veterans would continue to receive special treatment through the unique veterans benefits system.

Given their long and distinguished military service, General Bradley and President Eisenhower were clearly sensitive to the needs of veterans who were, in many cases, the soldiers who had served under them. If ever two men were pro-veteran, these two were. As part of its special studies, the Bradley Commission conducted a survey of veterans attitudes toward the VA and its benefits system. It found that veterans themselves shared the priorities reflected in the report. "Merely 1 in 8 of those interviewed was in favor of pensions."[29]

The major veterans organizations, however, were not satisfied. The American Legion called the Bradley Commission report a "scare document." The VFW charged that "the underlying philosophy of the Bradley Commission report is an attempt to reverse the traditional national policy of the United States." It thought the report should be filed and forgotten.[30] Congress concurred. The report's recommendations were never implemented.

When General Bradley became administrator of Veterans' Affairs, he brought with him a cadre of young World War II veterans. One, William (Bill) J. Driver, stayed for the duration. Nineteen years later, after service as chief benefits director and deputy administrator, he was nominated to be VA administrator by President Johnson in January 1965.

Driver's nomination came in the midst of controversy. In an effort to upgrade the VA hospital system, the VA was building new facilities that would expand the number of beds by thousands. Matching the expansion, the VA proposed in January 1965 that 11 hospitals and four domiciliary units be closed.

Closing the old facilities was an integral part of the plan for upgrading care. Those slated for elimination were either old and unable to provide an adequate range of specialized care, or located in areas where there were not enough veterans to justify the costs. The list of targeted hospitals contained horror stories of outdated, decaying facilities.

One facility, in Bath, New York, had been constructed in 1878. Its obsolete physical plant required a half-million dollars a year in repair work. Another facility, in McKinney, Texas, had been built during World War II as a "wartime containment, brick veneer hospital over wood frame and [was] non-fire-resistant."

The Brecksville, Ohio facility, slated for closure, had been opened in 1938 as a tuberculosis facility. Medical progress had brought new treatment for tuberculosis, making hospital care unnecessary. A new general medical and surgical hospital had been opened in the same town, limiting the need for the old facility.[31]

The major veterans organizations were no more swayed by the merits of the arguments on hospital closings than they were by the quality of the Bradley Commission. They saw only one fact. Beds were to be cut. It was irrelevant to them that new beds in better hospitals were also to be built. Veterans organizations were prepared to insist on the retention of the old beds, in addition to the construction of new facilities.

The major veterans organizations went to work, adopting resolutions opposing the closing of facilities. A massive letter-writing and telegram campaign was begun. Hearings were quickly held. A leader in the campaign was the national commander of the American Legion, Donald E. Johnson. Johnson "felt so strongly" about the closing "that it is a challenge to be concise." The nation, he was certain, "is chagrined, is dismayed, is incensed, and is aroused."[32]

The veterans organizations, however, did not stop with opposing the hospital reorganization directly. They insisted on personalizing the issue. As the man responsible within the VA during the development of the hospital reorganization (first as deputy administrator and then as acting administrator), the major veteran groups focused their attack on Bill Driver.

It is difficult to understand their choice of target. A veteran of World War II and Korea, Driver is the *only* administrator of Veterans' Affairs to rise through the ranks of the VA. His distinguished service had spanned both parties. He had been chief benefits director under Republican President Eisenhower and deputy administrator under Democratic President Kennedy.

Yet the major organizations were not impressed by his credentials and his past service to the VA. Senate confirmation of his nomination was to be held back until the plan to close the VA facilities was defeated. On January 26, 1965, the veterans groups won a brief victory. Driver's confirmation by the Senate was postponed.[33]

On February 1, 1965, another effort to postpone the confirmation was defeated after an extensive and often heated debate. Despite intense pressure on many senators, the Senate then confirmed Driver's nomination by a resounding 75 to 7 vote.[34] The proposed hospital reorganization did not fare quite as well. President Johnson appointed a special commission; and, upon its recommendation, five of the 11 hospitals and two of the domiciliary units were spared.

A major theme of the Bradley Commission report was the need for long-range programming. The VA needed to risk reform in the interest of quality services. As the commission noted, however, that would require "broadening and modernizing the Veterans Administration's concept of mission."

> The current role of the Administrator and the facilities supporting him, reflect the traditional Veterans Administration position — frankly stated by key executives throughout the agency — that its mission is to administer the distribution of veterans benefits in accordance with existing laws, nothing more.[35]

The fate of the Bradley Commission recommendations and the proposed hospital reorganization demonstrated that reform would not come easily. In the VA, the lobby works against progress. The result is an agency almost impossible to manage.

Because they were new veterans with new needs, the difficulty of reform had special meaning for Vietnam veterans. For the VA to meet their needs, it would first have to recapture the basic ability to adapt and to change. The task would clearly not be easy. The politics of VA management compounded the normal hurdles that stand in the way of any new program, making failure almost inevitable.[36]

CARE SECOND TO NONE

Priding itself on its unique medical program, the VA claimed to offer care second to none, but for Vietnam veterans, this claim was a hollow promise. If the VA did provide quality care, it was care for someone else. To Vietnam veterans, the VA hospital program was not an ally, but an enemy whose many resources were almost consciously deployed against them.

The VA runs the largest medical program in the United States. In 1983, it contained 172 hospitals, 99 nursing homes, and 53 independent satellite clinics. It had a staff of just under 200,000 and a total operating budget of over $7 billion.

On its own, independent of the rest of the VA, the hospital program is larger than most federal agencies, yet the true measure of any program's size is the number of clients it must serve. The VA hospitals face a huge job. There are more than 25 million veterans in the United States, and a large share are eligible for VA medical care.

Veterans with disabilities resulting from their military service are, of course, eligible for care related to their disabilities; but all veterans over age 65 are also eligible for any care at all. All veterans under age 65 are also eligible, with just one restriction. The VA can treat them if the veteran cannot afford care elsewhere.[37]

The broad eligibility for VA health care has a significant impact. Although the general public assumes that the VA hospitals principally treat veterans with war-related wounds, in fact, only 30 percent of VA patients have service-related disabilities. Broken down by the individual treatment provided, the percentage is even smaller. Only 16 percent is service-related.[38]

The numbers involved are staggering. In 1983, about 1.4 million patients received hospital care from the VA. Another 18 million visited VA clinics for care that did not involve hospitalization. To measure only one dimension of the work involved, the VA ran over a quarter of a billion laboratory tests.

For the VA medical program, the largest single group of eligible veterans is from World War II. Numbering nearly 12 million, they place a special demand on the system. In 1981, their average age reached 60, pushing them further into that period of their lives where their medical problems increase sharply and where they are closer to the age of automatic eligibility.

With a medical complex this large, the VA is hard pressed to avoid meeting the demand for care through an assembly-line attitude. Any group of veterans who have a problem shared only by a minority risk being overlooked or mistreated. Women veterans are an example. There are more than 1 million female veterans, a sizable group by any standard; yet as late as 1982, the General Accounting Office (GAO) discovered that the VA was totally unprepared to meet even the most basic needs of women patients.[39]

Ruth Young, the assistant state director of Veterans Employment in New York, was one example. During a 1969 operation, she had to be housed in a male ward. In 1979, she sought help for an urgent gynecological problem after passing out in her car. She was diagnosed as being pregnant, despite her claims to the contrary, and was discharged. A second VA hospital put her on a four-month waiting list. In fact, she had a tumor and a hernia.[40]

This failure was not caused by prejudice alone. As the GAO's own staff noted when asked for an explanation of the problems, the fundamental issue was a lack of awareness. Despite the large number of women veterans, they were so small a percentage of the total population served that the hospitals simply overlooked their special needs. Women were treated as if they were men.[41]

Not surprisingly, most veterans seek care from their own physician if they can afford the cost. Excluding the small percentage with war wounds, those seeking care from the VA come from the fringes of society. Sixty percent of all VA patients are poor. Seventy percent have no health insurance, and they are old. In 1982, 62 percent of the hospital patients were over 55.[42]

The needs of VA patients are both severe and special. They suffer not only from acute health care needs, like broken bones, but also from the long-term consequences of poverty. A full 50 percent have chronic health care needs.

The result is a medical program with a particular focus. It is oriented toward the long-term care of the chronically ill. A VA hospital is more like a nursing home than an emergency surgical center. As a result, the VA system neither regularly tests, nor routinely requires the unique skills of specialized surgery.

For precisely that reason, however, the VA medical system offers few challenges to the medical community. "The VA is losing the interest of the top people. The best specialists are becoming harder to attract," noted former VA administrator Bill Driver. "They remain deeply committed, but the present VA patient load simply does not require their very special skills."

The flood of patients, accordingly, is only a part of the VA's problems, and perhaps the lesser part, because the VA is uniquely dependent on its ability to attract the interest of the medical community. At stake is the quality of its own permanent staff, and a great deal more.

Through a system begun under General Bradley, VA hospitals are affiliated with medical schools, which provide the skilled resources of their own teaching and hospital staffs. In 1981, the VA's own staff was augmented with nearly 100,000 affiliated doctors, nurses, and medical students.

The VA's declining ability to attract the finest in the profession creates a crisis when its hospitals are asked to shift focus abruptly from chronic to acute care. The Vietnam War did just that.

A half-million veterans were disabled as a result of their service. To the nation, the number seemed staggering — far too high a price to pay. To the VA hospital system, the numbers were small, half the size of the number of women veterans, and although Vietnam veterans should have been the VA's highest priority, they were nonetheless the wrong kind of patient. Equally important, they were transients. The acute care needs of the war wounded declined as the war ended. The bulge passed, and when it did, the decades-old VA hospital program returned to normal.

In its May 22, 1970 cover story, *Life* magazine documented an extreme case of the kind of care Vietnam veterans received through pictures of a rat-ridden ward at the Kingsbridge VA hospital on Long Island. The problem ran deeper, however, than isolated cases of shocking malpractice. The entire VA hospital system was simply not prepared to meet the acute health care needs of young, recently wounded veterans.

In 1977, the National Academy of Sciences released the results of a multiyear, Congressionally mandated study that found that VA surgical care was plagued by problems. The academy's study merely confirmed the results of earlier studies done by the General Accounting Office.[43]

The VA conceded many of the problems identified by the academy and the GAO. In fact, it sought corrective actions where possible; yet in its own defense, the VA argued that the problems were fundamentally beyond its control. If certain VA hospitals functioned less well as acute surgical care units than as nursing homes, that reflected the nature of their mission.[44]

The excuse was more than credible. It expressed the genuine fatigue of managers who know that in the end the VA medical program is governed by the patients it serves. Yet the VA managers' frustration was not necessary. The problems facing the VA hospital program were almost the conscious product of mistaken policies.

The VA desperately needed to retain a patient mix that could sustain a concentration on acute care needs. Yet during the crucial last years of the Vietnam War, Congress acted to expand significantly eligibility for outpatient care for nonservice-connected needs.

This change brought a staggering increase in demand. The number of outpatient visits increased by 64 percent. The result, in the words of the Senate Committee on Veterans' Affairs, was "serious overcrowding and long waiting lines." As the Senate Committee concluded, "the VA has not been sufficiently sensitive to the special needs of veterans seeking treatment for service-connected conditions."[45]

The VA was pressed to meet the needs of a large patient population, yet the academy found that the VA management policies in place in the mid-1970s were almost consciously designed to produce overcrowding. Funds were allocated among competing hospitals according to patient load. Hospitals that faced low demand risked budget cuts if they did not fill their beds.

The results were almost inevitable. As the academy noted, "In hospitals with few applicants per bed per year [i.e., little competition for admission], most applicants are hospitalized." The academy went on to point out that "when applications per bed are low, the stays are long." The academy also found that large hospitals were sometimes set in areas without a pressing demand for care, while peak areas sometimes had smaller facilities.[46]

The VA hospital program is a system of paradoxes. Overburdened with patients, it also has excess beds. Constantly battling for a bigger budget, it also has excess capacity. Like most political paradoxes, however, this one is intelligible from the inside.

From their perspective, the major veterans organizations have few options. Uncertain that any attempt to focus resources will be compassionately administered through the VA's suspect budget process, they must be wary of any cuts. The organizations' doubts, in turn, raise the price of any effort by VA managers, the White House, or Congress to improve the quality of care through better resource allocation.

The only safe course for all parties is ever-continued expansion that throws new resources at the crisis of the moment. Having opted for safety, it is hard to look back. Constant expansion makes budget issues the driving imperative of the VA medical system.

Unable to meet rising demand through better allocation of resources, there is no alternative but to provide more beds. Facing increasing difficulties in attracting and retaining the best in the medical profession, the VA sought better care in constant staffing increases.

The best motives of the VA and the veterans organizations are caught in a cycle that avoids the fundamental issues. Questions of quality of care are pushed into the background or are defined in terms of quantity of care.

THE MEN AT THE TOP

The VA, with 217,000 employees in 1983, is the second largest federal agency, exceeded only by the Department of Defense. In 1984, it will spend over $25 billion. Overseeing the VA is the counterpart of the secretary of defense, the administrator of Veterans' Affairs.

Reform came with difficulty to the VA, and the job of exerting the required leadership fell to the administrator. From 1963 until the official end of the Vietnam War in 1975, four men ran the agency.

For a few brief years at the beginning of the war, John S. Gleason ran the agency. He was followed in 1965 by Bill Driver. During the peak years, two men served as administrator: Donald E. Johnson and Richard L. Roudebush.

Of the four, three shared an important common characteristic. They had been former leaders of the nation's largest veterans organizations. Gleason and Johnson had been former national commanders of the American Legion. Roudebush had been commander-in-chief of the Veterans of Foreign Wars.

During his confirmation hearings, ex-Commander-in-Chief Roudebush was asked to comment on the importance of the major veterans organizations. Naturally, he exuded goodwill. "I can honestly say, Senator," he stated, "that the Veterans Administration could not operate if it were not for the great veteran organizations."[47]

The major veterans organizations were in control of the VA. For Vietnam veterans, the implication was clear. Abandoned by the major veterans groups, Vietnam veterans were not likely to find an ally in the administrator's office. Not surprisingly, in the continuing budget battle between programs for younger and for older veterans, the ex-commanders fought for the priorities of their old organizations.

During his confirmation hearings, Roudebush was asked to pledge his opposition to an earlier administration proposal that would have reduced nonservice connected pensions. He did, in the most unequivocal terms, concluding, "I do not know how I can say I am against something more clearly than I have just done."[48] Roudebush was as good as his word. The VA did not press for pension reform.

Asked if he could support a full increase in the Vietnam veterans GI Bill, however, Roudebush did little more than equivocate.[49] Two months after his confirmation hearings, President Ford vetoed the GI Bill increase over muted VA objections. It was the first and only veto in the history of the GI Bill.

Donald E. Johnson had been national commander of the American Legion in 1964 and 1965, and had helped lead the attack against the proposed hospital reorganization under Administrator Bill Driver. He was appointed VA administrator in 1969. In 1974, he resigned under pressure, following allegations of corruption and political pandering.

Appointed by newly elected President Nixon, Johnson became an eager participant in the generalized political abuses that surrounded Watergate and President Nixon's reelection in 1972. No fewer than 13 employees of the Committee to Reelect the President (CREEP) had found their way into the VA. Three were given key management positions. At least six others were given middle-management positions.[50]

In early April, the Disabled American Veterans, the Veterans of Foreign Wars, Senator Cranston, and Congressman Teague simultaneously called for Johnson's resignation. Senator Cranston scheduled comprehensive hearings on problems at the VA for April 23.[51]

On April 22, Cranston and Teague met with White House Chief of Staff Alexander Haig, Jr. Late the same day, Johnson announced his resignation, and Cranston canceled the scheduled hearings.[52]

The resignation could not have been better timed. Political featherbedding, it quickly emerged, was the least of Johnson's troubles. Allegations swirled.

- Johnson had apparently approved payment of a $10.3 million cost overrun claim under a federal contract without a government audit of the overrun and over the objections of the VA's ranking career employee, Associate Deputy Administrator Rufus Wilson.[53]

- Johnson had apparently hired a next-door neighbor as deputy controller, one of the VA's most responsible positions.[54]
- Another of Johnson's neighbors had apparently been awarded a VA management consulting contract without competitive bidding.[55]
- The former employer of one of the CREEP employees hired by the VA had also apparently received a contract without competitive bidding.[56]

Donald Johnson was administrator of Veterans' Affairs from 1969 through 1973. The peak years of the Vietnam War, they were also crucial years in the formation of Vietnam veterans programs. Benefit levels were set under the new Vietnam GI Bill. The Readjustment Counseling Program had been introduced and suffered its first defeat.

That VA administrators shared the outlook of the major organizations was barrier enough for Vietnam veterans. Tragically, for four crucial years, misplaced priorities were just a small part of the problem. Vietnam veterans programs were shaped not only by indifference but also by corruption.

Max Cleland was nominated by President Carter to be administrator of Veterans' Affairs in 1977. He replaced Richard L. Roudebush and served through early 1981.

Like his predecessors, Cleland brought the political credentials of service to the party in power. He had been a Democratic state senator in Georgia and had worked with then-Governor Jimmy Carter. There was, however, an important difference. Max Cleland was a Vietnam veteran.

He was the first Vietnam veteran to be appointed VA administrator. He had volunteered for Vietnam and been decorated with both the Bronze Star and the Silver Star for heroism. His service in the Army had ended with a wound that cost him both legs and one arm, giving him a tragically intimate understanding of the VA hospital and benefit system.

Both Cleland and Roudebush were asked during their respective confirmation hearings about the pressing need for expanded alcohol treatment centers in the VA hospital system.[57] The largest single diagnosis in VA hospitals, alcohol abuse was an especially severe problem among Vietnam veterans with extensive combat experience.

Yet after three years in office, Roudebush had added just seven new centers. In cities as large as Baltimore, Miami, and Portland, there were no specialized facilities. In just one year, Max Cleland added 15 additional centers, with a commitment to add still more centers in the future.[58]

Max Cleland understood the problems and seemed prepared to act, but he was not a member of the inner world of VA politics. Max Cleland was not an ex-Commander-in-Chief of a major veterans organization.

During the confirmation hearings for Roudebush, the American Legion, the VFW, the DAV, the Veterans of World War I, and the Jewish War Veterans each sent a top official to testify. As Cooper Holt, the executive director of the VFW was careful to note, his organization was the only one that bothered to appear at Max Cleland's confirmation hearing.

Cleland was careful to credit the cooperation he did receive from the major organizations. They worked together on improving the rehabilitation program for veterans disabled as a result of their service. As always, he noted, the veterans organizations were prepared to work with the VA in service to an ever larger budget.

In the end, however, as Cleland put it, his very appointment was a straightforward repudiation of politics as usual in veterans affairs. Looking at himself from the perspective of the major veterans organizations, Cleland could be honest about their ultimate conclusion: "He is not our guy. We cannot control him."

Cleland was an outsider. The problems that this created were magnified by the nature of the Carter administration in general. Whatever the reality, it was characterized as an outsider's government run by a "Georgia Mafia" indifferent to the subtle Washington traditions of power. As one more Georgian, Cleland seemed to fit this stereotype.

It was a bad time for an outsider's government to be involved in veterans affairs. Increasing concern with the seemingly ever-rising federal deficit was creating new pressures for the VA medical budget. The Carter administration supported increases in the VA medical budget, but it also insisted that the VA share in the general fiscal constraint. The increases were small.[59]

The veterans organizations were not satisfied. A new era of confrontation over the VA medical system began. Because Cleland was a severely disabled veteran, the Disabled American Veterans

— whose membership is limited to veterans injured as a result of their service — found itself in the midst of the controversy.

The dispute came to a head in mid-1979. A special article entitled "Disappointments" and printed under the national commander's byline was placed in the DAV's magazine.[60] At the group's national convention in August, Billy O. Hightower, the DAV national commander, and Cleland shared a podium. Hightower was blunt:

> In my view, Mr. Cleland has been used as a symbol by the Administration. The severity of his disabilities and the fact he's a hero of the Vietnam War give him a moral authority that's difficult to question. But, if the Administration uses that authority to the detriment of America's disabled veterans, the symbolism is empty.[61]

Cleland's response was equally strong. Abandoning a prepared speech, he stated, "I may be a symbol. Yes. And I hope I am a symbol, just like you, for what a human being can do when something traumatic has happened."[62]

The attacks from the major veterans organizations were matched by difficulties from within the VA itself. The prevailing attitude within the VA was that Vietnam veterans were, as Cleland put it, "social misfits." That attitude compounded the difficulties of meeting new problems. VA employees saw the Agent Orange claims of Vietnam veterans, according to Cleland, as a "big hoax, like witchcraft. The [VA] doctors said, 'Sure. Right.'"

The combination of pressure from the major veterans organizations and the prevailing attitudes within the VA made action difficult for VA Administrator Cleland. It required the new administrator to constantly retain his own counsel against advisers wedded to old beliefs, while at the same time protecting himself against determined opposition. Cleland had to fight a two-front war.

Able to effect a massive increase in alcohol treatment for Vietnam and other veterans, he was not so constant on GI Bill reform. During the early months of his appointment, Cleland had given his personal support for expanding college benefits. Six months later, he signed official VA positions opposing any significant change in the GI Bill.[63]

As Cleland himself was careful to note, his new job as VA administrator had brought new responsibilities. He was simply not free to turn his personal feelings into official position, yet he did more than offer reluctant cooperation in efforts to defeat GI Bill reform. He became the willing apologist for the existing GI Bill.

Cleland's appearance on ABC's *Issues and Answers* was characteristic. He argued forcefully for the status quo: "I would say that the present GI Bill provides a program of student loans, tuition assistance, other certain benefits that the World War II GI Bill never envisioned."[64]

The pattern of progress on one Vietnam veterans issue matched by retreat on another was frequently repeated. It was Vietnam veteran Max Cleland, not just any administrator, who signed the opinion dismissing the Swedish studies. Yet it was also Vietnam veteran Max Cleland, not just any administrator, who finally oversaw victory in the nearly decade-long effort to enact the Readjustment Counseling Program.

Throughout his term as administrator, Cleland seemed caught in a constant struggle to bring the truths he remembered from his own experience to bear on the VA. His appointment gave Vietnam veterans a last chance at reform within the VA system, but the barriers to reform were still too high. In the end, Cleland's administration was a draw for Vietnam veterans.

SLOW PROGRESS

In the federal penitentiary at Atlanta, Georgia, one veteran recalled the day he returned from Vietnam:

> Most of my time was in the field, and I stayed over there for seven months and about 20 some days, and most of my time was spent in the field. I left on the 3rd of July. . . . I got home, it was the 4th of July. Everybody shoots firecrackers on the 4th of July, and I would be just walking down the street, and people started shooting firecrackers, and then I would reflex, and I knocked all the skin off my knees and elbows on the asphalt concrete and stuff, and people looked at me like I was something you might go to the zoo to see. So people started coming around you, just throwing firecrackers around just to see you go through that so they would have something to laugh at. And this almost drove me out of my mind. So I would take some action to stop people from shooting firecrackers and started shooting at people's homes and stuff.

His story is not unique. Between 25 percent and 30 percent of all prisoners are veterans, a total of over 100,000. Half are veterans of the Vietnam era. A full 5 percent of all prisoners in the United States served in Vietnam.[65]

There is a broadly shared belief that, compared to other prisoners, Vietnam veterans are unique. They are better educated. The only comprehensive survey ever undertaken, done by the Department of Justice, found that 60 percent of the veterans in prison had a high school diploma. Only 40 percent of the nonveteran prisoners had graduated from high school.[66]

A special survey of prisoners in Massachusetts found that veterans also had better prison records. Although 39 percent of nonveterans had been in prison before their present sentence, only 12 percent of the veteran prisoners were returning offenders.[67]

Dr. Robert L. Carr has worked with veterans in at least four different prisons. In 1979, while serving as chief psychologist at the federal penitentiary in Lewisburg, Pennsylvania, he testified before the Senate Committee on Veterans' Affairs, describing the Vietnam veterans he had seen in prison:

> They are more flexible. They receive fewer incident reports. They are not into contraband and various other things that are illegal. In my written statement, I pointed out that for one sample that I had taken, there were 1,502 incident reports for the year written; and as I was able to track it down, the Vietnam veterans in that particular sample only received 33 incident reports.[68]

In the technical phrases of prison literature, Vietnam veterans have unusual rehabilitative potential. Equally important, veterans in prison retain their eligibility for the GI Bill. Its programs might have increased their chances of rehabilitation, yet the GI Bill proved to be little more than a false promise.

In 1974, at the request of Congressman Charles B. Rangel (D-New York), the General Accounting Office (GAO) studied the VA's outreach program for veterans in prison. They found no regular VA visits to prisons. The VA had, in fact, visited only one of the four prisons surveyed by the GAO, and it had visited that prison only once. Among the prisoners the GAO interviewed, 81 percent had never been counseled on veterans benefits. Not surprisingly, 53 percent falsely believed that their convictions ended their eligibility for veterans benefits.[69]

The VA did try to respond to the GAO's scathing study. In April 1975, a new program was established. Under that program, the VA mandated that each prison be visited twice each year by its counselors. In 1976, a special outreach effort was begun to alert probation officers to the range of VA benefits.[70]

In 1979, two independent studies were done on the effectiveness of the VA effort. As part of a special article, *Corrections Magazine* ran a survey of prisons in New England and found uneven performance.[71] The GAO, asked to review the VA's progress by Senator Cranston, reached the same conclusion.

Despite the continuing problems, the VA had made significant progress. Eighty-three percent of the veterans surveyed knew of their eligibility for benefits. A full 83 percent had actually been counseled, and 28 percent were using their benefits.[72]

Vietnam veterans in prison did not use their military service as a justification for their crimes. What they were saying is less simply stated, but perhaps more compelling. One veteran in the Atlanta penitentiary commented, "We do have a sense of rightness. We do feel we fought for the country." What they ask now is to find some way to turn that sense of rightness into another chance.

By 1979, the VA had made some progress in prison outreach, but it was slow progress at best. That progress can be recounted quickly in this narrative. It takes just a few paragraphs. To sit in the outer room of a prison, however, is to know that the long road to progress must be measured in the hard time of prison life.

The war, after all, had officially begun in 1963. U.S. combat involvement had officially ended in 1973. Only in 1975 did the VA even begin a prison outreach program, and then only under the pressure of an outside study. As late as 1979, major problems remained to be corrected.

A prison is an extreme situation, yet the perspective it gives to the passing of time applies as well to the whole range of Vietnam veterans issues. The veterans in prison were not the only ones waiting for someone to care. The hard price of passing time was felt as deeply by those Vietnam veterans whose lives were changed by unemployment or divorce, or by the inability to afford college and professional training.

In 1975, Congress could finally claim that the Vietnam GI Bill had been made at least adequate, if not generous. Yet the war had begun in 1963 — more than a decade had been lost. In 1979, the VA could point proudly to the finally expanded alcohol treatment program. Yet the war had begun in 1963 — a decade and a half had been lost. In 1980, the Readjustment Counseling Program was finally under way. Yet the war had begun in 1963 — nearly two decades had been lost.

As far back as 1956, the Bradley Commission had warned, as though it could have already foreseen the consequences of the nation's failed Vietnam veteran policy:

> An important lesson learned from our experience over the last 150 years is that the problems of veterans' benefits must be squarely and promptly met immediately at the end of a war. Timely and adequate assistance must be provided to alleviate the war-incurred handicap of servicemen as soon as possible after separation.[73]

The years spent making slow progress in Vietnam veterans policy were years lost to Vietnam veterans. For many veterans discharged in 1965 or 1969, the laboriously achieved programs of 1975 or 1980 came too late. The important decisions in their lives had already been made. Beginning again was only a romantic option.

Sitting in the outer room of a prison, it is clear that time may have turned the nation's debt to many Vietnam veterans into an unpayable obligation.

How can the VA — how can the nation — return those lost years?

NOTES

1. *Involuntary Exposure to Agent Orange and Other Toxic Spraying*, hearings before the Subcommittee on Oversight and Investigation of the Committee on Interstate and Foreign Commerce, House of Representatives, 96th Congress, 1st Session, June 25-27, 1979, Serial No. 96-139, p. 27.

2. Ibid.

3. The VA response was given in an NBC story on John Woods, Mike Ryan, and a third Vietnam veteran, Frank Moore, who subsequently died of cancer. See NBC Nightly News, June 25, 1979.

4. *Involuntary Exposure to Agent Orange and Other Toxic Spraying*, op. cit., p. 32.

5. Ibid., p. 40.

6. "Rebuttable Presumption Against Registration and Continued Registration of Pesticide Products Containing 2,4,5-T," Environmental Protection Agency, *The Federal Register*, Vol. 43, No. 78, Friday, April 21, 1978, pp. 17116-17157.

7. Letter from Bonnie Hill of Alsea, Oregon. 1978. 2,4,5-T RPAR Rebuttal Submission 30000/26: #363.

8. *Report of a Field Investigation of Six-year Spontaneous Abortion Rates in Three Oregon Areas in Relation to Forest 2,4,5-T Spray Practices*, (Alsea Report), Environmental Protection Agency, 1979.

9. "Decision and Emergency Order Suspending Registrations for the Forest, Right-of-Way, and Pasture Uses of 2,4,5-T," *Federal Register*, Vol. 44, No. 52, Thursday, March 15, 1977, pp. 15874-15893.

10. "Minutes of the V.A. Central Office Steering Committee on Toxic Effects of Herbicides," March 7, 1979, p. 3.

11. See, for example, the statements of Guy McMichael, general counsel, and Max Cleland, administrator of the Veterans Administration in a discussion with Congressman Andy Maguire on precisely this issue, *Agent Orange: Exposure of Vietnam Veterans*, hearings before the Subcommittee on Oversight and Investigations of the Committee on Interstate and Foreign Commerce, House of Representatives, 96th Congress, 2nd Session, September 25, 1980, pp. 222-224.

12. Letter of the Honorable Eula Bingham, assistant secretary of Labor, Occupational Safety and Health, to the Honorable Thomas P. Daschle, September 11, 1980, printed in *Oversight Hearing to Receive Testimony on Agent Orange*, hearings before the Subcommittee on Medical Facilities and Benefits of the Committee on Veterans' Affairs, House of Representatives, 96th Congress, 2nd Session, July 22, 1980, pp. 394-395.

13. The studies received early public attention. See *New York Times*, Richard Severo, "2 Studies for National Institute Link Herbicide to Cancer in Animals," June 27, 1980, p. A10.

14. The cancers related to exposure were soft-tissue sarcomas and lymphomas. Two separate case-control studies focused on the correlation with soft-tissue sarcomas. Hardell, L. and Sandstrom, A., "Case-Control Study: Soft-tissue Sarcomas and Exposure to Phenoxyacetic Acids of Clorophenols," *British Journal of Cancer*, 39: 711-717. Ericksson, M., Hardell, L., Berg, N. O., Moller, T., and Axelson, O., (in Swedish) "Case-Control Study on Malignant Mesenchymal Tumors of the Soft Tissue and Exposure to Chemical Substances," *Lakartidninger*, 76: 3872-75, 1979, (EPA translation available). A third study related exposure to malignant lymphomas. Hardell, L., Ericksson, M., and Lenner, P., (in Swedish) "Malignant Lymphoma and Exposure to Chemical Substances, Especially Organic Solvents, Chlorophenals and Phenoxy Acids," *Lakartidninger*, 77 (4): 208-210, 1980, (EPA translation available).

15. *Oversight Hearings to Receive Testimony on Agent Orange*, hearings before the Subcommittee on Medical Facilities and Benefits of the Committee on Veterans' Affairs, House of Representatives, 96th Congress, 2nd Session, February 25, 1980, p. 103.

16. Letter of the Honorable Max Cleland, administrator of the Veterans Administration to the Honorable David E. Bonior, April 16, 1980. A copy of the

letter, as well as the Swedish studies and the correspondence bringing the studies to the VA's attention, is printed in *Oversight Hearing to Receive Testimony on Agent Orange*, July 22, 1980, op. cit., pp. 71-166.

17. Letter of Richard D. Remington, Ph.D., dean of the School of Public Health, University of Michigan, to Dr. Michael Gough, project director, Office of Technology Assessment, Congress of the United States, June 19, 1980. A copy of the letter and the attached review of the Swedish studies were inserted in *The Congressional Record – Senate*, August 6, 1980, S. 10911-12, by Senator Alan Cranston (D-California).

18. See, for example, the statement of Guy McMichael, general counsel to the Veterans Administration, *Agent Orange: Exposure of Vietnam Veterans*, op. cit., p. 224; or the statement of Max Cleland, administrator of Veterans' Affairs, *Oversight Hearing to Receive Testimony on Agent Orange*, February 25, 1980, op. cit., p. 6.

19. *VA'S Agent Orange Examination Program: Actions Needed to More Effectively Address Veterans' Health Concerns*, General Accounting Office, HRD-83-6, October 25, 1982, p. 3.

20. Statements abound. See, for example, three statements of Guy McMichael, general counsel to the Veterans Administration: (1) *Scientific Community Report on Agent Orange*, hearings before the Subcommittee on Medical Facilities, and Benefits of the Committee on Veterans' Affairs, House of Representatives, 96th Congress, 2nd Session, September 16, 1980, p. 137, "That is a judgement for Congress to make."; (2) *Agent Orange: Exposure of Vietnam Veterans*, op. cit., p. 224, "It is clear that Congress can establish presumptions. Congress has established the presumption with respect to multiple sclerosis. If Congress wanted to establish other presumptions, such as any cancer developing at the present time, we could pay as well." (3) *Agent Orange Update and Appendix: Agent Orange Activities (Part II)*, hearings before the Committee on Veterans' Affairs, United States Senate, 96th Congress, 2nd Session, September 10, 1980, p. 71, "I might mention that it has generally been our practice in the past, when considering the establishment of a presumption for which there may be some question, it has been our practice to seek legislative amendment to title 38. I would suspect that that would probably be our approach in this case."

21. In 1981, the VA opposed providing health care to veterans with Agent Orange-related concerns. The provision was later enacted into law as part of P.L. 97-72. See *Veterans' Health Care Act of 1981*, May 19, 1981 – Committed to the Committee of the Whole House on the State of the Union and ordered to be printed, 97th Congress, 1st Session, Report No. 97-79, pp. 31-32. In 1983, the VA also opposed H.R. 1961, the compensation measure. See *H.R. 1961 – Vietnam Veterans Agent Orange Relief Act*, hearings before the Subcommittee on Compensation, Pension, and Insurance of the Committee on Veterans' Affairs, House of Representatives, 98th Congress, 1st Session, April 26, and April 27, 1983, Serial No. 98-18, pp. 10-15, and pp. 230-263.

22. *William G. White, et al., v. Max Cleland, et al.*, Civil Action No. 70-1426 (D.D.C. filed May 31, 1979). In general, see Thomas A. Daschle, "Making the Veterans Administration Work for Veterans," *Journal of Legislation*, Winter, 1984, pp. 1-14, and especially, Dean K. Phillips, "Subjecting the Veterans

Administration to Court Review," in *Strangers at Home: Vietnam Veterans Since the War*, edited by Charles R. Figley and Seymour Leventman (Praeger: New York, 1980), pp. 325-341. Phillips discusses procedures governing regulations at pp. 326-327.

23. The bar covered "any question of law or fact" in benefit decisions and is contained in 38 U.S.C. 211(a). Dean K. Phillips discussed the major cases interpreting the bar, which have created limited opportunities for judicial review, ibid., pp. 331-338.

24. Presently, 38 U.S.C. 3404 limits a claimant's attorney fees to $10.

25. The history of judicial review legislation in the Senate is briefly outlined in *Veterans' Administration Adjudication Procedures and Judicial Review Act*, report of the Committee on Veterans' Affairs, United States Senate, to accompany S. 636, May 18 (legislative day, May 16) 1983. – Ordered to be printed, 98th Congress, 1st Session, Senate Report No. 98-120, p. 16. In the House, Congressman Don Edwards (D-California), the ranking Democratic member of the Committee on Veterans' Affairs, led efforts to enact legislation granting Vietnam veterans fuller due process.

26. *Veterans' Benefits in the United States: A Report to the President by the President's Commission on Veterans' Pension*, Parts I and II, Findings and Recommendations, (hereinafter, the Bradley Commission), April 23, 1956, House Committee Print No. 236, 84th Congress, 2nd Session, pp. 9-10.

27. Ibid., p. 10.

28. Ibid., "Letter of Transmittal."

29. Ibid., p. 371.

30. *Findings and Recommendations of the President's Commission on Veterans' Pensions (Bradley Commission)*, hearings before the Committee on Veterans' Affairs, House of Representatives, 84th Congress, 2nd Session, on the report of the President's Commission on Veterans' Pensions, April 23, May 8, 9, 10, 11, 16, 17, 18, and 22, 1956, pp. 3635-3583 for the statement of the American Legion, and pp. 3695-3734 for the statement of the VFW.

31. *Proposed Closing of Veterans' Hospitals*, hearings before the Subcommittee on Veterans' Affairs of the Committee on Labor and Public Welfare, United States Senate, 89th Congress, 1st Session on the proposed closing of veterans' hospitals, January 22, 25, and 28, 1965. The hospitals are individually discussed at length. The VA's rationale for closing most of the facilities is summarized on pp. 417-428.

32. Ibid., p. 404.

33. *The Congressional Record – Senate*, January 26, 1965, p. 1291.

34. Ibid., February 1, 1965, pp. 1762-1826.

35. *Bradley Commission*, op. cit., p. 401.

36. The stories of both the Bradley Commission and the 1965 proposed hospital reorganization have been told in Gilbert Y. Steiner's seminal work, *The State of Welfare*, op. cit., pp. 250-264.

37. Care for veterans over 65 is prescribed in 38 U.S.C. 610(a)(4). Care for all veterans "unable to defray the expenses" is provided in 38 U.S.C. 610(a)-(1)(b) and 610(b)(2).

38. The figures have varied only slightly with time. See *Study of Health Care for American Veterans*, a report prepared by the National Academy of Sciences, National Research Council (Pursuant to Section 201(d) of Public Law 93-82), submitted to the Committee on Veterans' Affairs, United States Senate, June 7, 1977, Senate Committee Print No. 4, 95th Congress, 1st Session, pp. 24-29; and *Administrator of Veterans' Affairs Annual Report 1982*, p. 63.

39. *Actions Needed to Insure that Female Veterans Have Equal Access to VA Benefits*, GAO, HRD-82-98, September 24, 1982.

40. *VA Health Care for Women and H.R. 1137*, hearings before the Subcommittee on Hospitals and Health Care of the Committee on Veterans' Affairs, House of Representatives, 98th Congress, 1st Session, March 3, 1983, Serial No. 98-4, pp. 28-30 and 83-84.

41. Ibid., p. 46-47.

42. *Study of Health Care for American Veterans*, op. cit., pp. 28-29; *Administrator of Veterans Affairs Annual Report 1982*, p. 62.

43. *Study of Health Care for American Veterans*, op. cit. The GAO testified, summarizing the results of its individual studies, in hearings held in response to the NAS Study. See *National Academy of Sciences Study of Health Care for American Veterans and the VA Response*, hearings before the Committee on Veterans' Affairs, United States Senate, 95th Congress, 1st and 2nd Sessions, September 30, October 17, Washington, D.C.; November 16, 1977, Los Angeles, California; January 11, Beckley, West Virginia; February 6, and March 6, 1978, Washington, D.C., pp. 371-406.

44. See *Veterans' Administration's Response to the Study of Health Care for American Veterans*, a report prepared by the Veterans Administration (pursuant to section 201(c)(2) of Public Law 93-82), submitted to the Committee on Veterans' Affairs, United States Senate, September 22, 1977, Senate Committee Report No. 7, 95th Congress, 1st Session, for example, pp. 89, 93, 97, 112, 126-129, 210, and 222.

45. *Veterans' Omnibus Health Care Act of 1976*, report of the Committee on Veterans' Affairs, United States Senate to accompany S. 2908, September 3 (legislative day, August 27), 1976 — Ordered to be printed (filed under authority of the Senate) on September 1 (legislative day, August 27), 1976, 94th Congress, 2nd Session, Report No. 94-1206, p. 71.

46. *Study of Health Care for American Veterans*, op. cit., p. 125 and p. 123. See also pp. 35-49.

47. *Nomination of Richard L. Roudebush to Be Administrator of Veterans' Affairs*, Hearings before the Committee on Veterans' Affairs, United States Senate, 93rd Congress, 2nd Session, on the nomination of Richard L. Roudebush to be administrator of Veterans' Affairs, September 19, 1974, p. 19.

48. Ibid., p. 45.

49. Ibid., pp. 38-41, 45-46.

50. For the allegations against Johnson, see the Copley News Service piece of April 6, 1974 by Benjamin Shore, "Troubles Mount for VA Chief," and the April 1974 Scripps Howard piece by Lee Stillwell, "Nixon Campaign Aides Got VA Jobs." Johnson's defense was covered in a Copley News Service piece

of April 11, 1974 by Benjamin Shore, "VA Chief Replies to Cranston Criticism," and by Don Irwin of *Los Angeles Times*, April 11, 1974, "VA Chief Answers Hill Criticism."

51. See Lee Stillwell's piece for Scripps Howard, April 19, 1973, "All-Out Attacks Hurled at VA's Johnson."

52. See "VA Chief Johnson to Resign," Richard Harwood, *Washington Post*, April 23, 1974; and, "Controversial VA Chief to Step Down," Norman Kempster, *Washington Star-News*, April 23, 1974.

53. See Lee Stillwell's piece for Scripps Howard, April 23, 1974, "Johnson Resignation Linked to Publicity."

54. See Lee Stillwell's piece for Scripps Howard, April 23, 1974, "VA Chief Gave No-Bid Contracts."

55. Ibid.

56. Ibid.

57. *Nomination of Richard L. Roudebush to be Administrator of Veterans' Affairs*, op. cit., pp. 30-37; and, *Cleland Nomination*, hearings before the Committee on Veterans' Affairs, United States Senate, 95th Congress, 1st Session, on the nomination of Joseph Maxwell Cleland to be administrator of Veterans' Affairs, February 25, 1977, p. 20.

58. See *Veterans' Health Care Amendments of 1977*, hearings before the Subcommittee on Health and Readjustment of the Committee on Veterans' Affairs, United States Senate, 95th Congress, 1st Session on S. 1693 and H.R. 6502, June 22, 1977, p. 54; *Veterans' Health Care Amendments of 1979*, hearing before the Committee on Veterans' Affairs, United States Senate, 96th Congress, 1st Session, on S. 7, January 25, 1979, p. 85.

59. See the appendix to *The Budget of The United States Government*, fiscal year 1980, pp. 833-837 and 1060.

60. See *DAV*, June 1979, "Disappointments," Billy O. Hightower, national commander, p. 2. The DAV's offensive was early and sustained. See "Our Stand," Billy O. Hightower, national commander, *DAV*, January 1979, p. 2 and the accompanying "Special Report" on pp. 3 and 18; "New Initiatives," Billy O. Hightower, national commander, *DAV*, February 1979, p. 2; "DAV Offensive Is Causing Controversies!" *DAV*, March 1979, pp. 8 and 10; "The Evidence!" Norman B. Hartnett, national director of services, p. 9; and, "We Speak Out!" Billy O. Hightower, national commander, pp. 2-3, 10-12, 14.

61. *DAV*, August 1979, p. 12.

62. Ibid.

63. For his early statements, see *Cleland Nomination*, op. cit., p. 53; hearings before a Subcommittee of the Committee on Appropriations, House of Representatives, 95th Congress, 1st Session, Subcommittee on HUD – Independent Agencies, p. 20; and his statement during the *Oversight Hearings on All Forms of Federal Student Financial Assistance*, oversight hearings before the Subcommittee on Postsecondary Education of the Committee on Education and Labor, House of Representatives, 95th Congress, 1st Session, May 25, June 1, 8, 9, and 16, 1977. On his subsequent opposition to GI Bill reform, see the two letters of the Honorable Max Cleland, administrator of Veterans' Affairs to the Honorable Ray Roberts, chairman, Committee on Veterans'

Affairs, of July 29, 1977, and September 12, 1977, *H.R. 2231 Proposing Accelerated Entitlement and Other Changes in Veterans Education and Training Programs; H.R. 8419 Proposing Tuition Assistance; and Related Measures,* op. cit., pp. 17-34, and pp. 101-107.

64. *Issues and Answers,* Sunday (Memorial Day), May 28, 1978. A similar defense, for example, was made in an interview for the Memorial Day issue of *U.S. News and World Report,* May 29, 1978.

65. Figures vary among the different studies. See, generally, "Veterans in Prison," *Bureau of Justice Statistics Bulletin,* February 1981; Part Five, "The Incarcerated Veteran," of the Presidential Review Memorandum (PRM) on Vietnam Veterans, October 1978, and the PRM's "Summary of Findings Concerning the Status of Vietnam Era Veterans;" and the two GAO studies cited below. The PRM led to a message to Congress, printed on pp. 1737-1742, *Public Papers of the Presidents of the United States, Jimmy Carter, 1978,* Book II, June 30 to December 31, 1978.

66. "Veterans in Prison," op. cit., p. 2.

67. "The Incarcerated Veteran," op. cit., p. 6.

68. *Oversight on Issues Related to Incarcerated Veterans,* hearings before the Committee on Veterans' Affairs, United States Senate, 96th Congress, 1st Session, July 11, 1979, p. 177.

69. *Need for Improved Outreach Efforts for Veterans in Prison or on Parole,* General Accounting Office, MWD-75-48, December 30, 1974, pp. 1 and 3.

70. The new program is described in the VA's Xeroxed report, "Veterans Administration Services to Incarcerated Veterans," April 1975 – May 1976.

71. The article played a significant role in focusing attention on incarcerated Vietnam veterans. "Inmate Veterans: Hidden Casualties of a Lost War," Edgar May, *Corrections Magazine,* Volume V, Number 1, March 1979, pp. 3-13.

72. *Letter Report to the Chairman, Senate Committee on Veterans' Affairs,* HRD-79-97, June 29, 1979, pp. 5 and 8.

73. *Veterans' Benefits in the United States,* op. cit., p. 11.

8   Conclusion: On the Road Home

On February 10, 1978, the *Washington Post* printed a column by Colman McCarthy, who, along with the editor of the editorial page, Phil Geyelin, had written the *Post*'s editorial series on Vietnam veterans. The column heralded the formation of a new advocacy group specifically for Vietnam veterans, headed by Robert O. Muller.[1]

An experienced observer of Washington politics, McCarthy was careful to note that a new interest group alone, "in a city already dense with interest groups," did not automatically promise change, but he was also clear about the need:

> The closed world of veterans affairs — the trinity of the VA, Congressional committees, and traditional organizations like the American Legion, the Veterans of Foreign Wars and the Disabled American Veterans — often created pacts of joint protection, at the expense of many veterans excluded from the decision-making process.[2]

Muller's group was called the Council of Vietnam Veterans. In February 1978, its small staff consisted of just Muller, Stuart Feldman, and Mary Lane. Over the next five years, however, the group would grow, change its name to the Vietnam Veterans of America, and become a national membership organization with more than one hundred chapters and with thousands of members.

Colman McCarthy's column attracted the attention of a new member of Congress, David E. Bonior, a Democrat from Michigan. Bonior had served stateside in the Air Force during the Vietnam

War. He called the Council of Vietnam Veterans and volunteered to help.

Moreover, Bonior proposed that the members of Congress who were also Vietnam-era veterans be brought together as an active caucus working on Vietnam veterans issues. Working with John P. Murtha (D-Pennsylvania), he formed the Vietnam Veterans in Congress.

Nine months earlier, the *Washington Post* had run a special essay by another Vietnam veteran, Jan Scruggs. Entitled "Forgotten Veterans of 'That Peculiar War,'" the essay reviewed the results of a study Scruggs had done on the effects of the war on college veterans.[3]

The divorce and separation rate among combat veterans, the study found, was 30 percent. Among those who had served in units with casualty rates above 25 percent Scruggs found especially severe problems. Those veterans were 11 times more likely to report combat nightmares than were veterans who had served in combat units with lower casualty rates.[4]

At the end of the article, almost as if it were an aside, Scruggs suggested that "perhaps, a national monument is in order to remind an ungrateful nation of what it has done to its sons." In April 1979, Scruggs formed the Vietnam Veterans Memorial Fund.[5]

With the strong support of Senators Charles Mathias, Jr., (R-Maryland) and John W. Warner (R-Virginia), legislation was introduced in November 1979 to set aside a piece of ground near the Lincoln Memorial for the project, which was to be funded by private contributions. The legislation was passed on July 1, 1980. The money was raised, and in November 1982, the nearly completed Vietnam Veterans Memorial was dedicated.

On May 24, 1973, nearly a decade earlier, President Nixon and his family hosted a dinner for the U.S. prisoners of war who had just returned from Vietnam. The guest list was the largest in the history of the White House. It included the POWs, their families, political figures, and Hollywood stars.

In Washington, where nearly all events have political implications, the dinner was a carefully exploited moment of relief and triumph for a president approaching the edge of a gathering storm that would bring his resignation just 14 months later. Yet the dinner was also a rare moment of national recognition.

Despite heavy rains, which made the canopied dinner party messy underfoot, the president seemed truly jubilant. He seemed to honestly appreciate the great sacrifice his guests had made for their country. The POWs, in turn, were admiring of their commander-in-chief and thankful for the once-in-a-lifetime opportunity to enter the White House as honored guests.[6]

It was a remarkable night. It was a night when Lt. Colonel Lewis Shattuck, awaiting a cornea transplant, donned an eyepatch appliqued with an American flag and tried to explain its meaning to a cynical Washington press corps:

> "I only wear this one when I'm among people who know what it's all about. What is it all about? I don't know if my feelings could be framed in words." He waved his arm toward the marble staircase leading up to the White House foyer. "There's a guy who lives here who understands what it's all about."[7]

It was a night when the president declared, "Never has the White House been more proud because of the guests we have tonight." It was a night when actor John Wayne told the former POWs, "I'll ride into the sunset with you anytime."[8]

It was also a night in sharp contrast to the events that were to come one year later on Vietnam Veterans Day. On that day, there was no dramatic White House ceremony. Instead, the president spoke at Fort McNair's National War College. As the *New York Times* noted, "Few other formal ceremonies were scheduled elsewhere in the nation."[9]

Vietnam veterans noticed the slight. The *New York Times* reported:

> Several hundred veterans jammed into the Capitol hearing room of the Veterans Committee to press [their] demands. They booed at the mention of President Nixon and booed Veterans Administration officials who testified. They shouted "Lies, lies, lies" when Senators on the committee promised to push hard for higher benefits.[10]

As *Washington Post* writer William Greider noted, "The one-time nonholiday was meant to compensate for the emotional fanfare showered . . . on 566 returning prisoners of war while the nation virtually ignored the other 2.5 million men who served in Vietnam."

The compensation, however, proved impossible. Neither the nation nor its leaders were ready to recognize Vietnam veterans.[11]

In 1978, the Vietnam Veterans in Congress proposed that the nation try again. They asked President Carter to take the initiative with a presidential proclamation, but the Carter White House demurred. Left to its own, the caucus enacted House Joint Resolution 1147, declaring May 29 through June 3, 1979 as Vietnam Veterans Week.

The Carter administration was hesitant in its implementation of the resolution. The new administrator of Veterans' Affairs, Vietnam veteran Max Cleland, taped a public service announcement, and a memo was sent to each federal agency encouraging its participation. The Vietnam Veterans in Congress proposed a White House dinner. Instead, the Carter administration held an afternoon reception.

Yet a commemorative postage stamp was issued, and the private sector moved to fill the gap in federal action. Stuart Feldman, then working on the Week with the United States Conference of Mayors, helped arrange events across the country. Ed Figueroa, Yankee pitcher and Vietnam veteran, made a public service announcement.

The Week meshed with a rising tide of interest by the media and the general public. Almost spontaneously, hundreds of special stories and editorials appeared. CBS and the producers of *Lou Grant* arranged for a repeat of their special Vietnam veteran show, "Vet." Some ABC affiliates ran a public service announcement.

The Week was a milestone, but its tone seemed strangely restrained in contrast to the outpouring of emotion in early 1981, when the U.S. hostages returned from Iran. Then President Reagan closed down the federal government in Washington, and hundreds of thousands of people were on the streets to cheer the embassy staff and Marine guards.

The hostages themselves noted the contrast in treatment, and some were quick to reject any claim to special honor. Vietnam veterans were glad to see the hostages welcomed home. Knowing from their own experiences the personal problems the hostages might have to face over time, Vietnam veterans were hesitant to raise their own concerns.

Yet voices began to speak out. A retired army colonel, whose son had served in Vietnam and had been cruelly burned, wrote a letter to the *Washington Star*:

Returning Vietnam heroes — true, combat heroes — have been spat on, figuratively and literally, by their countrymen on their return home. The excesses about the detained, inconvenienced and maltreated ex-hostages today is in crass contrast.

If I were a returning Marine or State Department person, I would say, "You will make no circus animal of me! I knew there were risks when I signed aboard. Let me now alone, so that I will be free!" . . .

Do we have any values, proportion or balance not manipulated by professional tubthumpers. Think of my boy, now going on 29 years old, in the burn ward. He was carrying igniters on his back as he was ordered to.[12]

The nation could be led, but not rushed. The loud rush of welcoming joy for Vietnam veterans would have to wait until November 1982, when the Vietnam Veterans Memorial was dedicated through a week-long series of ceremonies in Washington.

The president did not give federal employees in Washington any time off to join in the celebration. In fact, he did not attend either the dedication or the accompanying parade. The official absence, however, hardly touched the emotion that swept through the Week.

The names of those who had died in Vietnam, carved on the Memorial, were read in a continuous vigil at the Washington Cathedral. President Reagan paid a brief visit to the reading. A parade was held through the streets of Washington. There were few brass bands or floats. Mostly, there were just thousands of Vietnam veterans, organized into state delegations, walking proudly as tens of thousands cheered.

Asked to explain why he felt a memorial was important, Jan Scruggs frequently read a passage from Philip Caputo's autobiographical book about his years in Vietnam, *A Rumor of War*. In one passage, Caputo remembered the courage of a friend who never came home.

"These words," Jan Scruggs noted in introducing the reading, "are the true story of a young Marine killed in Vietnam." Scruggs read:

I knew I could not have done what Levy had done. Pulling himself up on his wounded legs, he had tried to save the corpsman, not knowing that the man was beyond saving. . . .

You died for the man you tried to save. You were faithful. Your country is not. As I write this, eleven years after your death, the country for which you died wishes to forget the war in which you died. Its very name is a curse. There are no monuments to its heroes, no statues in small-town squares, no plaques, nor public wreaths, nor memorials. For plaques and wreaths and memorials are reminders, and they would make it harder for your country to forget the Vietnam war.[13]

By the end of 1982, the time for forgetting had passed. The memories at least were free to return.

*   *   *

In October 1980, just a few months after Congress had set aside the ground for the Vietnam Veterans Memorial in July, the Memorial Fund announced a national design competition. More than 1,400 individuals and teams submitted proposals, the largest architectural competition of its kind in U.S. and European history.

A distinguished panel reviewed the designs and nominated a winning entry to the board of the Vietnam Veterans Memorial Fund. However, the board, composed principally of Vietnam veterans, reserved for itself the final decision. After careful consideration, it unanimously accepted the panel's recommendation.

The winning design was simple, yet expansive in scope. From a common point, each of two walls would stretch out nearly 250 feet. One wall would point to the nearby Lincoln Memorial. The other would point to the Washington Monument, which towered above an intervening hill.

Recessed into the ground, the Memorial walls would be approached by a gently declining slope of grass. The walls would be of polished black marble, reflecting the grass and surrounding trees. On the walls would be engraved the name of each Vietnam veteran who had died or is missing in action, listed according to the date of death.

Time selected the Memorial as one of the ten best designs of 1981. The *Army Times* called it "simple, honest and in good taste." Yet the winning entry had been designed by a Chinese student, Maya Ling, from Yale University. In her ancestry was already the beginning of a controversy.[14]

Maya Ling's parents had fled from Communist China, yet she was nevertheless yellow-skinned like the Vietnamese. Sounding the alarm, Tom Carhart, a decorated Vietnam veteran whose design had not been selected, called the Memorial "a black gash of shame and sorrow, hacked into the national visage that is the Mall."[15]

In the *National Review*, the design was dismissed as an "Orwellian glob." "The design," the editorial suggested, "says that the Vietnam War should be memorialized in black, not in the white marble of Washington." "The mode of listing the names," the editor complained, "makes them individual deaths, not deaths in a cause." The preferred alternative was to list the names in alphabetical order.[16]

Jim Webb, a Vietnam veteran and member of the Memorial Fund involved in the design selection, opposed the design vehemently. He wrote an op-ed piece for the *Wall Street Journal*. At one point, his article compared the Memorial to the "ovens at Dachau."[17]

Resigning from the Memorial Fund National Sponsoring Committee, Webb wrote General Westmoreland, asking him to resign from the committee as well. The general wrote back:

> With an open mind and careful consideration of all factors, my verdict is not in agreement with yours. [The Memorial] is in no way a "trench," black polished granite is far more handsome than any other possible stone, the chronological listing of names is not inappropriate, the structure reflects dignity and good taste and blends in aesthetically [with] that beautiful area of Mall.[18]

The *National Review* and the *Wall Street Journal* are both conservative publications, but the issue did not divide on ideological lines. James Kilpatrick, one of the nation's most distinguished conservative columnists, wrote, "Let me venture my own opinion: this will be the most moving war memorial ever erected."[19]

The major veterans organizations, in an act of courage that reflected their growing attention to Vietnam veterans issues, supported the Memorial, several with financial contributions. The American Legion gave a staggering total of over $1,000,000 to the Memorial, becoming the largest single donor.

The Memorial Fund tried to find a common ground with its critics. The simple design seemed too stark for some. They wanted symbolism that would add meaning to the names. The Memorial Fund agreed. It accepted the suggestion that a sculpture be designed and incorporated with the Memorial.

Few think of the problem, but, in fact, employees have to be hired to raise and lower the flags at the many national monuments.

Over the years, the cost mounts up, and therefore government officials had opposed including a flag at the Memorial. When critics complained, the Memorial Fund secured permission for a flag.

On March 24, 1982, following months of debate and negotiation, Senator Warner proudly announced that compromise had been reached. Within a few short months, the consensus dissolved. Having won so much, the critics now took issue with the exact location of the statue.

The critics' list of complaints was potentially unending. If they won on the issue of the statue's exact location, that victory in hand, they could then return to the issues of the Memorial's color, or the method of listing the names, or the decision to recess the walls with a gentle approach slope. They could even raise their continuing opposition to the basic concept of the walls themselves.

The alleged issues were merely the surface symbols for an underlying and emotional concern. The Vietnam Veterans Memorial Fund had consciously decided to avoid a political statement about the war itself, either pro- or antiwar. Instead, it had sought to focus national attention on honoring the service of the veterans themselves.

The critics, however, wanted a memorial that would declare explicitly that the Vietnam War had been right. Rather than move past the divisive debate of the early 1970s, they wanted to resume it and to use the Memorial as their vindicating last word. The critics concluded that Maya Ling's design was not the necessary proud assertion.

At best, they viewed the design as an invitation to reflection. At worst, the very idea of reflection was suspect, implying that the nation had reason to pause and consider not only the service of Vietnam veterans but also the war itself.

Given these perceptions, no compromise could be struck. Throughout the long debate, the Memorial opponents turned to vicious and apparently unsubstantiated attacks. The opponents' tactics included portraying the Memorial Fund as communist controlled by suggesting that one member of the design jury was connected to the American Communist Party.[20]

The debate could only be silenced by seeing the quiet tears of mothers, who, finding their sons' names, accepted with joy the Memorial's grace. The debate could only be silenced by the hundreds of thousands of visitors — veterans and nonveterans — who paused in awe during the Memorial's week-long dedication.

Seeing the now completed monument, the *National Review* reversed its position. Finding the Memorial "unusual and beautiful," the *Review* wrote:

> Experienced directly, however, rather than in theory, the memorial possesses considerable power and even eloquence. Much of this comes from its high-gloss surface on which both the Lincoln Monument and the Washington Monument reflect — suggesting, if you wish, some of the ideals for which the men fought and died, and also joining their monument to American history itself. The spectator, moreover, sees his own reflection superimposed on the carved names, symbolically uniting him to them.[21]

Today, the Vietnam Veterans Memorial is one of the most visited monuments in Washington. Its place is secure, yet the opposition remains. In December, following the Memorial's dedication, its critics tried to sneak through Congress a resolution calling for design changes.[22]

Joseph Zengerle was an informed observer of the Memorial debate. He had gone to West Point and had served in Vietnam. Upon his return, he used his GI Bill benefits to earn a law degree. Already active in Vietnam veterans issues, he became one of the most active of a small group of Vietnam veterans who guided the formation of the Vietnam Veterans of America in 1978 and its subsequent growth.

In 1981, when President Reagan illegally froze the Vietnam veterans Readjustment Counseling Program, Zengerle volunteered his time, with the support of his firm, Bingham, Dana and Gould, to litigate the suit challenging the personnel freeze. In February 1982, he published in the *Washington Post* an article entitled "Vietnam: The Bone in Our Throat."

Referring to the stinging debate over the Vietnam Veterans Memorial Fund and to other controversial Vietnam veterans issues, the article reflected on the nation's inability to move past the bitter tone of controversy set during the Vietnam War:

> Despite its different guises . . . the beast is the same: our inability or unwillingness to assimilate compassionately our own history. . . . The foremost dilemma before the country respecting the legacy of the Vietnam War is how to close the divisions it opened in our society, between the doves and the hawks, unrepentant veterans and peace activists, the uniformed military and its civilian leadership, the Class

of '46 and those who fought in Vietnam, and so forth. What Arthur Miller said of people in his play "After the Fall" seems equally true of nations: "One must finally take one's life in one's arms."[23]

Both Bonior and Bobby Muller had been uncertain about spending time on either Vietnam Veterans Week or the Vietnam Veterans Memorial. There would be time enough for symbols, they thought, after basic benefits had been won.

Sensing, however, that "On this, too, I might be wrong," both men put their energies into the Week and the Memorial on the advice of others, like Jan Scruggs, who counseled that symbols might lead to national healing and to an atmosphere conducive to meeting the other needs of Vietnam veterans.

On more than one occasion, Bonior and Muller have acknowledged how lucky it was that they deferred to others. The symbols proved decidedly hard to win. Once won, they proved to be far more than just a parade. The Week, in part, and the Memorial, more fully, gave substance to the nation's evolving support for Vietnam veterans.

If the Vietnam War is today not quite as stuck in our throats as once it was, the symbols have made a large part of the difference. Yet laws are symbols, too. Even at this late date, the nation could take action that would acknowledge publicly its past failures and demonstrate its present commitment.

Veterans have been denied basic rights too long. It is time to pass judicial review legislation and to grant our veterans the right to counsel and open administrative procedures. Our government bought the entire town of Times Beach, Missouri, because it had been exposed to the dioxin in Agent Orange, but it has yet to compensate Vietnam veterans for those disabilities most clearly related to Agent Orange exposure. It is time to pay those claims.

This agenda is not expensive, and much more could be legitimately asked, but the demands of leadership do not fall on political figures alone. They fall on Vietnam veterans as well. As Bobby Muller has frequently said, "Vietnam veterans are not going to be another gimme generation." That claim will need proof.

The nation did not honor its debt to Vietnam veterans. That failure should be written deeply in our history books. It is easy to ask now, as public support seems to be building, that a final accounting be made, yet the demand for benefits must come ultimately to an end.

Times change even the most just of claims because, in the end, the past cannot be undone. Vietnam veterans, who were reaching age 30 when the Carter administration seemed to hold the promise of one last chance, are now reaching the average age of 35. At some point, the priority has to become not correcting old errors but preventing new mistakes.

Benefits alone will not give dignity to each Vietnam veteran's long years of waiting. It falls to Vietnam veterans to move ahead despite the nation. That is not a new challenge. It is the challenge Vietnam veterans have faced since the war began. They cannot let the nation's errors dominate their lives.

When veterans return from the next war — whether it is called good or bad, whether it is won or lost — Vietnam veterans must be in the forefront fighting for others. Let Vietnam veterans make the solemn vow that never again will one generation of veterans abandon another.

If Vietnam veterans must make a private peace, then those who make that peace will be the stronger because the job was the harder. Perhaps, this experience will produce leaders with a distinctive stamp of character. Long years of waiting may finally be justified by this — new leaders with a unique vision.

NOTES

1. Colman McCarthy, "An Advocate for Vietnam Veterans," *Washington Post*, February 10, 1978.

2. Ibid.

3. Jan Craig Scruggs, "Forgotten Veterans of 'That Peculiar War,'" *Washington Post*, May 25, 1977.

4. Ibid.

5. Ibid.

6. See William Claiborne, "Nixon Hits Security Leaks," *Washington Post*, May 25, 1973, which outlines events earlier in the day.

7. "Their Cheers, Their Tears, Their Day," *Washington Post*, May 25, 1973.

8. Ibid.

9. *AP*, "Nixon Hails Veterans' Efforts in Vietnam," *New York Times*, March 30, 1974.

10. Ibid.

11. William Greider, "Viet Vets Press for Jobs, Tuition Aid," *Washington Post*, March 29, 1974.

12. Howard Wickert, lieutenant colonel, U.S.A., retired, "Who Bled for Real Heroes?" *Washington Star*, March 10, 1981.

13. Statement of the Honorable John Warner, "The Groundbreaking Ceremony for the Vietnam Veterans Memorial," *Congressional Record — Senate*, April 13, 1982, S. 3375-3378, transcript of the statement at the groundbreaking by Jan C. Scruggs, president, Vietnam Veterans Memorial Fund.

14. See Jan C. Scruggs, "In Defense of the Vietnam Veterans Memorial," *Wall Street Journal*, Thursday, January 14, 1982.

15. Tom Carhart, "Insulting Vietnam Vets," *New York Times*, October 24, 1981.

16. "Stop That Monument," *National Review*, September 19, 1981.

17. James H. Webb, Jr., "Reassessing the Vietnam Veterans Memorial," *Wall Street Journal*, December 18, 1983.

18. Jan C. Scruggs, "In Defense of the Vietnam Veterans Memorial," op. cit.

19. James J. Kilpatrick, "Finally, We Honor the Vietnam Dead," *Washington Post*, November 11, 1981.

20. Patrick Buchanan, "An Insulting Memorial," *Chicago Tribune*, December 26, 1981.

21. "That Vietnam Monument," *National Review*, November 26, 1982.

22. See *Congressional Record — House*, December 20, 1982, H-10511-10512, for passage of H. J. Res. 636 and H. Con. Res. 437, and the statement of the Honorable Don Bailey, "Vietnam Veterans Memorial Completion," December 21, 1982, H-10661.

23. Joseph C. Zengerle, "Vietnam: The Bone in Our Throat," *Washington Post*, February 19, 1982.

Name Index

Subject Index

Agent Orange, and the American Legion, 116-17; need for compensation legislation, 188; history of Congressional action, 142-43; Oversight and Investigation Hearings, 140, 147-49; and the Reagan administration, 78; 2,4,5-T and the Environmental Protection Agency, 149-50; Veterans Administration evaluation of Animal Evidence, 150-51; Veterans Administration evaluation of epidemiological evidence, 151-52; Veterans Administration reaction to Environmental Protection Agency actions on 2,4,5-T, 150; Veterans Administration Agent Orange research program, 152; and the Veterans of Foreign Wars, 116-17

American Legion, and Agent Orange, 116-17; attitude toward proposed closing of VA facilities in 1965, 157-58; membership, 101; power, 99-101; priorities, 105-06; and the Readjustment Counseling Program, 131, 134; and Special Discharge Review Program established by President Carter, 108-10; support for Vietnam Veterans Memorial, 185; traditional position on less-than-honorable discharges, 107; Vietnam veterans in key staff positions, 114

Apocalypse Now, 64-65.

Barney Miller, "Agent Orange", 22
The Boys in Company C, 63
Bradley Commission, 155-56

Carter administration, 86-87, 88-90; and pardon for draft resisters, 86-87; and the Readjustment Counseling Program, 90, 132-33; and the Special Discharge Review Program, 108-12; speech before the American Legion, 87; and the Vietnam GI Bill, 89-90; and Vietnam Veterans Week, 182

Coming Home, 64

Committees on Veterans' Affairs - House, Chairman Montgomery, 138-43; House, Chariman Rankin, 121-25; House, Chairman Roberts, 130-35, 135-36, 138-40; House, Chairman Teague, 121-30, 137; Senate, 135-36

The Deer Hunter, 65-67

Disabled American Veterans, The Forgotten Warrior Project, 113, 114; membership, 101; power, 99-101; and the Readjustment Counseling Program, 134; and the Special Discharge Review Program, 109; own special outreach efforts to Vietnam veterans, 113; Vietnam veteran elected to leadership position, 115; Vietnam veterans in key staff position, 113-14

discharges, less-than-honorable, 106-12

documentaries, See "film documentaries" and "television documentaries"

draft resisters, Carter pardon program, 86-87; Ford conditional pardon program, 85-87

Falkland Islands, British Invasion,

About the Authors

David E. Bonior is a member of the U.S. House of Representatives. He served stateside in the Air Force during the Vietnam War and was the Founding Chairman of the Vietnam Veterans in Congress, the Congressional Advocacy Group for Vietnam veterans. A member of the prominent House Committee on Rules, he was first elected to Congress in 1976 following four years in the Michigan State Legislature. During his off-duty hours in the Air Force, Congressman Bonior earned a Master's Degree in history from Chapman College.

Steven M. Champlin, the nonveteran among the authors, became active on Vietnam veterans issues while at Yale Divinity School. He worked for the Vietnam Veterans of America from 1978 through 1980, becoming the Director of its Washington office. In 1981, he joined Congressman Bonior's staff. He earned a Master's Degree in religious studies from Wesleyan University and a Master's Degree in divinity from Yale Divinity School.

Timothy S. Kolly served in Vietnam in 1969 and 1970. He was the original Staff Director to the Vietnam Veterans in Congress and has also served on the professional staff of the Committee on Rules. He lives in Florida, where he is now running for Congress. He has a Master's Degree in international economics from Johns Hopkins University.